DUKE · UNIVERSITY · PUBLICATIONS

JONES VERY

JONES VERY

EMERSON'S "BRAVE SAINT"

WILLIAM IRVING BARTLETT

DUKE UNIVERSITY PRESS

DURHAM, NORTH CAROLINA

1942

PRINTED IN THE UNITED STATES OF AMERICA BY
THE SEEMAN PRINTERY, INC., DURHAM, N. C.

To

JOHN CALVIN METCALF
inspiring teacher
dependable scholar
and Virginia gentleman

PREFACE

ANY STUDENT OF American transcendentalism will occasionally en-
counter the name of Jones Very, of Salem, Massachusetts, friend of
Emerson, member of the Transcendental Club, and a mystic of
such unusual intensity that he was considered insane by many who
knew him. And sometimes, too, a reader of transcendental poetry
will discover a little of the remarkably mystic verse of this man.
But ready information concerning him is scant. His poems have
seldom appeared in print, save in anthologies, since 1886; and only
a few scholars are qualified to discuss him with any degree of
impressiveness. Believing that some of Jones Very's nature sonnets
and religious poems are among the best pieces of their kind that
have been contributed to American literature, the author determined to search for material dealing with Very's life. The task
was arduous, but the results were oftentimes astonishingly enlight-
ening and sometimes genuinely thrilling.

The fact that most of Very's letters were burned after his death
served to discourage many interested students, and led them to
overlook other sources of information: viz., the newspaper files and
genealogical material in the Essex Institute; the Essex County
Court records; the material in the Archives of the Widener Library,
at Harvard University; the manuscripts in the Andover Theological
Library and in Brown University; and Emerson's unpublished
letters and the unindexed matter in his *Journals*.

A study of these and other unexploited materials revealed that
Very was an intensely interesting man, so pure as to be saintly,
thoroughly unworldly, supremely transcendental, even mystical;
that he early suffered a severe religious excitation that shattered his
nervous system and left him often so unimpassioned as to appear
a devotee of quietism; that he was intimate with Emerson and
influenced his thought and, to a certain extent, his works; that
he considered his work divinely inspired; that Lowell, Dana, Bryant, Elizabeth Peabody, and Margaret Fuller were deeply impressed

with his verse, and that Emerson predicted for him a "very large" audience; and that he deserves a more substantial and popular recognition than that which is often accorded him. To prove these facts by acquainting the reader with Very as a man, a mystic, and a poet, and to further his reputation as an important minor American poet, rather than an inconsequential appendage to the transcendental group, are the objects of this study.

This study of the life and works of Jones Very represents the co-operation and helpfulness of many exceedingly kind people. It is a pleasure for me to acknowledge my gratitude to them at this time, and to state that the work could never have been accomplished without their aid.

I am exceedingly grateful to the officials of the following libraries: the Library of Congress, Washington, D. C.; the New York Public Library; the Antiquarian House, Concord, Massachusetts; the Alderman Memorial Library, of the University of Virginia, at Charlottesville; and the Bittle Memorial Library, of Roanoke College, at Salem, Virginia.

To Houghton Mifflin Company, who furnished me with records concerning the editions of Jones Very's works published in 1883 and 1886, and to Dr. W. Franklin Wood, of the McLean Hospital, Waverly, Massachusetts, who supplied me with dates concerning Very's illness, I express my obligation.

To Miss Marjorie Very, of Westwood, Massachusetts, and to Mrs. Edmund R. Brown, of Sharon, Massachusetts—grandnieces of Jones Very—who graciously entertained me in their homes, permitted me to use portraits, and supplied me with information from letters, I shall always be grateful.

To the Clerk of the Court of Essex County, Massachusetts, to Miss Carrie Martin, Miss Jennie Dale Fuller, Miss Charlotte Nichols (now deceased), and Miss Harriet I. Wilkins—all of Salem, Massachusetts—I wish to express my thankfulness for relating to me their recollections of the Verys. Miss Wilkins has been especially kind, having accompanied me on many drives in and around Salem to spots frequented by Jones Very, having presented me with books once belonging to him, and having exerted every means at her disposal to further my research.

In addition, I am grateful to the following:

The Andover-Harvard Theological Library, for permission to quote from the sermons and to quote from and print the poems in the collection of Jones Very's manuscripts now in the possession of the library.

D. Appleton-Century Company, for permission to quote from the article "An Inspired Life," by William Page Andrews, which first appeared in *The Century Magazine*.

Mr. Carlos Baker and *The New England Quarterly*, for permission to quote from Mr. Baker's article "Emerson and Jones Very," published in *The New England Quarterly*, March, 1934.

The Public Library of the City of Boston, for permission to quote from Sarah Freeman Clarke's manuscript "Impressions and Recollections of Miss Peabody."

Mr. Van Wyck Brooks and E. P. Dutton & Co., Inc., for permission to quote from *The Flowering of New England* and *The Life of Emerson*.

Mr. Henry B. Van Hoesen, Librarian, and the Library Committee, of Brown University, Providence, Rhode Island, for permission to print certain manuscripts of Jones Very now in the Harris Collection of Poetry and Plays; and Miss Elizabeth Spicer, curator of the collection, who assisted in the preparation and classification of the manuscripts.

The Ralph Waldo Emerson Memorial Association, for permission to quote from *Records of a Lifelong Friendship*, by Horace Howard Furness, published by Houghton Mifflin Company in 1900.

The Essex Institute, Salem, Massachusetts, for use of their library, newspaper files, and museum, and for permission to quote from their publications and manuscripts and to reproduce a portrait of Captain Jones Very and a letter from Emerson owned by the Institute. To Miss Florence Osborne and Miss Harriet S. Tapley, of the Institute, I acknowledge my especial indebtedness.

Harcourt, Brace and Company, Inc., and Mr. Louis Untermeyer, for permission to quote from Mr. Untermeyer's *American Poetry from the Beginning to Whitman.*

Mr. K. D. Metcalf, Director, and other officers of the Widener Library, at Harvard University, for permission to use and to quote from the *Records of the College Faculty,* Volume XI; *Harvardiana,* Volume II (1835-1836); *Exhibitions and Commencement Performances, 1834-1835; Bowdoin Prize Dissertations,* Volume VI (1835-1836); James Russell Lowell's copy of Very's *Essays and Poems,* published by Charles C. Little and James Brown in 1839, and now in the Treasure Room of the Widener Library; and the typed copies of Emerson's complete *Journals,* also in the Treasure Room of the Library.

Houghton Mifflin Company, for permission to quote from: *The Journal of Gamaliel Bradford,* edited by Van Wyck Brooks; *James Freeman Clarke: Autobiography, Diary and Correspondence,* edited by Edward Everett Hale; *The Complete Works of Ralph Waldo Emerson* (Centenary Edition); *Journals of Ralph Waldo Emerson,* edited by Ralph Emerson Forbes and Edward Waldo Emerson; *Nathaniel Hawthorne and His Wife,* by Julian Hawthorne; *Among My Books, Second Series,* by James Russell Lowell; *Henry D. Thoreau,* by Franklin Benjamin Sanborn; *Poems by Jones Very; Poems and Essays,* by Jones Very; and *A Memoir of Ralph Waldo Emerson,* Volume I, by James Cabot.

Little, Brown & Company, for permission to quote from *Essays and Poems of Jones Very.*

The Methodist Book Concern, for permission to quote from "Jones Very—A Son of the Spirit," by G. M. Hammell, and published in *The Methodist Review,* for January, 1901.

Library of Middlebury College, Middlebury, Vermont, and Miss Viola C. White, of the library staff, for permission to use a bookplate in a volume formerly owned by Jones Very but now in the Abernethy Library of American Literature, at Middlebury College.

The Rowfant Club, Cleveland, Ohio, for permission to quote from George Willis Cooke's *An Historical and Biographical Introduction to The Dial.*

Professor R. L. Rusk, the Columbia University Press, and the Ralph Waldo Emerson Memorial Association, for permission to quote from *The Letters of Ralph Waldo Emerson,* edited by Professor R. L. Rusk, in six volumes, 1939.

Mrs. Beatrix Hawthorne Smyth, for permission to quote from *Memories of Hawthorne,* by Rose Lathrop Hawthorne, and published by Houghton Mifflin Company, 1897.

The Yale University Press, for permission to quote from *The American Notebooks of Nathaniel Hawthorne,* edited by Randall Stewart.   W. I. B.

CONTENTS

ILLUSTRATIONS

JONES VERY

CHAPTER I

EARLY YEARS

SATURDAY, August 28, 1813, was a bustling and exciting day in Salem, Massachusetts, for the War of 1812 not only was creating further anxiety for Salem folk but was also exacting greater responsibilities of them. Since the earlier days of the American Revolution, when Boston and New York were occupied by the British, the patriotic merchants of Salem had proved their worth to the American people. They had not failed in the earlier crisis, and they should not fail now. Boston might have a deeper harbor, but Salem had better seamen and older maritime prestige. During the Revolution had not Salem merchants turned 158 sailing vessels into privateers, carrying 2,000 guns? And had not these privateers captured 445 prizes? Larger and swifter vessels should be built on lower Derby Street; perhaps a ship even larger than the 860-ton frigate *Essex* might be launched in the harbor. The pluck and ingenuity of Salem's citizens had enabled them to survive the detested Embargo of 1807 until its repeal in 1809, and Yankee persistency should defeat another embargo now proposed for immediate effect. Trade with Russia, the Cape of Good Hope, India, China, Java, Sumatra, the Fiji Islands, and the West Indies should somehow or other be continued. Yes, Salem had more than her ghosts of witches on Gallows Hill, her tales of loose women doomed to wear scarlet letters on their sinful bosoms, her eccentric old men and women, croaking in melancholy behind spider-webbed shutters because of the curses hurled on their proud, selfish forbears. Federal and Chestnut and Essex streets could boast of mansions as spacious and beautiful as any in America, for that eminent wood carver and architect, Samuel McIntyre, had lavished his genius on both interior and exterior of many a private residence and public building. Salem had its own culture fostered by wealth from foreign trade. One had only to examine the records in the customhouse to prove the importance of the old Massachusetts port. Had not the ship *Eliza,* under the mastership of James Cook, brought from Sumatra a cargo of 1,012,148 pounds of pepper, on which a duty of $66,903.90 had been paid? Yes, Salem was proud of her history, of her commerce, and of her wealth.

On that Saturday morning in late August, 1813, most of the men and women of Salem rose courageously from their comfortable beds and walked briskly and confidently about their morning duties. In the journeyman's shop on Essex Street, in the shipman's gambrel-roofed cottage on the harbor, in the counting room of the customhouse above Derby Wharf, and in the elegant parlor of the Peirce-Nichols mansion on Federal Street, Salem men and women talked of America's war with Great Britain and longed for the time when the East Indian trade and the whaling industry would be unmolested.

The boys—yet free from school but conscious of a vacation almost spent—caught the spirit of their elders. In their games they substituted the British for the Indians, and wondered when they themselves should master sailing vessels or proudly await cargoes for their own mercantile establishments. Young Nathaniel Hawthorne, his nine years already acquainted with the ghost of a seafaring father, sauntered from his home on Herbert Street down Long Wharf, staring with childish wonder at the strange figureheads on the bowsprits of the schooners, and watching the bronzed and iron-muscled sailors unloading their fragrant cargoes of spices.

But in the household of the Verys at old Buffum's Corner, the bustle and excitement of war and commerce had subsided temporarily, and a tense, muffled expectancy gripped the occupants. Lydia Very, the young wife of Captain Jones Very, was in her first travail. Finally, the cry of a newborn man child rose above the stillness of the house, and when the neighbors learned that the baby had been named Jones Very after his father, most of them supposed that another seafarer had been born. Not one of them had the audacity to suggest that a poet and a mystic had begun his strange life in the proud New England town.

The child's parents were cousins, both having descended from Bridget Very, a widow, who, with her sons, Samuel and Thomas, and her daughter, Mary, came to New England from Salisbury, England, and settled on the north side of Cedar Pond, near Danvers. She early attached herself to the First Church in Salem, and sought the physical protection and the comradeship of a second husband in the person of Edward Giles, a neighbor who had belonged to the Salem church as early as 1636. They christened the first of their children in 1640, and before Bridget Giles died in 1680 she had seen her son Samuel Very marry Alice Woodice and had been assured of the perpetuation of the Very name through the birth of their eight sons and four daughters, only one of whom had died in childhood.[1]

The Very family early established itself as one of brave and stable character, marked by patriotic and religious zeal and enough of Yankee tenacity and thrift to prove that it would be comparatively free from the worries of financial embarrassment. Samuel Very fought against the Narragansett Indians and received a grant of land on the Sowhegan River as compensation. Jonathan Marsh, who married Samuel Very's daughter Mary, and John Giles, grandson of Bridget (Very) Giles, were wounded in battle against the Indians at Haverhill, August 29, 1708. Later members of the Very family were Revolutionary soldiers. Their readiness to defend their homes was only a part of their demonstration of the love they bore to the large holdings of farm and pasture lands in the vicinity of Cedar Pond and the well-known Ship Rock. The Very descendants lived on in this locality until the end of the eighteenth century, and their name clung to the soil and was recorded in many of the Essex County Register of Deeds books in such terms as "Very's lot" and "Very's plain."[2]

But by the middle of the eighteenth century some of the younger Verys were turning their eyes toward the bustling neighboring port of Salem, and were leaving the farm to take to the sea. In 1736 Isaac Very, great-grandson of Bridget and great-grandfather of Jones, the poet, married into the Palfrey family, well-known sailmakers, and from that time the Verys seemed destined to follow the sea.[3] A son, Daniel, died while on a voyage to some foreign land. The elder Isaac's fifth child, also named Isaac, became a

[1] *Bulletin of the Essex Institute*, XII (Jan.-June, 1880), 74-75.
[2] See an article written by Jones Very for the Essex Institute and titled "The Very Family," *Essex Institute Historical Collections*, I (1859), 116 ff., and II (1860), 33-38.   [3] *Ibid.*

shipmaster and later a customs officer, and lived on May Street in Salem, next door to his mariner brother Samuel's household and mercantile establishment. Samuel had left the sea after gaining his captaincy and had opened a large store at the busy junction of Boston and Essex streets, familiarly known as Buffum's Corner, These brothers were the grandfathers of Jones Very, the poet, for Isaac Very's son Jones married his cousin Lydia, daughter of Captain Samuel Very.[4]

The father of the poet was a fine product of New England seamanship. Taken by his own father on voyages at an early age, he quickly responded to the appeal of the sea, and became skilled in managing sailors and in manipulating even the larger vessels. In fact, he seemed destined to enjoy the vigor and old age of his sire, Isaac Very, who during his eighty-six years married four times, and begot twelve children.[5] But during the War of 1812 the elder Jones Very was captured in a privateer, the *Montgomery,* and carried by the British into Halifax, Nova Scotia, where he was kept a prisoner for several months.[6] The harsh and cruel treatment inflicted upon him by his enemies undermined his health; consumption slowly fastened its grip upon him. But the young seaman was at first not conscious of the nature of his disease, and he believed that he should rally quickly from a weakness occasioned, as he thought, by confinement, cold, and malnutrition. On his release from prison and on his return to Salem he felt so much recovered from his former physical weakness that he renewed his courtship of his cousin Lydia Very and received her promise to marry him. The ceremony was performed on the thirteenth of February, 1813, and the young bridegroom (he was then twenty-two years old) escorted his nineteen-year-old bride to his father's home only a few feet away from old Buffum's Corner, where she had spent her girlhood.[7] Here she remained while her husband continued his voyages, and here, six and a half months later, her first child was born on the twenty-eighth of August and was christened Jones after his father. A second son, born two years later, was

[4] *Ibid.*   [5] *Ibid.*
[6] "The Father of Jones Very," Salem *Register,* May 17, 1880.
[7] *Essex Institute Historical Collections,* II (1860), 37.

PORTRAIT OF CAPTAIN JONES VERY

(From a drawing made by an unknown artist in Paris, before 1820. The
original hangs in the library of the Essex Institute, Salem, Massachusetts.)

called Washington, and a third child, who died in 1822 when only
four years old, was given the name of another great American—
Franklin. A fourth son, Horace, lived only a month, but the two
youngest children, who were girls and were named Frances Eliza
and Lydia Louisa Ann, respectively, enjoyed long and useful lives.[8]

The grandfathers of the baby Jones looked with pride upon the
child and already began to plan for his early career as a mariner;
and even the father longed for the time when he might take his
own son with him as cabin boy. But perhaps the mother had
different plans, for she was a silently patient but determined young
woman, combining in her nature a generous share of the Very
pluck, thrift, and religious zeal, and an equal proportion of artistic
temperament from her Putney ancestry.[9] Intensely fond of nature,
she spent long hours out of doors and tended her flowers and her
vegetables with a care so assiduous that it suggested a passion.
But she also loved books and, like her husband, had a turn for
rhyming.[10] When he returned from a voyage, she often greeted
him with verses made during his absence, and he, in turn, presented her with stanzas composed while he waited patiently for
his vessel to reach port. Lydia Very enjoyed hearing her husband
read his carefully kept journals of his long voyages, but she felt
no compelling desire to journey to strange lands. Her religion
intensified her gentle nature, made her humane and generous in
her treatment of both animals and men; it sustained her through
the long months when she awaited anxiously the return of her
husband from a voyage to Russia or to the East Indies, and it
flooded her being with thankfulness when the familiar masthead
of his sailing vessel at length appeared on the horizon of the Salem
harbor. But she knew him to be a capable mariner, and she con-
gratulated herself on her marriage to a man whom William Gray
selected to master his brig *Concord* in 1817 and his barque *Aurelia*
from 1821 until September, 1824.[11] In later years she often read
to her children the following clipping from the Philadelphia *American Daily Advertiser,* and in so doing instilled into them, not only

[8] *Ibid.*   [9] Her mother was Hannah Putney.
[10] "The Life and Services to Literature of Jones Very, a Memorial Meeting,
Tuesday, Dec. 14, 1880," *Bulletin of the Essex Institute,* XIII (1881), 5.
[11] "The Father of Rev. Jones Very," Salem *Register,* Monday, May 17, 1880.

reverence and admiration for their father, but also pride in the fact that they were sons and daughters of a man who was both brave and good:

Humanity and Benevolence, In whatever shape or circumstance they appear, deserve to be held up to the public eye, and to meet with public gratitude. It is with the highest pleasure that the citizens have witnessed some unusual instances of this kind in Masters of vessels with crowded passengers from foreign ports.

Notwithstanding the severity which is too frequently observable in captains, often arising from the peculiarity of their situation, we find some exceptions so laudable and philanthropic, that whilst we admire them, we are also bound to give them that publicity which they merit.

The arrivals of vessels from Europe with passengers have, within two or three years past, been frequent; and the treatment which many of these wretched people experienced from unfeeling captains has often excited the most painful sympathy. We trust, however, abuses of this kind will seldom occur again, to pain the feelings of humanity.

These remarks have obtruded themselves upon the mind by the recent arrival in this port of two brigs, one from Amsterdam, and the other from Hamburg; to wit, the brig Concord of Boston, Jones Very, Master; and the brig Susan, Captain Arnold.

The extreme attention which these worthy gentlemen have paid to the accommodation and comfort of their passengers, in every respect, deserves to be mentioned with the highest encomiums. And whilst every candid and feeling member of society will strongly reprobate the barbarous treatment, which has been often displayed to passengers in the many crowded vessels from Germany, we are also happy to contrast the above mentioned gentlemen, with former instances; and hope their conduct will become a pattern for imitation with future captains.

Sept. 17, 1818. Frederick Schwickard.[12]

In 1822 Captain Very was master of William Gray's *Aurelia* and was sailing between New England and Spanish ports. He brought to Boston from Malaga, with his cargo of fruit and wine, two grapevines, a White Hamburg and a Muscat of Alexandria, or Royal Muscadine. Taking them home to Salem, he rooted them in large earthen vessels and expected to keep them for his family; but finding it inconvenient and difficult to preserve them, he at length sold them to his neighbor, Mr. William Dean, who had just built a greenhouse at his home across the street. These vines were

[12] Philadelphia *American Daily Advertiser,* Sept. 17, 1818.

reputed to be the parents of all the White Hamburgs and Royal Muscadines in the United States.[13]

But the summer of 1822 meant more to the Verys than the bringing home of grapevines. It was then that Captain Very decided his eldest child should go to sea. The boy was nine years old, and it was high time he became acquainted with a sailor's life. For surely he would be a mariner. Had not his grandfathers been sea captains? Yes, young Jones should follow in the steps of his father, learn the flow of tides, the behavior of ocean currents, and determine the location of a vessel from observation of the heavens. He should accustom his body to sun and wind, to the tang of salt spray, and to the surge of mighty waters. When he reached his twenty-first year, he would know how to manage both men and sailing vessels; then, no doubt, he would become "Captain" Very, would marry a Massachusetts girl and become the father of other sons, who, in turn, would take to the sea. Yes, the Verys had the sea in their blood; a seaman's life was manly, natural, and vigorous: it was time the boy left his mother's apron strings and felt a father's discipline. Whether Lydia Very protested openly is not known. Doubtless, she said little, wishing in her heart of hearts that her eldest child might remain with her, yet trained by family custom and influenced by community environment to believe that sea folk's sons should follow the sea. So, in January, 1823, when she stood on the threshold of the May Street home and bade farewell to the younger and the elder Jones, she needed all the fortitude of her staunch faith to sustain her. In July her four-year-old son, Franklin, had died, and only two and a half years before, almost to the day, the infant Horace, for the preservation of whose life she had almost exhausted her strength, had died a short month after his birth. Now that Jones had gone with his father, only Washington, aged six, and the two-year-old Frances were left to her. But birth and death were frequent visitors to Salem homes, and Lydia Very took up her knitting with a determination to bear her lot bravely and unprotestingly. She must not question the ways of Providence, and she prayed God's for-

[13] *Bulletin of the Essex Institute*, IV (Jan.-June, 1873), 117; also Salem *Register*, Monday, May 17, 1880.

giveness even for her silent rebellion and asked especial protection for the *Aurelia* on the long journeys to and from Russia.

The voyage was made successfully, and were Captain Very's journals still in existence one might glean much interesting material concerning young Jones's reaction to his new life. But all the facts available come from a few poems and from statements made by the poet in later life; and these are rare and meager. One does know, however, that the boy Jones suffered from homesickness. As the familiar landmarks of Salem slowly faded from view, Jones crept to his father—a man, who, as a boy, had also been taken from his home and put to sea, who had suffered, and who bore the marks of pain in his handsome face and in the grey streaks of his raven hair. The man understood the boy's misery and sought to comfort him. Part of the conversation Jones Very recorded later in an unfinished poem:

> The sun was shining on the deck
> The stars looked out upon the sea
> The sail had dwindled to a speck
> That was upon our lea.
>
> I crept beside the grey-locked man
> Whose words I loved to hear so well
> He knew my wish and thus began
> His ocean tale to tell.
>
> The ship from Hamburgh held her way
> And playing round her stately form
> The waves curled bright their wreaths of spray
> All heedless of the storm
>
> .   .   .   .
>
> And I was young my boy as thou
> And all around seemed strange and new
> I watched the ocean's deep green brow
> I watched the heavens so blue.
>
> I looked behind—my home had fled
> And seemed afar like distant cloud
> My mother all I loved seemed dead
> I wept and sobbed aloud.[14]

[14] This poem, with the exception of one omitted stanza, is reproduced here as it occurs in manuscript (hence the lack of punctuation) in the Harris Collection of American Poetry, at Brown University. It is one of approximately sixty of Very's

The *Aurelia* docked at Kronstadt, and there it remained in the ice-coated harbor until the following spring. It was this voyage that decided the fate of Captain Very. Exposure to the intense Russian cold irritated the old and arrested tubercular condition. The strength he had succeeded in accumulating through careful and temperate living supported him for months, but gradually his reserve weakened. Young Jones often awoke in the dead of night to hear his father's violent coughing, and he noticed at times the hectic flush of his thin cheeks and the unnatural luster of his eyes. But finally spring came, the ice thawed, and the *Aurelia* slowly moved out of the harbor. They landed in Boston the latter part of August,[15] having been away from home about seven months. The voyage across the Atlantic had proved beneficial to Captain Very's health, but he wanted no more northern voyages. William Gray believed that a southern journey would restore his captain's health, so the *Aurelia* was loaded with a cargo destined for New Orleans. When Lydia Very bade good-bye to her husband and son, she was reconciled to her life, for her sixth child was stirring within her. The autumn days were so crisp as to make a fire desirable, and she sat by the cheerful hearth singing hymns and knitting baby clothes. "The Lord giveth," she repeated quietly.

Meanwhile the *Aurelia* sailed southward, the breezes becoming warmer day by day. Off Key West a pirate vessel came out and gave chase, but the barque continued on in her course, her crew openly making preparations to retaliate if an attack were made.[16] At length, when within an eighth of a mile of the freighter, the pirate ship turned back, its captain evidently convinced that his enemies were too ready to receive him. Arriving in New Orleans, Captain Very was greeted by his friend, Captain Samuel Cook of the *Delphos,* who had sighted the *Aurelia* from the harbor and had come down the river in his boat to greet his fellow seaman. The boy Jones remembered this incident, and fifty years later,

poems in manuscript owned by Brown University, no one of which is included in any edition of the poet's works.

[15] *Bulletin of the Essex Institute,* IV (Jan.-June, 1873), 117; also Salem *Register,* Monday, May 17, 1880.

[16] *Ibid.*

upon the death of Captain Cook, paid a tribute to him in the
sonnet, "Captain Samuel Cook."[17]

Soon after docking his vessel, Captain Very discovered that he
must wait several months for a cargo; so he put young Jones to
school. But the boy had barely acquainted himself with his master
when he had to set sail again. When he left the quaint old city
in Louisiana, he carried only faint impressions of its luxurious
vegetation, its languid, lackadaisical life, and its slave market.[18]
Captain Very loaded his barque with cotton and sailed in the
spring for Corves and Havre. After discharging his cargo, he went
to St. Ubes for salt.[19] Then he set sail for Boston. His illness by
this time was so painful as to make it exceedingly difficult to discharge his duties, but he apparently failed to realize the extreme
seriousness of his condition. When he arrived in Boston the latter
part of August, 1824, his employer realized that he was dangerously
ill and quickly sent him home to Salem. But when Captain Very
and Jones walked down the gangplank and climbed into the stage-
coach, neither of them suspected that his sea voyages were over.
They arrived home amid great excitement, for the Marquis de
Lafayette was expected the same day for his second visit to Salem.
Sailors in uniform moved cheerfully about the town; crowds of
children filled with the holiday spirit shouted gleefully as they ran
up and down Essex Street. Jones and Captain Very alighted at
Buffum's Corner and greeted their family. Both looked for the
first time upon the new Lydia, who greeted her father as lustily as
her nine months' voice permitted. But Captain Very was too ill to
make a cheerful response. His lank body shook with paroxysms
of coughing, and his flushed cheeks and parched lips bore unmistakable evidence of the ravages of consumption. He kept his bed
until his death three days before Christmas.[20]

[17] *Poems and Essays by Jones Very*, complete and revised edition, with a
biographical sketch by James Freeman Clarke and a Preface by C. A. Bartol
(Boston and New York: Houghton, Mifflin and Company, 1886), p. 513. This
edition hereinafter is referred to as *Clarke*.

[18] One unpublished poem, dated 1871, records the life in New Orleans. The
poem was sent to Captain Samuel Cook, and expresses the boyhood reaction of
both Jones Very and William Hooper to their experiences in New Orleans. See
Brown University MSS.   [19] Salem *Register*, Monday, May 17, 1880.

[20] *Essex Institute Historical Collections*, II (1860), 37; also, *Bulletin of the
Essex Institute*, XII (Jan.-June, 1873), 74-75.

As Lydia Very rode back from the old Danvers burying ground, where she had seen the body of her husband interred with Masonic honors, she drew her two sons close to her and thought of the past. Her years of married life had been filled with conception, with birth, and with death. Of the six children she had borne, one son, Franklin, had been blind throughout his short life of four years; another, Horace, had lived only a month. Within the year death had claimed her father, Captain Samuel Very, and now her husband. The words of the minister again sank into her consciousness: "The Lord giveth, and the Lord taketh away." But her religion sustained her, and she added forcibly, "Blessed be the name of the Lord."

Early next morning old Isaac Very came in to talk of money matters and to settle his son's slender estate.[21] Lydia Very was not on too friendly terms with her husband's family, and even before the birth of her youngest child in November of the previous year, she had sometimes lived in her father's home at Buffum's Corner.[22] But she respected old Isaac's grey hairs and she admired the sturdy carriage of his firm body, which eighty years on sea and land had failed to weaken greatly. It was his fourth wife who had caused the slight rupture in family relationship. But for the moment a mutual sorrow reunited them, and they read with moist eyes the last will and testament of Jones Very (No. 325, Salem Marine Society), Master Mariner:

In the name of God amen. I, Jones Very, of Salem, a citizen of the United States, do make, ordain and declare this instrument, which is written with my own hand, to be my last will and testiment, revoking all others, viz.—
To my beloved wife Lydia Very I give and bequeath the income of fifteen hundred dollars as long as she remains my widow and no longer; the principle I give to my children, Jones V., Jr., Washington V., Franceis L. V. and Lydia Ann V., one thousand dollars each; the remainder of my property of whatsoever name or nature, I give and bequeath to the following persons, viz.—my father Isaac Very, my

[21] Essex County, Mass., *Probate Book* 405, pp. 482-485.
[22] See sketch by Lydia L. A. Very, sister of the poet, preserved in the Essex Institute. The pencil sketch is designated as "Birthplace of Lydia L. A. Very," and is different from another sketch bearing the inscription "Birthplace of Jones Very."

brothers Nathaniel V. and Abraham V., and sisters Sarah Herelton, Margret Harwood, Mary Very, and my *neice* Nancy Manning.

Salem, 8 Oct., 1824   Jones Very

P. S. I appoint my father Isaac Very, executor of the within: the situation of my property is as follows, viz.

One note against William Gray					$4000
Two do	do	Benj. Chever	$500		
			$500	1000	
One do	do	Wm. G. Very		500	
One do	do	John Very		250	
				5750	
Cash on hand to be let				1250	
				7000[23]	

"Where is the twelve hundred and fifty dollars mentioned here?" asked Captain Isaac when he had finished reading the will.

"I do not know where it is," came Lydia Very's hasty reply.

"Jones also owned a quadrant and sextant and spy glass. You should also deliver them to me, for I am my son's executor."

"Yes, but I am your son's wife, and these are his children; it seems to me that we have the best right to them."

"There is no proof that you are his wife," retaliated the old man.

Lydia Very's cheeks burned with indignation; her eyes flamed with anger. But she did not rail against her kinsman. She bit her lips to keep back the tears and to hide her shame at such a charge. Then she said calmly: "For twelve years I have had a marriage certificate in my chamber upstairs. I will show it to you."

"You needn't trouble yourself to go for it, for you shan't find it there."

His threat proved true.[24] Her search was fruitless; she knew she had been outwitted. As she came back downstairs, her face was seared with humiliation and thwarted vindication. But she stood her ground and yielded no point. Stirred to the very depths of her womanhood, she gathered her four children around her and resolved to protect their interests with all her intellect and, if need be, even with her physical strength. When old Captain Isaac again

[23] Essex County, Mass., *Probate Book* (Wills), 404, p. 337.

[24] Essex County, Mass., *Probate Book* 405, pp. 482-485. The conversation corresponds with the questions and answers recorded at the trial which followed the quarrel. For a complete record, see Appendix I.

demanded the money, his daughter-in-law in a voice stern and icily calm answered: "I know nothing of the gold, but I suspect that your wife has taken it. As for the quadrant, sextant, and spy glass, I have been advised by my attorney, Mr. Foster, not to give them up until they have been appraised."

The old sea captain realized that he had met his match. It was Very against Very. This woman was no shrinking, yielding, irresolute dependent. Her abundant common sense and her keen intellect were equaled only by her indomitable spirit. Her father had called her "plucky"; but Captain Isaac thought her provokingly obstinate. He resolved to show her, however, that Massachusetts law was stronger than mere female stubbornness, and as he strode out of the room his mind was already formulating plans for legal action. In the months that followed, the estate of Jones Very, Master Mariner, was appraised, but since the whereabouts of the twelve hundred and fifty dollars was unknown, that amount was not included in the appraisal. In fact, the matter was not settled until the following year (1826), when at the July term of the Essex County Probate Court, the administrator made complaint and accused Lydia Very of concealing, embezzling, or conveying away the money, and accordingly petitioned that the defendant be examined upon oath. But Lydia Very was victorious. The court could find no fault with her testimony. Her answers were quick, direct, and pertinent, and her statements corroborated her original version of the story related to her father-in-law at the time of her husband's death.[25]

This experience established a local reputation for Lydia Very as a woman of marked poise, intelligence, and capability. Her neighbors came to realize that she could not be imposed upon; all of them respected her, and some even feared her. In fact, a few of the older Salem citizens muttered under their breaths that she had always been a fiery soul, stirred deeply by religious zeal, and that she was a bit too fearless and aggressive for a normal woman. But one might expect as much, for she had a surplus of Very courage in her blood. Her own mother had been the daugh-

[25] See records of Essex County, Mass.: *ibid.,* pp. 482-485, 503-504; *Probate Book* 58, p. 99; *Probate Book* 35, No. 205.

ter of Bridget Very's great-grandson, John Very, and her Putney
blood certainly could not dominate the Very streams of both her
parents. And now she, in turn, had married her first cousin. No
wonder that one child had been born blind and another had been
too weak to survive longer than a month. One might do well to
watch the four living children; they certainly would be either
geniuses or fools.

Lydia Very heard such rumors, but her hours were so completely filled with household duties and the formulating of plans
for the coming years that she paid little heed to wagging of tongues.
Three of her children were too small to be of any immediate
assistance in providing for the family, and Jones, if she had her
way, should not jeopardize his future by neglecting his books. And
so she kept the boy in school, jealously watching his phenomenal
progress and his keen interest in all his studies.

It was during these years immediately following the death of
Captain Jones Very that young Jones was stamped indelibly with
his mother's influence. Almost desperately concerned with the wel-
fare of her children, Lydia Very gave to them all her physical
strength, all the power of her intellect, and all the product of her
resourceful spirit and her decisive character. Mutual sorrow
strengthened and intensified the tender love between widow and
children and between brothers and sisters, and love produced a
delight and even eagerness in sacrifice for each other. Thus, the
young widow was able to preserve her family intact in spite of her
slender means. They lived simply but happily together, each work-
ing to the interest of the others, their resourceful natures and keenly
alert minds compensating for material comforts which their neighbors found indispensable. The mother's fondness for all natural
objects took root in the lives of all her children, and though this
nature-love expressed itself mainly as a sensuous delight in Lydia
and Frances, it inspired a scientific interest in Washington, and a
deeply spiritual feeling in Jones. The Verys became noted for their
flowers. Even the tenderest plants responded quickly to their care,
and in the coldest Massachusetts winter geraniums bloomed in their
living room. The Salem folk often sought Mrs. Very's advice concerning the nurture of flowers, the curing of plant diseases, and

the preparation of the soil. They watched her move about her garden and noticed the gentle yet capable care she lavished upon even the most insignificant shrub or common perennial.[26]

The assiduous protection of the weak members of her garden was occasioned only partly by her love of plants; in addition, it was an entirely natural outgrowth of Lydia Very's hatred of oppression. Her own recent experiences with her husband's relatives had fanned the flame of resentment against persecution of any living thing. She looked back over her married life, remembered the valiant struggle her husband had waged against consumption, and realized that his intense suffering and early death had resulted from the effects of imprisonment in Nova Scotia. She was a widow and her children were orphans because of such cruelty. And then she recalled the humiliating scene with her father-in-law and the further harassment when she was summoned to court and questioned at length concerning the disappearance of Captain Very's gold. The fact that men could be cruel and unjust had impressed itself deep in her consciousness and had seared her spirit; only a deluge of kindness and fair dealing could ever free her memory from its unhappy burden or wash away the stains from her wounded heart. And, consequently, she bestowed her protection on every weak and hurt thing she found: first, upon her children, and, afterwards, upon her flowers. But even then the fountainhead of her love stream ran full and strong, and overflowed to succor animals. She tenderly cared for wounded birds, and she offered a home to all the stray cats and forsaken kittens in her neighborhood.

This excess of love for plants and animals was shared in large measure by all the Very children, but especially by Jones. Love of nature, in part, also accounted for the poet's satisfaction with only the simple and natural, and his absolute disinterestedness in anything approaching the artificial. It was also responsible for his habitual long walks throughout the Essex countryside and up and

[26] For information concerning the domestic life of the Verys, the author is indebted to the following residents of Salem: Miss Harriet I. Wilkins, who, when a young girl, moved to her present home just opposite the house occupied by the Verys; Miss Carrie Martin; Miss Jennie Dale Fuller; and Miss Charlotte Nichols (now deceased), who lived in the Very house immediately following the death of Miss Lydia Very.

down the seashore near Salem, and for his familiarity with the spots where the hepatica, the bloodroot, and the violets first appeared and where, in the pasture lands, the Mayflowers grew in greatest abundance. But it also inspired his sympathy for injured birds or for creatures imprisoned from their natural habitat.

In an environment saturated with this atmosphere of nature and dominated by his mother's decisive and liberally expressed personality, Jones Very spent the most plastic period of his life. For three years after his father's death he attended the Hacker Grammar School on Dean Street, where he became known for his seriousness, his marked reserve, and his studious habits.[27] The latter won recognition at least once, for on August 28, 1826, when Jones Very was quietly celebrating his thirteenth birthday, the School Committee of the Town of Salem presented to the boy as a prize a copy of *Biographia Americana; or a Historical and Critical Account of the Lives, Actions and Writings of the Most Distinguished Persons in North America,* written "by a Gentleman of Philadelphia," and published in New York the previous year. In the front of the book was pasted a neatly printed plate, reading as follows:

At a Meeting of the School Committee of the Town of Salem, at the Town Hall, August 28, 1826, (being the day of the Annual Examination)— This Book was presented to *Jones Very,* a pupil in the *West* School, in testimony of the approbation of his Master and of the Committee, for his diligence and proficiency in his studies, and for his exemplary conduct and strict attention to the regulations of the School.

A. L. Peirson, Chairman.

Oliver C. Felton, Instructor.[28]

But though Jones Very undoubtedly was secretly proud of his school record, he was ever an extremely modest, even shy boy; and

[27] William P. Andrews, "Memoir," p. 5, *Poems by Jones Very;* hereinafter referred to as *Andrews.* Also letter from the Rev. Chas. T. Brooks, in *Bulletin of the Essex Institute,* XIII (Jan.-June, 1881), 29. Brooks, born in Salem, in 1813, was a lifelong friend of Jones Very.

[28] This book is preserved in the Abernethy Library of American Literature, of Middlebury College, Middlebury, Vt. The curator, Miss Viola C. White, kindly furnished the author with a copy of the plate referring to Jones Very. The plate is printed, except for the names (in italics above), which are written in in ink. An interesting feature is a penciled scrawl near the bottom of the plate: "My birthday AE 13 yrs," and at the very bottom, also in pencil, "AE 13."

he entered into few of the sports and recreations of his fellows. Yet with a playmate he sometimes walked the short distance down the hill to North River, left his clothes on Cook's Wharf, and plunged into the small, clear stream.[29] And in midsummer he often rambled through the Great Pasture in search of berries, and in autumn he gathered nuts from Pope's Pasture. For in those years of the early nineteenth century the Hacker School was in a secluded and quiet neighborhood, surrounded by pleasant pasture lands and refreshed by breezes from wood and field and unpolluted river.[30] Such idyllic charm was remembered by Jones Very, and just at the close of the Civil War, when the citizens of Salem were clamoring for a new structure to replace the worn-out Hacker schoolhouse,[31] he wrote in a reminiscent mood the following bit of verse:

THE HACKER SCHOOLHOUSE

Swift fly the years! Men call thee mean and old,
But I behold thee still as in thy prime;
The scroll of Memory quickly is unrolled,
Wherein I read of childhood's early time;
Of that first morn, when, finished, bright, and new,
We took our seats within thy well-built walls;
The master's voice I hear, his form I view,
As to his place, in order, each he calls.
Again I see,—it was a beauteous sight!—
Adorned with evergreen and summer flowers;
The parents sharing in their sons' delight,
And gay the schoolhouse looked as garden bowers.
Thus ever stand, flower-wreathed and fair and new,
A picture bright for Memory to view![32]

The concluding lines of the poem undoubtedly refer to the close of the session in 1827, for in that year Jones Very entered an auction room in Salem as errand and store boy, and sought to assist his mother in providing for her family.[33] By this time he was a tall lad for his fourteen years, fairly robust in physique, and unusually mature in his intellect. He found his new duties exceedingly dis-

[29] For Very's poetizing of such experiences, see "The Song," *Clarke,* p. 77; it is also found in the other editions.
[30] "Reminiscences of the Hacker School," Salem *Gazette,* March 19, 1875.
[31] Salem *Register,* June 25, 1865.
[32] *Clarke,* p. 495. [33] *Andrews,* pp. 5 ff.

tasteful, but his determined character and persistent ambition were
sufficient to compel a conscientious discharge of even the most
irksome of his duties. For already he desired to lead a literary
life. He read many of the books that were brought to the auction
room, purchased those his limited means would permit, and spent
most of his spare hours in study. One day while browsing among
some boxes of old books, he found a copy of Shakespeare and
bought it. Later, having discovered it to be a rare and valuable
edition, he exchanged his Shakespeare for the textbooks needed to
fit him for college.[34] In the preparation of his studies he was
greatly assisted by J. Fox Worcester, an erudite gentleman engaged
in fitting young men for Harvard, who had become very much
interested in the precocious boy in the auction room. Through the
influence of his tutor, young Very secured an assistantship in the
private Latin school presided over by Henry K. Oliver, and, along
with his own duties of preparing boys for entrance to the freshman
class at Harvard, pursued the studies of the first and part of the
second collegiate years under that gentleman.[35]

Meanwhile Lydia Very was making preparation for her family's social as well as economic future. In 1827 she had persuaded
Benjamin Cheever, guardian for her children, to purchase a dwelling on River Street,[36] but by 1833 the family had bought a plain,
comfortable home at 154 Federal Street, where Mrs. Very and her
four children lived until their deaths.[37] And the life on Federal
Street was full and happy. The house was attractively situated on
a plot of ground which, though narrow, extended for several hundred feet down a gentle slope to North River. Such a natural
location offered excellent possibilities to a family so fond of the
out-of-doors as were the Verys, and in a few years visitors to the
Federal Street home were shown the terraced garden, planned and
lovingly tended by Lydia Very and her children. A brick walk
bordered with boxwood extended down the center of the garden
to the edge of the stream below. White clematis and purple wis-
taria clambered over arbors on either side of the walk, and many

---

[34] *Ibid.*, p. 6.   [35] *Ibid.*
[36] Essex County *Deeds* (Grantees), 244, p. 195.
[37] *Ibid.*, 268, p. 281.

beds of brilliantly hued flowers attracted humming birds at the close of day. Here Jones Very spent much of his spare time reading and studying, and here he sought inspiration for many of his nature sonnets.[38] He had felt the urge to create verse even in the days spent in the auction room, and acquaintance with poets gained through his own reading and through the inspiration of Worcester and Oliver inspired him further. He modestly showed his early efforts to these gentlemen, and by the summer of 1833, he was occasionally offering his poems to the Salem *Observer*.

The first of these to be published had no title, and appeared on August 10, 1833, under the caption "Original Poetry for the Salem Observer." The name of the author was concealed, the poem being followed by the date of composition (July 24, 1833) and by the letter "I."[39] This poem is clearly an early attempt; in form and diction it is plainly imitative of those late eighteenth-century poets whose works reflect the transition from the Augustan to the Romantic era. It is written in the heroic couplet,[40] suggests the "landscape" scenes of James Thomson's and of Cowper's verse, and in spirit shows sympathy with nature and man and the acceptance of events as divinely ordained. The opening lines are representative:

> The earth is parched with heat, flowers droop and die,
> The clouds of dust fly whirling through the sky;
> The cattle lowing seek the friendly shade,
> By lofty rock or some dark forest made.
> The traveller spent with toil, by heat oppressed,
> Near some tall oak, exhausted, sinks to rest;
> And dreams of home, of all his soul holds dear,
> Dreams not, alas! of fatal danger near.[41]

Three days after the appearance of this poem, Very wrote a stirring forty-line protest against slavery, which the *Observer* published on August 24. It, too, is in the heroic couplet, but the spirited hatred of cruelty and oppression and the genuine sympathy

---

[38] See n. 26; also Lydia L. A. Very's *An Old-Fashioned Garden*.

[39] Jones Very thus signed all his verse in the *Observer* until after the publication of his *Essays and Poems* in late September, 1839. From October 5 of that year, the poems which he published in the Salem newspapers bore his name.

[40] The first and last lines, however, have six iambic feet.

[41] Salem *Observer*, Aug. 10, 1833. Cf. the passages describing the storm in "Autumn" of *The Seasons;* also ll. 340-352 of Book IV of Cowper's *The Task*.

with the lowly and oppressed are in the vein of pure romantic
literature.[42] Indeed, a number of lines recall Goldsmith's "The
Deserted Village" and Crabbe's "The Village," and, though differ-
ing in form, remind one strongly of the passages against slavery in
Book II of Cowper's *The Task*.

By December, 1833, the youthful poet had essayed blank verse,
his subject being the neighborhood cemetery of Mount Auburn.[43]
The serious, didactic lines are heavy with the graveyard atmosphere
and suggest portions of Young's "Night Thoughts" and Blair's
"The Grave."[44] At Christmastide, melancholy temporarily gave
way to a feeling of wonder at the birth of Christ. In the simple,
fragmentary "Lines Suggested by Hearing the Beach at F. Peabody's Mills, South Salem," one senses the mystic rapture felt by
a spirit already hypersensitive to the voice of nature and of God:

> The silent moon is rising
> O'er the hills of purest snow;
> The river silent flowing
> In its deep bed below.[45]

Jones Very's melancholy was due partly to his dissatisfaction
with his station in life. He was unwilling to be a mere town-
rhymster or a petty tutor, and he yearned to fit himself for great
works. All the while his heart was set on Cambridge, but his
slender means afforded little encouragement. At length, early in
1834, an uncle offered to supplement his meager savings sufficiently
to enable Jones to enter Harvard.[46] Perhaps in the few days immediately preceding his removal to Cambridge, he wrote the following stanza:

> Home of my youth! Where first my lot was cast,
> To Thee I dedicate my feeble song.
> Upon whose hills how swift the moment passed,
> As linked with flowers the days moved easily on.

[42] Salem *Observer*, Aug. 24, 1833.

[43] The poem bears the title, "Lines on Mount Auburn, December, 1833." See
Brown University MSS.

[44] Cf. ll. 487-536 of "Night III. Narcissa" from Young's "Night Thoughts," and
ll. 714-767 of Blair's "The Grave."   [45] See Brown University MSS.

[46] *Andrews*, p. 6; also, by the same author, "An Inspired Life," *The Century
Magazine*, II (Oct. 1, 1882), 852-862.

Though hills more fair and streams more bright than thine
May lure my eye, as from thy paths I stray,
While memory's ray shall on their summits shine,
What spot shall seem more fair to me than they?[47]

Certainly, at the time Very left Salem he wrote "Haunts of my youth, farewell!" and succeeded in expressing with marked sincerity his devotion to old Salem. The poem closes with a pledge of undying love:

. . . for there's no winter in my love
For thee, no age but death. Amid the snows
Of age 'twill like the evergreen appear
As fresh as in my vernal prime.[48]

The young aspirant went to Cambridge in February, 1834, and because of his studies under Oliver was allowed to enter the second term of the sophomore year.[49]

This marked the great turning-point in Jones Very's life and in that of his family. The old links that connected the Verys with the sea were definitely broken when Jones made his pilgrimage to Cambridge and matriculated at the college founded through the generosity of John Harvard. Henceforth, the Verys were to be scholars, preachers, artists, teachers, and scientists. Only ten years had passed since Captain Jones Very had died, believing that his son would continue in the family's heritage of seamanship, but the maritime prominence of Salem and the Verys declined simultaneously, and just as the city of Salem sought to sustain its life through participation in varied industries independent of its waning ocean commerce, so the Verys in the person of Jones turned

[47] See Brown University MSS. [48] *Ibid.*
[49] Andrews in the "Memoir" and in "The Life and Services to Literature of Jones Very," *Bulletin of the Essex Institute,* XIII (Jan.-June, 1881), 5, states erroneously that Very entered Harvard in the last term of the sophomore year. The catalogue of Harvard University for 1833-34, p. 24, states: "The academical year is divided into three Terms and three Vacations." Since Very matriculated at Harvard in February, 1834, he entered as a second-term sophomore. Most subsequent commentators on Very have used Andrews as a source and have thus repeated his error. Griswold, in *The Poets and Poetry of America* (Philadelphia, 1852), p. 404, states that Very entered Harvard in 1832; Emerson furnished this information, reasoning erroneously, because he knew that Very graduated in 1836, that the date of entrance had been four years earlier.

their eyes inland, felt the pulse beat of a changing New England life, and threw away quadrant, sextant, and spyglass. Henceforth, their voyages were to be inland, through that quiet and mystic land of the spirit, where one hears the voice of nature in all its variety of tone and harmony, and where one sometimes comes face to face with the clear, white lightning of truth.

CHAPTER II

LIFE AT HARVARD

WHEN JONES VERY entered Harvard, he appeared somewhat older than his twenty years would warrant. His boyish shyness had disappeared, but his reticence had clung to him persistently.[1] Yet he possessed an abundance of self-reliance, confidence, and fearlessness inherited from his forbears and developed by his experiences in auction room and school. For eight years he had earned his own living and had assisted his mother in caring for the younger children. The bearing of such responsibilities not only had made him conscious of material values, but had intensified his seriousness and had quickened his responsiveness to the opportunities offered for intellectual advancement. When he came to Cambridge, therefore, he was charged with mental energy and was spurred on by the curiosity of youthful genius and the hunger of unsatisfied ambition. He knew that his college training had been delayed, that he was older than his classmates, and that in order to compensate for his delayed entrance at Cambridge he must waste[2] no time and must pursue all of his prescribed tasks diligently. This he did, but he also kept faith with his kindred and friends at home. They expected verse from him, and he was determined that they should not be disappointed. In April he sent to the Salem *Observer* a thirty-one-line poem[3]—his third published work—of particular significance. In this piece he forsakes the heroic couplet for a sometimes imperfect blank verse, and discusses the relationship of God and nature. Though crude, the poem clearly indicates the influence of Wordsworth. The opening line— "Hast thou ever heard the voice of nature"—indicates, even at this early stage of Very's poetic career, the ultimate trend of his love for nature; and the concluding lines—

[1] *Andrews*, p. 7.

[2] "Jones Very, the Finest Song Writer in America . . . ," Boston *Sunday Herald*, May 16, 1880.

[3] See Appendix II, No. 3. The poem was published in the Salem *Observer*, April 26, 1834, but it bears the date of April 7, 1834.

. . . learn oft' as upon thy sight or
Ear they fall to think of him who made them—

show his lamentable fondness for the moral tag, and his occasionally objectionable seriousness.

But in spite of his serious attitude, Jones Very soon encountered difficulty in the form of the famous Dunkin rebellion. This demonstration of student opposition to the authorities at Harvard began on May 19, 1834, when one Maxwell, a student in the freshman Greek class, refused to recite in the manner his tutor, Mr. Dunkin, required. After several interviews between President Josiah Quincy and the rebellious students had resulted in the support of Dunkin by the administration of the College, the entire freshman class created great disturbance and commotion by smashing the furniture in the Greek recitation room and by breaking dormitory windows. Ultimately, the entire student body was drawn into the controversy. On May 21 the sophomore class expressed its disapproval of the stand taken by the faculty by attending morning prayers in a body and by such persistent groaning and scraping of feet that services could not be completed. After commons, the entire class, with three exceptions, was dismissed. This action was immediately followed by a demonstration of sympathy by the other classes, when, according to the Steward's estimate, property of the College was damaged to the extent of three hundred dollars. On the same day the juniors and seniors made further disturbance at evening prayers, and when one junior was dismissed the class voted to wear crepe on the left arm for three weeks, to publish articles in the papers relative to President Quincy, and "to burn him in effigy."[4] So intense was the feeling of dissatisfaction among the students, and so prevalent was rebellion to authority that on June 2 the faculty voted to appeal to the tribunals of the State of Massachusetts.[5]

It appears from the records of the faculty at Harvard that Jones Very was one of three sophomores not immediately dismissed, his

---

[4] *Circular* of the Senior Class in 1834, Relative to the Rebellion in that Year, the Boston Public Library, *Circular* 4483.121; also, *Tracts by Josiah Quincy, President,* in the Boston Public Library, C in 4394.109.
[5] *Ibid.*

companions being James Chisholm, of Salem, and a student named Scates. Since Chisholm was a monitor for another class, his duties prevented his march of protestation into chapel with the rest of the sophomores;[6] he was, therefore, exonerated. Scates and Very apparently found it difficult to escape the organized rebellion and were, consequently, listed among those sophomores to be dismissed. They both protested, however, as the minutes of the faculty for June 16, 1834, clearly show: "The case of Scates and Very having been considered and long discussed, it was finally voted that they must be considered among the dismissed sophomores."[7] Thus Jones Very experienced during his first year at Harvard a short period of rustication. But the days in Salem and the surrounding country-side were happily spent, as lines from a poem dated June 8, 1834, prove:

> What more delightful than to wander forth
> In spring, before the sun has chased away
> The freshness of the morn; or shook the dew
> From off the tender grass?[8]

In this poem, even though the vehicle for expression be a somewhat crude and prosaic blank verse, one senses a spontaneity of emotion, a lively imagination, and a communion with nature and God enjoyed most by him who is both a mystic and a poet. Another blank verse poem, "Death of Lafayette,"[9] appeared in the Salem *Observer* for June 28. The poem is dated June 21, 1834, and was, therefore, also written during the enforced vacation. Undoubtedly Very recalled Lafayette's second visit to Salem on August 31, 1824, the same day he and his ill father arrived from Boston after their last voyage. The tone of this poem is dignified, mellowly sonorous; the feeling of grief is strong but restrained; and the expression of love of liberty and hatred of tyranny is worthy of a mature poet.

The *Observer* by the close of the summer had published five other poems by Very. The first three of these—"Old Age,"[10] on

---

[6] David Holmes Conrad, *Memoir of Rev. James Chisholm, A.M.* (New York, 1856), p. 14.

[7] *Records of the College Faculty*, XI (1829-1840), 50. This volume is preserved in the Archives of the Widener Library, Cambridge, Mass.

[8] See Chapter VIII, Poem 8, in Brown University MSS.

[9] See Appendix II, Poem No. 4.   [10] See Appendix II, Poem No. 5.

July 5; "Lines—Suggested by Seeing a Butterfly Sculptured upon a
Tomb,"[11] on July 12; "Kind Words,"[12] on July 19—were inferior,
unimportant, and uninteresting poems. The fourth, "Pleasure,"[13]
published on August 2, is significant. It is an attempt to incor-
porate in blank verse, so irregular that it seriously threatens to be
free verse, the pleasures of retirement and introspection. The subject matter is undoubtedly the result of Very's temporary absence
from Cambridge; the diction suggests late eighteenth-century influ-
ences—a blending of Classicism and Romanticism—; and certain
lines indicate Very's acquaintance with Satan's speech to Beelzebub
in Book I of *Paradise Lost.* The following lines are indicative:

> Goddess of pleasure, where thy golden car? . . .[14]
> Ask him, who led astray o'er the treach'rous bogs,
> Is wandering; ask of him where shines the light,
> Which that he follows seems:—"At home," he says,
> There, pleasure, rest thy golden car. The mind
> Is its own home.[15]
>
> .   .   .   .
>
> It is the mind, communing with itself,
> That casts a sunshine on the paths of life.

The fifth poem in question bore the title "Stanzas,"[16] and showed
Very's preference for manly, yet nature-loving, gentle, and kind
friends. Surely, there is a flavor of Burns in the opening and closing stanzas:

> Give me an eye that manly deeds
> Shall kindle up with living fire;
> That rolls enraptur'd at the strains
> Resounding from the heroic lyre.
>
> Is there who has an eye like this,
> To dwell forever next my heart;
> To share my joy, to share my grief,
> And to my breast his own impart?[17]

[11] See Appendix II, Poem No. 6.
[12] See Appendix II, Poem No. 7.   [13] See Appendix II, Poem No. 8.
[14] Cf. John Gay's "The Fan," Bk. I, ll. 140-176.
[15] Cf. *Paradise Lost,* Bk. I, ll. 252-255.
[16] Salem *Observer,* Aug. 16, 1834; *Clarke,* pp. 165-166.
[17] Cf. Burns's "Lines to John Lapraik," ll. 73-78; and "A Man's a Man for
A'That."

The closing days of August, Very spent in writing a poem of autobiographic significance. This was "My Brother Franklin,"[18] another blank verse piece and an excellent example of Very at his best and his worst. Already a lover of the Greek language, he had saturated his mind with passages from Greek literature and had absorbed phrases so completely that certain words had become a part of his being, even as the word *Endymion* had sunk into the very life of Keats. Is not the following passage reminiscent of Keats?

> . . . his voice—sweet as nightingale's,
> That in some lone vale of Attica,
> 'Midst ivy dark, sits warbling her plaintive
> Notes. Entranced, the shepherd, as he
> Hies him home with quicken'd pace, unconscious
> Of delay, lingers to hear her evening
> Song.

One would choose to prolong the spell of other-worldliness, to retain the lyric rapture of these lines; but Very's sense of the artistic is seldom equal to his stern obedience to duty. He must, if possible, draw a moral; and this he does, completely spoiling the poem. Recalling his blind brother's capturing of a bee in his chubby hands, and the sting which resulted, Very concludes: "Let us from this / A moral draw." In the closing lines of the poem, Very's allegory necessitates the changing of the blue-eyed, golden-haired boy Franklin—blind from his infancy—into seeing men; the bee becomes vice; and the child's experience in his mother's garden becomes symbolic of human life. The treatment of subject matter in this poem is, unfortunately, representative of much of Very's verse: the sensuous and the saintly often did not mix artistically.

"My Brother Franklin" marked the close of Very's poetic efforts for the summer of 1834. The succeeding few months were to be filled with academic duties. On August 23, he and his dismissed classmates were voted by the faculty to readmission to the college "after the Commencement," upon a new examination and a certificate of "good conduct"; and on August 30 Very was one of sixteen "admitted to the Junior Class on probation."[19]

[18] Salem *Observer*, Aug. 30, 1834; *Clarke*, pp. 169-171.
[19] *Records of the College Faculty*, XI (1829-1840), 179; also *Tracts of Josiah Quincy, President*—in Boston Public Library, Catalogue No. C 4394.109.

Having conformed to these provisos, Jones Very entered upon his junior year at Harvard. He quickly gained a reputation for serious, prolonged study and thorough scholarship. Though he excelled in ancient and modern literature, his chief interest was religion. Feeling that the college administration failed to offer sufficient opportunity to the students for religious worship, he and his roommate, Thomas Barnard West, also of Salem, encouraged the organization of a society for religious improvement. In their senior year, when, with James Chisholm,[20] they occupied the whole upper story of the third entry of Holworthy, they often gathered together a small group of students on Sunday evenings and spent an hour or so singing hymns.[21]

Such activities in a college environment naturally marked Jones Very as a student too sedate and earnestly religious to be widely popular; yet his simple modesty, his genuine sympathy, and his quiet cheerfulness won for him a small group of warmly attached friends. And even those who were not intimate with him respected and reverenced him, for there was in his face the reflection of purity of character and serenity of spirit which stamped him early as a saint. In fact, his sweet benignity marked him as a young man of intuition and mysticism. Even in those days he did not hesitate to reveal to his intimate friends that he felt himself chosen to impart a great message to mankind,[22] and that, like Milton, he

[20] This young man afterwards migrated to Virginia as a tutor, later entering the Theological Seminary at Alexandria. After his confirmation by Bishop Meade in October, 1840, he was associated for a time with the family of Senator Rives, of "Castle Hill," Albemarle County, in a tutorial capacity. While awaiting a regular pastorate, he also acted as tutor for the children of Senator Rives's sister, at "Bentivoglio." He died of fever, in Portsmouth, Va., in September, 1855, having sacrificed his life in seeking to succor his parishioners during the epidemic of that year.

[21] See letter from Jones Very to David Holmes Conrad in *Memoir of Rev. James Chisholm, A.M.*, pp. 12-13. Referring to Chisholm, Very wrote: "He was a member with Thomas Barnard West, of Salem, now deceased, and myself, of a small Society for religious improvement, which held meetings once a week, during most of my college course. I remember these meetings with great satisfaction, as hours well and happily spent; and I doubt not that they were so remembered by all who participated in them. During the senior year, Mr. Chisholm, Mr. West, and myself occupied the whole upper story of the third entry, in Holworthy. James was fond of singing, and often on Sabbath evenings he would enter my room and say: 'Come, let us sing some hymns'; and we spent many Sabbath evenings in singing together."   [22] *Andrews*, pp. 8-9.

must keep himself pure and unspotted from the world, so that he might himself "be a true poem, . . . a composition and pattern of the best and honorablest things."[23] He, therefore, participated in none of the sports or revels of his classmates, but stuck strictly to academic duties and his own religious and literary pursuits.

The latter, having been inactive for about four months, revived at the turn of the year. On January 3, 1835, the *Observer* published Very's "The New Year,"[24] in which he expressed his delight in struggling with the snow and wind of a winter storm in New England. The same storm furnished material for one of the few exceptions to Very's serious verse, for "The Sleigh Ride,"[25] dated January 5, 1835, is a joyous, full-throated lyric, saturated with the vigorous and zestful spirit of lighthearted youth.

With the coming of spring, Very wrote "The Snow Drop,"[26] which, in spite of its very obvious imitation of Burns's "To a Mountain Daisy" in both its stanza form and its diction, has a personal, individual flavor about it which is so charming and sincere as to make it approach freshness and originality. The same stanza form was used for "To the Humming Bird,"[27] but the spirit and the diction are Very's own. Happy is he who becomes acquainted with Very by reading first a lyric so characteristic of the poet's best verse. It is not strange that Emerson later chose it to lead the poems appearing in the edition which he sponsored—that of 1839. This poem is intensely romantic in its lyric expression of sympathy with animal life. Less lyric is another bird poem, "The Snow Bird," the manuscript of which reads "Cambridge, 1836." The resemblance in tone and thought to William Cullen Bryant's "To a Waterfowl," published eighteen years earlier, is noticeable. The poem represents Very in a mood more religious than artistic. As he sat in Holworthy Hall contemplating the Divine Spirit, he saw spiritual significance even in the coming of the snowbird to his window. To him the event revealed God's constant love and con-

[23] Milton, *Apology for Smectymnuus.*
[24] Also in *Clarke*, pp. 167-168.   [25] See Appendix II, Poem No. 9.
[26] Salem *Observer*, April 11, 1835; *Clarke*, pp. 173-174.
[27] Salem *Observer*, Aug. 8, 1835. The poem is included in the three editions of Very's works.

cern for all his creatures; and when the bird had flown away, he wrote:

> Thou'st fled—and gone, perhaps to find
> Thy playmates of the blast;
> I bless thee—for thou left'st behind
> Thine image ere thou passed,
>
> And bid me feel that He, whose eye
> Thy wants doth pitying see
> And through the wintry time supply,
> Will surely succor me.[28]

Doubtless, a kindred mood, though tinged with nostalgia, occasioned the contemporary poem, "My Mother's Voice."[29] Spring again provoked a nature poem; this time, the columbine—though only a painted one—offered inspiration.[30] By June, Very had written his "Hymn" to be sung at the dedication of the New Stone Church of the North Society in Salem.[31]

During Very's senior year at Harvard, eight of his poems appeared in *Harvardiana*, a literary magazine published by the students and lasting from 1834 to 1838. Six of these pieces had already appeared in the Salem *Observer*, but "King Philip" and "Lines to— on the Death of a Friend" owe their first printing to the Harvard magazine.[32] Very, therefore, came to be known at Harvard as a student-poet of more than average ability.

But he never allowed the creation of verse to offer an obstacle to the fulfilment of his academic duties. His close and regular attention to the routine of study enabled him to participate in three Public Exhibitions,[33] to win twice the coveted Bowdoin prize[34]—a

[28] Salem *Observer*, Jan. 2, 1836; also *Clarke*, pp. 168-169.

[29] Salem *Observer*, June 4, 1836; also *Clarke*, p. 157.

[30] "The Painted Columbine"; it appeared in the *Observer* on April 23, 1836. Also, see *Clarke*, p. 157.

[31] Salem *Observer*, June 25, 1836; *Clarke*, p. 334.

[32] See *Harvardiana*, II (1835-1836), 133-139, 377. For the other poems, see the Bibliography.

[33] See, in the Harvard College Archives, *Exhibition and Commencement Performances—1834-1835*. Jones Very participated as follows: April 28, 1835, "A Greek Version. Extract from Webster's 'Oration at Plymouth' "; Oct. 20, 1835, "Mathematical Exercises"; May 3, 1836, "An English Oration,—'The Heroic Character.' "

[34] The manuscripts of Very's prize dissertations are in the Archives of the Widener Library at Harvard University: *Bowdoin Prize Dissertations*, VI (1835-

feat which had never previously been accomplished[35]—and to tie
with Robert Bartlett, of Plymouth, in achieving the highest scholas-
tic average in the senior class. But, in view of the fact that Very
had entered as a second-term sophomore and had not pursued the
entire four-year course, Bartlett was declared by the faculty to be
entitled to first honors and Jones Very to second.[36] This apparent
difference in honor, however, was partly compensated for on class
day, when Very's "Song"[37] to the tune of "Auld Lang Syne" was
sung as a valedictory by the seniors. At the Commencement on
August 31, 1836, Jones Very delivered an English oration, "Individuality." The piece contains much that suggests those views of
excessive intellectual independence and intense religious fervor
expressed by Very later in life.[38]

But of far more value than honors to be formally recognized
at commencement time was Very's reputation for independent
thought. Both students and faculty members were sometimes
startled by the sheer clarity of his statements and the striking originality of his interpretation. Such contributions to classroom recita-
tions and to intimate personal discussions in the old yard contra-
dicted the impression held by some of the Cambridge community

---

1839), Nos. 2 and 4. Very won the first prize of $40 offered the junior class in
1834-1835, with a splendidly written piece entitled "The Practical Application in
This Life, by Men as Social and Intellectual Beings, of the Certainty of a Future
State." He won $50 in his senior year for the essay "What Reasons Are There
for Not Expecting Another Great Epic Poem?"

[35] See letter from Lydia L. A. Very to the editor of the Boston Sunday Herald,
published in that newspaper on June 6, 1880, under the heading "Jones Very
Again."

[36] Records of the College Faculty, XI (1829-1840), 281, under heading of
"Faculty Meeting, July 12, 1836." The minutes read, in part, as follows: "The
committee on the subject reported the following distribution of parts for Commencement: First English Oration, Bartlett; Second English Oration, Very."

Robert Bartlett was a brilliant youth. He became a tutor at Harvard and
received his Master's degree from that institution in 1839. He was a younger
member of the Transcendental Club and strongly expressed his faith in transcendentalism in his oration delivered upon receipt of his graduate degree. He died
in 1843, and in the next to the last number of The Dial Charles A. Dana, by way
of elegiac tribute, addressed a sonnet to him. (See Emerson's Journals, VI, 214;
also George Willis Cooke, An Historical and Biographical Introduction to Accompany The Dial, I, 166.)

[37] See Chapter VIII, Poem No. 11, in the Andover Theological Seminary MSS.

[38] The manuscript is found in Exhibition and Commencement Performances—
1834-1835.

that the unusual Salem student was rabidly bookish, and won for
him the friendship and admiration of his teacher, Professor Edward
Tyrrell Channing.[39]

This gentleman, more than any other at Harvard, exerted a
profound influence on Jones Very.[40] In the fifteen years he had
served as Boylston Professor of Rhetoric and Oratory, he had taught
hundreds of students and had come in contact with what he had
believed to be the gamut of youthful emotions and intellectual
interests; but shortly after Very entered his lecture room, the sea-
soned teacher realized that he had a student possessing a personality and a mind entirely unlike any he had known before. He,
therefore, carefully watched his new discovery, gradually led him
into literary discussions, learned of his interest in Shakespeare—
particularly in *Hamlet,* suggested readings to further the young
enthusiast's knowledge of world literature, and helped him toward
the unfolding of his own independent interpretation of both the
English and the classical writers. Jones Very responded eagerly and
strongly to Professor Channing's leadership; Homer, Vergil, Shakespeare, Milton, and Wordsworth became to him more intensely
alive, more vibrant with thought, with reason, and with emotion.
He saturated himself with readings from the works of these poets,
and added their names to his older acquaintances, such as Thomson,[41] Young, Blair, Campbell, Goldsmith, Crabbe, Cowper, Gray,
and Burns.[42] So eager was he to demonstrate his understanding of
verse and his facility in creating it, that he actually composed a
number of his required themes in verse. These exercises, as well as
his prose essays, demonstrated to a marked degree a further influence of Professor Channing—the influence of style. For Professor
Channing had always stressed the value of simple diction, clarity of
thought, and direct, natural, unadorned expression. He urged his

[39] Younger brother of the elder William Ellery Channing, and noted Unitarian
minister and abolitionist, and uncle of the poet, William Ellery Channing.

[40] See letter from R. C. Waterson, in *Bulletin of the Essex Institute,* XIII (1881),
28; also, *ibid.,* p. 29, letter from Charles T. Brooks.

[41] The author has in his possession Very's copy of *The Seasons,* printed for
Richard Scott, by D. and G. Bruce, New York, 1811; the little volume was pre-
sented to him by Miss Harriet I. Wilkins, of Salem, Mass., who acquired it from
Miss Lydia L. A. Very, after the death of Jones Very.

[42] Very was influenced strongly by Burns, as has already been shown.

students to think, to arrange their thoughts logically, and to write even to the point of exhaustion when, and only when, they felt compelled to express themselves. The latter condition he himself undertook to create. Such instruction naturally succeeded with Very, for every characteristic of his personality and every natural inclination of his mental processes fitted perfectly into such a system of literary creation. He composed carefully, simply, and slowly; he revised little; and his diction was strongly Anglo-Saxon, with some Hebraic borrowings.

Another influence, though a less powerful one, was that exerted by Edward Everett, professor of Greek literature. His oratorical and histrionic talents incited in Very an admiration less extravagant than that inspired in the youthful and impressionable Emerson a few years earlier,[43] but in the teacher's eloquence Very sensed the Greek spirit and responded to its appeal. In fact, his record in Greek at Harvard was so satisfactory that, upon his graduation on August 31, 1836,[44] he was appointed freshman tutor in that subject.

When Jones Very received his Bachelor of Arts degree, he had already made up his mind to enter the ministry He had been encouraged toward this decision by his appointment as tutor in Greek, the emolument from which would enable him to defray part of his expenses at the Divinity School. He returned to Salem for his vacation, happy that he had felt the urge to preach, and humbly proud that he had won the confidence of the faculty at Harvard. When he went back to Cambridge in the autumn, the reserve and reticence of his undergraduate days had disappeared. In their place was a quiet confidence in his own ability which quickly impressed all his associates. His energy seemed inexhaustible; from early morning until late at night he stuck doggedly to his assignments, both as a student in the Divinity School and as a tutor in the College. In fact, the teaching methods of Very and Longfellow, who also had just entered upon his career at Harvard, somewhat astonished the elder members of the faculty. Both men were friendly and sympathetic, and took a personal interest in their

[43] Emerson, at the age of sixteen, had recorded this resolution: "To make myself acquainted with the Greek language and antiquities and history with long and serious attention and study."

[44] Very's diploma is now in possession of the Essex Institute.

students. Such a change from the cool reserve and even austerity generally associated with the academic life of Cambridge was a great relief to the students, and made both men exceedingly popular. In 1863 one of Emerson's visitors recalled his indebtedness to Very and so impressed the Concord sage with Very's ability that Emerson made a significant entry in his *Journals:* "Abraham Jackson, Esq., was here yesterday, and speaks of his old experience of the College at Cambridge. He owed more to Jones Very, who was Greek tutor, than to almost any or all others in the faculty. Any enthusiasm, any literary ambition or attempt was sure to be snubbed by teachers, as well as by public opinion of the classes. Only expense, only money, was respectable."[45]

One of Jones Very's students, writing in 1880 to show his appreciation for the tutoring he had received forty-two years earlier, said:

You were my teacher of Greek in 1837-38, and your manner of instructing made a favorable impression on my mind, and produced a leaning to that language which still lasts. You were unwearied in drawing our attention to tenses, and making us translate literally—two important points in learning languages, of which, however, Mr. Felton quite lost sight. The charm with which you surrounded Greek vanished from Harvard with you. You felt the spirit of the Greek people, and were ready to communicate it to such as had ears to hear. I often used to regret your departure, and think how different it could have been could we have continued under your guidance, instead of undergoing that superficial and heartless course under the professor.[46]

It was during this second year of tutoring that Very and Thoreau, then a senior in the College, were probably drawn to each other through their mutual love of Greek literature.[47] Little did they realize then, how often they should be meeting afterwards

---

[45] IX, 504. The date is April 20, 1863.

[46] Letter, dated from Bologna, April, 1880; printed in the Salem *Gazette,* Friday morning, May 21, 1880, under the heading, "A Pupil's Testimony to Mr. Very as a Teacher." The same letter is quoted, in part, by Lydia L. A. Very in her letter to the editor of the Boston *Sunday Herald,* which appeared in that newspaper on June 6, 1880, under the title "Jones Very Again." It is regrettable that the former student's name was not given in either case.

[47] Franklin Benjamin Sanborn, *Henry D. Thoreau* ("American Men of Letters Series," Boston: Houghton, Mifflin and Co., 1882), p. 51.

in Concord at the home of Emerson, who was soon to stir Cambridge with his Phi Beta Kappa address.

Meanwhile Very claimed no great honor for his successful teaching, and in answer to compliments offered him merely said that he "only let the Greek grow." It appears, however, that the young instructor watched his students very closely and taught them diligently. He often visited them in their rooms to talk, first of Greek, but ultimately of religion. For shortly after Very entered upon his teaching duties his religious zeal became more pronounced and more self-absorbing. He conceived of God as an all-enveloping, ever-present Spirit, thoroughly and actively alive, flooding and saturating all nature and all personality, and flowing into the receptive soul with continuous enrichment. He became more and more a mystic, firm in his resolution to be pure and will-less because he felt that the Spirit communed only with him who was pure of heart and devoid of will. Often, quiet and passive, he sat in his room, contemplating the Divine Spirit. At such a time, he wrote "The Voice of God," the concluding lines of which express his deep faith in the near and constant presence of God:

> God dwells no more afar from me,
> In all that lives his voice is heard;
> From the loud shout of rolling sea
> To warbled song of morning's bird.
>
> In all that stirs the human breast,
> That wakes to mirth or draws the tear,
> In passion's storm or soul's calm rest,
> Alike the voice of God I hear.[48]

Very scattered copies of his poems among his students, or wrote them on the backs of their exercises, hoping that such verse might serve as an incentive to exalted spirituality.[49] Toward the close of the session of 1836-37, his demeanor became so serious and his conversation so thoughtful and earnest that even the least studious members of his Greek class were impressed. Soon, he very frankly

[48] *Andrews*, p. 127.
[49] *Ibid.*, p. 8; see, also, letter from one of Very's students, in *The Unitarian Review*, XXVII (Feb., 1887), 111-112; and letter from R. C. Waterson, in *Bulletin of the Essex Institute*, XIII (1881), 28.

expressed his profound conviction that God had revealed something specially to him, a message for New England youth, and he became more intent upon saving the souls of Harvard undergraduates than teaching them Greek roots and interpreting Greek literature.[50] Often, in company with a group of students, he would take long walks into the surrounding countryside, rhapsodizing on nature, truth, and goodness.[51] When his first year of tutorage had passed, he had won the reputation of being a thoroughly original and independent instructor, a man so singularly pure in thought and deed that he deserved the appellation of "saint."[52]

Indeed, there was something about Jones Very which suggested that he belonged to a life and a world different from those of his fellows. His tall, slender figure seemed too delicate for an ordinary, mundane existence, and one marveled that he had enough muscle in his gaunt legs to carry him on the seventeen-mile walks between Salem and Cambridge. His thin-lipped, sensitive mouth responded quickly to his varying moods of love and tenderness and religious ecstasy. His dark, expressive eyes fixed their trustful gaze intently on everything they encountered, and often seemed to penetrate even to the very soul of a man. His face, though angular, was sculpturesque and suggested majesty, but his high brow was too pale and accentuated his thick, black hair. Yet the features of Very bore the stamp of serenity which comes from long and deep communion with holy thoughts. For there was undoubtedly a spirit about this man, a spirit pure and noble that had been kindled at the very altar of God; and it burned with a flame so strong and beautiful that it had purged the flesh of all its worldliness and had left on the countenance an expression of rapt benignity. At times the spirit flamed up in the man's eyes, making them brilliant with inspiration and urging him on to speech; yet it was not the beauty of his voice but the mystical message carried in his words that drew men to him and startled them with a new depth of meaning.

[50] *Andrews*, p. 8.

[51] See a letter from Will Orne White, in *Bulletin of the Essex Institute*, XIII (1881), 31-32; also "Jones Very, the Finest Song Writer in America . . .'," Boston *Sunday Herald*, May 16, 1880.

[52] Emerson called him "our brave saint" (*Journals*, V, 110, under date of Oct. 30, 1838).

No wonder, then, that James Cabot, writing years later of his remembrance of his tutor, said of Jones Very: "I well remember the tall, angular figure and the solemn, fervent face that made one turn and look when he passed."[53]

[53] *A Memoir of Ralph Waldo Emerson* (2 vols.; Boston and New York: Houghton, Mifflin and Co., 1890), I, 348.

CHAPTER III

ELIZABETH PEABODY AND EMERSON
DISCOVER GENIUS

WHEN JONES VERY returned to Salem at the close of his first year as tutor and Divinity School student, he had been preceded by the intellectually and physically vigorous Elizabeth Peabody,[1] who had returned from Boston and had settled with her parents, her invalid brother George, and her two sisters in a large house at 53 Charter Street. This residence was bordered on the east and south by "Burying Point," the oldest cemetery in Salem, and was used by Hawthorne in his melancholy *Dolliver Romance* and *Dr. Grimshawe's Secret*. Because of the energetic and dynamic personality of Elizabeth Peabody, the house soon became the rendezvous for a small, happy circle of Salem folk, brought together by interest in art and literature, and strongly stirred by the New England Renaissance. The flowing tide of transcendentalism, abolition of slavery, and Unitarianism had already passed beyond the precincts of Boston and Cambridge into Concord; and even before Elizabeth Peabody's return to the "Dr. Grimshawe House" in 1836, the new ideas had penetrated the solemn conversation of Salem folk and had stimulated the dormant culture of the once prosperous seaport town. But the movement needed dynamic leadership and human urge. Miss Peabody immediately furnished them. When she had studied Greek under Emerson, fresh from his graduation at Harvard, she had so much impressed him that he refused to accept payment for his services, declaring that he had taught her nothing. But their friendship had continued, and even in the trying days of his unhappy ministry at the "Old North Church," when some of his parishioners had whispered that their pastor was deranged, she had felt that he was a great man, certain to achieve ultimate victory. When he gave up his pulpit in 1832 and sailed on Christ-

[1] For a general sketch of Elizabeth Peabody's life, see *The National Cyclopaedia of American Biography*, XII, 350; and *D. A. B.*, XLV, 335-336. For interesting detailed matter, see Julian Hawthorne's *Nathaniel Hawthorne and His Wife* (2 vols.; Boston and New York: Houghton, Mifflin and Co., n.d.).

mas Day for Europe, she followed him in her thoughts and eagerly awaited his return to Concord that she might hear from his own lips his opinion of Carlyle, of Wordsworth, and of Coleridge—all of whom he had visited. Meanwhile she had become for a short time literary assistant to William Ellery Channing and had accepted wholeheartedly his doctrine of Unitarianism and his belief in the necessity for the abolition of slavery. But the most interesting experience of her early sojourn in Boston had been gained through her friendship with Amos Bronson Alcott when she taught for a short time in the extraordinary Temple School. This experiment in kindergarten work led to her friendship with Margaret Fuller and other transcendentalists, and inspired her to further activity in the field of child education. Though naturally studious and mentally alert, Elizabeth Peabody was never completely satisfied with ideas accumulated only from books. She had a passion for human contact, for conversation, and for the personal exchange of ideas. This abundance of the social instinct, combined with her indomitable moral zeal and philanthropic interest, directed her efforts to help everybody she met. In fact, a few of her friends sometimes resented her interference and spoke of her as a woman who liked to manage other people's lives.[2] But they always forgave her, and recognized that she was a woman of almost omnivorous interests, inexhaustible energy, and strong intellect.

When she came back to Salem in 1836 to make her home, she quickly found congenial companionship and alert minds eagerly responsive to her fondness for social organization. Having been accepted in October, along with Margaret Fuller, as a member of what was named in derision by its enemies the Transcendental

[2] *The American Notebooks by Nathaniel Hawthorne,* ed. Randall Stewart, pp. 327-328, n. 539: "Miss Peabody, it seems, sometimes disturbed her brother-in-law with suggestions which she thought would be helpful. In May, 1851, she urged upon Hawthorne the importance of life insurance. Later she suggested that Mrs. Hawthorne ought to show a greater regard for her father's well-being. It must have been an especially annoying intrusion which called forth the following pronouncement from Hawthorne in a letter to Miss Peabody dated Liverpool, April 20, 1855: 'I sometimes feel as if I ought . . . to endeavor to enlighten you as to the relation between husband and wife. . . . But the conjugal relation is one which God never meant you to share, and which therefore He apparently did not give you the instinct to understand; so there my labor would be lost.' (This letter is in the Morgan Library.)"

Club,[3] Elizabeth Peabody immediately allied herself with the Salem Lyceum and became one of the most faithful and active members of that group which met on Saturday evenings at the home of Miss Susan Burley, the sponsor. Soon she heard about Jones Very and read some of his verses, which, she was told, had been appearing for several years in the Salem *Observer*.[4] Always on the alert for the discovery of genius, she eagerly if not impatiently awaited the young poet's return to Federal Street, formed friendships with Mrs. Very and her two daughters, and through their agency contrived at length to meet Jones Very. She asked to see his verses, read them with genuine delight, recognized their unusual quality, and inspired him through her unfeigned appreciation and enthusiastic admiration to write more. Thus began that constant pilgrimage between Federal Street and the "Grimshawe House" on Charter Street. During one of these visits Very was introduced to Nathaniel Hawthorne, whom Elizabeth Peabody had met shortly after the publication of *Twice-Told Tales* in February, 1837, and whose friendship she had also cultivated. Sometimes the two men went together to visit Elizabeth Peabody and her sister Sophia and to talk with the invalid brother George. Sarah Freeman Clarke tells of such a visit when she herself was a guest of the Peabodys: "That evening I saw Hawthorne for the first time. He came with Jones Very, both new treasures of Elizabeth's discovery, to go with her to a lecture. Hawthorne, shrouded in a coat, Byronic and very handsome, looked gloomy, or perhaps only shy. Mr. Very had written poems which were remarkably spiritual and savored of Swedenborg."[5]

Elizabeth Peabody was the first person who made Very thoroughly conscious of his own poetic ability; she aroused in him the old though somewhat dormant wish to imitate Milton in writing

[3] G. W. Cook, *An Historical and Biographical Introduction to Accompany The Dial*, I, 49; II, 73.

[4] See, in the Essex Institute, Dr. Wheatland's notes in *Dr. Henry Wheatland Manuscripts*, XXVI, Genealogical: R-W. Speaking of Very, Dr. Wheatland states: "From 1835-1839 he was a contributor to the Salem *Observer*, since 1839 to the Salem *Gazette*, and since 1860 to the Boston *Christian Register*." The list of *Observer* poems in the Bibliography ("Primary Sources") may also be consulted.

[5] Sarah Freeman Clarke, "Reminiscences concerning Elizabeth Peabody, Written for the Memorial Meeting, 1894," in the Boston Public Library MSS: MS 622, *Impressions and Recollections of Miss Peabody*.

NATHANIEL PEABODY HOUSE, OR "DR. GRIMSHAWE HOUSE"
53 Charter Street, Salem, Massachusetts

nobly. Under her stimulus, the urge to sing began again to pulsate through his being. His mother afterwards recalled his habits during that summer of 1837, when his eyes often shone with a strange and brilliant light, and when he returned after a morning's stroll into the countryside to eat a scanty meal at noon and then retreat into an arbor in the garden. There, through the long afternoon, she could hear his monotonous droning and his regular tapping against the lattice-work, as he composed his sonnets,[6] often at the rate of two a day.[7] Sometimes he wrote them down in pencil on a large sheet of paper neatly folded to pages of small note size.[8] When he had filled a sheet, he took it to Elizabeth Peabody for criticism, and later he sometimes legibly copied her favorites for her in ink on small sheets of paper.[9] Among these was the sonnet which he called "Nature":

> The bubbling brook doth leap when I come by,
> Because my feet find measure with its call;
> The birds know when the friend they love is nigh,
> For I am known to them both great and small;
> The flowers that on the lovely hill-side grow
> Expect me there when Spring their bloom has given;
> And many a tree and bush my wanderings know,
> And e'en the clouds and silent stars of heaven:
> For he who with his Maker walks aright
> Shall be their lord, as Adam was before;
> His ear shall catch each sound with new delight,
> Each object wear the dress which then it wore;
> And he, as when erect in soul he stood,
> Hear from his Father's lips, that all is good.[10]

As Elizabeth Peabody read the poem, she immediately thought of Emerson. In the previous September the Concord lecturer had

[6] Miss Wilkins, and other residents of Salem mentioned before, recall such incidents in Very's later life, and remember remarks made by Lydia and Frances Very.

[7] *Andrews*, p. 12; the statement is quoted from Miss Peabody.

[8] Among Very's manuscripts in the Andover Theological Library, at Cambridge, is a sheet somewhat similar. The sheet is 16 x 24 inches, and is folded once so as to make four pages. There are eight poems, written neatly in small letters, on each page, making thirty-two poems (sonnets) for the one large sheet.

[9] In August, 1933, the author saw a copy of Very's "The Windflower" (*Clarke*, p. 72) among a collection of Elizabeth Peabody's correspondence, owned at that time by W. H. Lowdermilk & Co., Washington, D. C.

[10] *Clarke*, p. 91.

published anonymously a little book bearing the title *Nature*. Although nearly all of its few readers were mystified by it or else openly hostile to its message, Elizabeth Peabody was enthusiastic in her praise. Frequently she reread the "Introduction," and delighted in the independent spirit and the American gusto with which Emerson proclaimed that a New World had come of age. She agreed with his statements: "The foregoing generations beheld God and Nature face to face; we through their eyes. Why should we not also enjoy an original relation to the universe? Why should not we have a poetry and philosophy of insight and not of tradition, and religion by revelation to us, and not the history of theirs? . . . There are new lands, new men, new thoughts."[11] Was not Jones Very one of these new men, with new thoughts. And was not he traversing new lands—the ever-beckoning, peaceful lands of the spirit, where one saw nature and truth through the medium of mystical communion with God? Yes, he was undoubtedly a genius, a unique product of the religious, social, and academic life of Massachusetts, with a song and a spirit which combined in a strain so pure, original, and independent as to serve for the poetic expression of American transcendentalism itself. Emerson's lectures were fairly satisfactory, but his poetry was too vague for popular approval. Jones Very should be the poet of the Transcendental School, and he should achieve distinction through the clarity and purity of his verse, not only for himself, but also for the new group of philosophers with whom Elizabeth Peabody was in sympathy. She, therefore, took pride in introducing Very to the Salem Lyceum group and finally persuaded him to read to them his prose essay "Epic Poetry." This he did during the last week of December, 1837,[12] when the Lyceum was conducting its ninth course of lec-

[11] *The Complete Works of Ralph Waldo Emerson*, Vol. I, *Nature, Addresses, and Lectures*, p. 9.

[12] In the Salem *Observer* for Saturday morning, Dec. 23, 1837, one finds Very's "The Windflower," signed as usual only with the letter "I." In the column to the right is a notice, reading as follows: "Salem Lyceum. Lecture next week by Jones Very, Esq., of Harvard University."

Very was the eighth speaker. Oliver Wendell Holmes appeared as the thirteenth speaker, using as his subject "English Versification." See *Historical Sketch of the Salem Lyceum*, with a list of the officers and lecturers since its formation in 1830 (Salem: Press of the Salem Gazette, 1879), p. 42.

tures. His audience was charmed. Immediately, Miss Peabody sent off a letter to Emerson, acquainting him with the event and advising him to meet her discovered genius. From Concord, under date of January 20, 1838, Emerson, in a letter to Sophia Peabody, showed his marked interest: "Tell your sister Elizabeth that her account of Mr. Very interested me much, and I have already begged Mr. Whiting to bring him to our Lyceum, and he promised his good offices to get him here."[13]

In the meantime, Elizabeth Peabody kept in frequent communication with Very, and furnished him with Emerson's biographical lectures in order that her protégé might be acquainted with the elder transcendentalist's views and enter comfortably into conversation with him. Writing on February 26, 1838, to Robert C. Waterson, a student at Harvard, Miss Peabody stated: "I mean to get more of those biographical lectures from Mr. Emerson when I make my visit. . . . But when you see Mr. Very tell him that I am not sure of any but that one on Biography which is in my possession."[14] Thus Very was prepared for his initial visit to Emerson, made only a few weeks later.

Early in April, Jones Very, fortified with his copy of Emerson's *Nature*[15] and his own essay on epic poetry, walked out from Cambridge to Concord to meet Emerson. Perhaps seldom before had a pilgrimage in search of friendship and mutual spiritual inspiration met with more immediate responsiveness. Emerson was at the height of his ardor in his search for American genius; he was eager to discover living witnesses to prove his prediction made the previous August that America's sluggard intellect was about to "look from under its iron lids and fill the postponed expectation of the world with something better than the exertions of mechanical skill." America's literary Declaration of Independence had been written,

[13] Rose Hawthorne Lathrop, *Memories of Hawthorne,* p. 183.

[14] See letter from Elizabeth Peabody to Robert C. Waterson, in the *Essex Institute Autographs,* Margaret W. Brooks Collection.

[15] Very's copy of *Nature* (a first edition) is now in the possession of Mr. Parkman D. Howe, of Needham, Mass. The small blue volume contains Very's signature ("Jones Very, September, 1836, Salem") and a note in Emerson's handwriting ("Har[mony] Of Man With Nature Must Be Reconciled With God"). See Kenneth Walter Cameron's *Nature* (New York: Scholars' Facsimiles & Reprints, 1940), p. xviii.

read aloud to a Cambridge audience, and approved. But where were the volunteers to swell the ranks of American scholarship and free this continent from the shackles which bound it to the intellect of Europe? The recruits came slowly, mustering themselves at Concord under the leadership of Emerson. And though they were few in number, their zeal was so pronounced as to enkindle a nation's spirit and quicken its literary, social, and religious life. From Concord and its vicinity the world was destined to hear the report of a second revolution, and its purport should be hardly less significant than the shots fired by the "embattled farmers" on that April morning in 1775.

Very's visit heartened Emerson greatly. Here was a young tutor and student of divinity, modest but frank in his statements, unembarrassed in the presence of a man ten years his senior and already famous as a lecturer, writer, and independent thinker. The conversation flowed freely; thought rushed out to join thought, quick to recognize and embrace its kindred in an environment as yet hostile to its reception. They read and discussed Very's "Epic Poetry," and at length parted with expressions of hope for the development of warm friendship and mutually helpful literary relations. Immediately (April 5, 1838) Emerson wrote a letter to Elizabeth Peabody, effusive in its appreciation: ". . . But what I write for is to thank again your sagacity that detects such wise men as Mr. Very, from whose conversation and lecture I have had a true and high satisfaction. I heartily congratulate myself on being, as it were, anew in such company."[16] Two weeks later (April 19) Emerson's enthusiasm had not waned, as his journalistic entry proves: "I have been to New York and seen Bryant and Dewey, and at home seen young Jones Very, and two youthful philosophers who came here from Cambridge,—Edward Washburn and Renouf,—and who told me fine hopeful things of their mates in the senior class. . . . And I begin to conceive hopes of the Republic."[17]

But hopes were mixed with misgivings. The contrast between the indifference of the masses toward religion and the sincere devotion of young men like Jones Very was so great as to provoke astonishment. Emerson brooded over the state of American society,

[16] *Andrews*, pp. 18-19.   [17] *Journals*, IV, 432.

and on April 26 wrote in his *Journals:* "Have I said it before in these pages? Then I will say it again, that it is a curious commentary on society that the expression of a devout sentiment by any young man who lives in society strikes me with surprise and has all the air and effect of genius; as when Jones Very spoke of 'sin' and 'love' and so on."[18]

Meanwhile Very was surprising the students and faculty members of Harvard by the further expression of "devout sentiments." His conviction that he was an especial messenger from God grew more and more pronounced, and his interest in religion became so extreme and absorbing as to arouse in some of his friends the suspicion that he was slightly insane. Like Madame Guyon and Fénelon,[19] he contended that all sin consists in self-will and that holiness is the result of unconditional surrender to the will of God. The more complete the surrender, the more perfect was the state of holiness; Very, therefore, modestly and humbly announced that because of his will-lessness God used him as an instrument of communication to a sinful humanity and that the words which flowed from his mouth and the verses which came from his pen were not his own, but God's.

At length, the Reverend Henry Ware, Jr., one of Very's professors in the Cambridge Divinity School, heard of his student's peculiar views and decided to interview him in an effort to clarify his mind and lead him into a more conservative view of religion. But the discussion was a total failure. Very reiterated his belief with strong conviction, and when the amiable and more elderly gentleman frankly stated that he did not believe the younger man entirely inspired of God with living truth, Very burst into tears.[20]

Reports concerning Very circulated so rapidly and created so much discussion that they aroused the interest of Dr. William Ellery Channing, who invited Very to come to interview him.

[18] *Ibid.*

[19] For an excellent discussion of these mystics, see Chapter IX, "The Mystics of All Religions," in James Freeman Clarke's *Events and Epochs in Religious History;* also William James's "Mysticism," in *The Varieties of Religious Experience* (New York: Longmans, Green and Co., 1917), pp. 379-429. For a general treatment of mysticism, see Evelyn Underhill's *The Essentials of Mysticism.*

[20] "Jones Very, the Finest Song Writer in America, the Earth Life of a Mystic, Lately Ended," Boston *Sunday Herald,* May 6, 1880.

The following account of the meeting is recorded by James Freeman Clarke:

I was one day at Dr. Channing's house, when he had just had a visit from Jones Very. Dr. Channing, like Emerson, was always looking for any symptoms of a new birth of spiritual life in the land. Having heard of Mr. Very, he invited him to come and see him, and inquired what were his views on religious subjects. Having listened attentively, he asked him, whether it was in consequence of his invitation or in obedience to the Spirit that he came to Boston that morning. Mr. Very answered, "I was directed to accept your invitation." Then Dr. Channing said, "I observed that during our conversation you left your chair and went while speaking to the fireplace, and rested your arm on the mantel. Did you do this of your own accord or in obedience to the Spirit?" Mr. Very replied, "In obedience to the Spirit."[21]

But though the Cambridge and Boston folk might wound Very with their refusal to accept him as the Messenger of the Divine Spirit, Emerson reassured him with his interest and confidence. He had soon induced Very to align himself with the Transcendental Club and to attend a meeting at Medford in May, 1838. The subject discussed was: "Is Mysticism an Element of Christianity?" Apparently Jones Very's poems had prompted the subject, for not only Emerson and Elizabeth Peabody were familiar with his verse, but also other members of the club, among whom some of the sonnets had been circulated. Undoubtedly Very was a leader in the discussion and so impressed Bronson Alcott that he recorded the meeting in his journal and made the following reference to it in one of his "Conversations": ". . . as if, in answer to the inquiry whether Mysticism was an element of Christianity, here was an illustration of it in a living person, himself present at the club."[22] Indeed, to Emerson, Very was the most heartening of all that strange company he now knew. He was the living proof, the vibrant personification of transcendental humanity, a partaker of Universal Reason, a sharer in the Over-Soul. He, more than any other of his contemporaries, seemed to Emerson to rely on intuition, and not on history or social customs as a source of truth.

[21] *Clarke*, p. xxv.

[22] George Willis Cooke, *Ralph Waldo Emerson: His Life, Writings, and Philosophy* (Boston: James R. Osgood and Co., 1882), p. 57; also Cooke's *An Historical and Biographical Introduction to Accompany The Dial*, I, 52.

JONES VERY, AGE 24 YEARS
(From a daguerreotype owned by Mrs. Edmund R. Brown
and Miss Marjorie Very)

His very will-lessness identified him as an individualist, self-reliant because God-reliant, Nature-loving because God-loving. To Emerson he served as a tonic force and helped, by his example of living, to classify into more orderly arrangement that chaotic mass of thought and idea which he was seeking to formulate into an expressible philosophy or even into a creed. The sermon which Emerson delivered on July 15 to the graduating class of the Harvard Divinity School, therefore, owed something to Jones Very; and the fact that this sermon, as Alcott said, came nearer to the "center and core of things" than almost anything else spoken or written, was perhaps as much the result of Jones Very's conversations with Emerson as of the latter's interpretative study and original thinking. Though the two men from the very first did not entirely agree concerning religion, each nevertheless found in the other that intellectual stimulus which he needed during a great spiritual crisis.

During the summer and early autumn of 1838 Very diligently studied Shakespeare and began two essays concerning the dramatist; one dealt generally with Shakespeare, but the other was limited to a discussion of *Hamlet*. Very had been intensely interested in Shakespeare ever since his discovery of the rare edition in the auction room at Salem, and while an undergraduate at Harvard had developed a strong friendship with Professor Edward Tyrrell Channing mainly through their mutual enthusiasm for Shakespeare. Now, however, having reached the belief that he was the mouthpiece of the Divine Spirit and that "It is the necessity of the spirit to speak with authority,"[23] he determined to study Shakespeare, not from a purely literary viewpoint, but rather from a transcendental one. Very discussed the matter with Emerson, and the latter, after the conversation, recorded in his *Journals:* "What led him to study Shakespear was the fact that all young men say, Shakespear was no saint—yet see what genius! He wished to solve that problem."[24] The task Very set for himself was difficult and exhausting, but the impulse was so great that by the time of his return to Cambridge for the session of 1838-1839 he had almost completed his work. Emerson was kept notified of the progress,

[23] Emerson's *Journals*, V, 105.   [24] *Ibid.*

for on September 1 he wrote to his aunt, Mary Moody Emerson: "There is a young man at Cambridge named Jones Very who I think would interest you. He studies Shakespear now & will presently finish & probably publish an Essay on S. and from a point of view quite novel & religious. He has been here twice yet be not uneasy on that account for he does not agree to my dogmatism."[25]

Truly, Very at this time was agreeing to nobody's dogmatism. His mind had reached a state of such excitation that even the Harvard authorities seriously doubted his sanity.[26] His body was emaciated from lack of recreation and food, his nerves frayed and broken by super-excitement and abnormal exertion. Only the spirit seemed thoroughly and constantly alive. One day early in the term, as he stood before his Greek class, the increasing consciousness of his prophetic powers outgrew all further restraint. His eyes burned with a strange and intense light. Suddenly he startled his students with the apocalyptic cry, "Flee to the mountains, for the end of all things is at hand."[27]

[25] *The Letters of Ralph Waldo Emerson,* ed. R. L. Rusk (6 vols.; New York: Columbia University Press, 1939), II, 154.

[26] James Elliot Cabot, *A Memoir of Ralph Waldo Emerson,* I, 349.

[27] G. Bradford, Jr., "Jones Very," *The Unitarian Review,* XXVII (Feb., 1887), 111. The editor quotes from a letter received from one of Jones Very's former students.

One of Very's sonnets, "Flee to the Mountains," seems definitely to be the product of this experience; see Chapter VIII, Poem No. 22, in Brown University MSS.

CHAPTER IV

EMERSON'S BRAVE SAINT

INDEED, all things—at least at Harvard—were at an end; not for
the astonished Greek students, however, but rather for Very. The
more kindly disposed of the Cambridge authorities were now certain that he was on the verge of a nervous collapse; the more
orthodox and those susceptible to sensationalism were convinced
that the young tutor was positively insane. At any rate, his presence at Harvard was considered undesirable, and he was asked to
withdraw. He attended no meetings of the faculty after September 10.[1] Returning to his home in Salem, he immediately astonished his neighbors by his wild enthusiasm, and he disconcerted
and, in some instances, shocked the staid ministers of his city by
calling them sinful and spiritually barren. Obsessed by his mission of savior and prophet, he begged some of the Salem preachers
to repent of their dead formalism, to accept unhesitatingly and
literally the precepts of Christ as recorded in the New Testament,
and to pray with him that they also, through their submission to
the Holy Ghost, might become will-less and unified with God.
Such radical evangelism was so annoying that some of the Salem
folk demanded that Jones Very be sent to an insane asylum. His
mother, however, seriously opposed his forcible removal, and
again, as in her battle with old Isaac Very thirteen years before,
she was victorious. She consented, by way of compromise, to his
temporary and voluntary sojourn at the McLean Asylum, in
Somerville, where he was placed under the care of Dr. Bell.

Jones Very entered the asylum on September 17, 1838. Two
days before,[2] he had sent to Emerson his essay on Shakespeare,[3]

[1] *Records of the College Faculty,* XI (1829-1840), 287.

[2] For proof of the date, see Emerson's letter to Margaret Fuller, quoted a few
lines below.

[3] The statement made by Andrews in the 1883 edition of *Poems by Jones Very,*
p. 18, is incorrect: "While under Dr. Bell's care he finished the paper on Shakespeare, included in the collection made by Mr. Emerson, together with the other
admirable papers on Hamlet and on Epic Poetry."

Van Wyck Brooks, *The Flowering of New England,* p. 204, is also incorrect with the following note: "I am glad at last to be able to transmit what has been told me of Shakespeare—'tis but the faint echo of that which speaks to you now. . . . You hear not mine own words, but the teachings of the Holy Ghost. . . . My friend, I tell you these things as they are told me, and hope soon for a day or two of leisure, when I may speak to you face to face as I now write."[4] The contents of the letter worried Emerson a great deal. At first he wondered whether the reports concerning Very might not be true, but after a careful reading of the essay he was convinced that its author was sane. On September 20 he wrote to his friend, William Henry Furness: "There is a young man at Cambridge, a tutor, Jones Very, who has written a noble paper on Shakespeare, which I have just been reading. Yet I am distressed to hear that he is feared to be insane. His critique certainly is not."[5] Emerson's contemporary letter to Margaret Fuller also clearly reflects his concern at the time:

Concord, 28 Sept. 1838—
. . . Have you heard of the calamity of poor Very, the tutor at Cambridge? He is at the Charlestown Asylum & his case tho't a very unpromising one. A fortnight ago tomorrow—I received from him his Dissertation on Shakespeare. The letter accompanying it betrayed the state of his mind; but the Essay is a noble production: not consecutive, filled with one thought; but that so deep & true & illustrated so happily & even grandly, that I account it an addition to our really scanty stock of adequate criticism on Shakespear. Such a mind cannot be lost.[6]

It was not lost; neither was it idle, for Very completed his second Shakespearean essay, "Hamlet," and revised his "Epic

---

in making a similar statement: "In the McLean Asylum, where he dwelt for a while, he had written an essay on Shakespeare, which had been 'told' him by the Holy Ghost." In *The Life of Emerson*, p. 87, Brooks further states: "He [Very] went of his own accord and placed himself in the asylum at Somerville; he was sane enough, however, to write while there an essay on epic poetry and two papers on Shakespeare that had much in common with Emerson's thought."

Both Mr. Andrews and Mr. Brooks apparently did not have access to Emerson's letters to Margaret Fuller and to William Henry Furness, and to the newspaper files of the Essex Institute, in Salem, Mass. The essay, "Epic Poetry," had been read before the Salem Lyceum in December, 1837.

[4] *Andrews*, p. 20.
[5] *Records of a Lifelong Friendship*, ed. Horace Edward Furness, p. 8.
[6] *The Letters of Ralph Waldo Emerson*, ed. R. L. Rusk, II, 164-165.

Poetry" while under Dr. Bell's care.[7] Then, too, he wrote verse and spent much time comforting the other patients, who, as he later pleasantly related to Emerson, "thanked him when he came away, and told him that he had been of great service to them."[8] The McLean authorities dismissed Very on October 17, exactly one month after his entrance to the hospital.[9] He went back to his home on Federal Street in Salem, where under the tender care and sympathetic understanding of his mother and sisters he entirely regained his physical health and, at length, his mental balance. But the latter come only after some violent outbursts against conventional religion.

Very had been in Salem barely a week before he set out to Concord to spend a few days with Emerson. The latter received him gladly but anxiously and, through long conversations, took great pains to learn for himself the exact state of Very's mind. A thorough examination of the *Journals* from 1838 through 1841 affords ample proof of Emerson's concern.[10] Under date of October 26, 1838, he writes: "Jones Very came hither two days since, and gave occasion to many thoughts on his peculiar state of mind and his relation to society. His position accuses society as much as society names it false and morbid; and much of his discourse concerning society, the church, and the college was perfectly just."[11] Yet immediately following this apparent agreement with Very is a

[7] The original manuscript of "Epic Poetry" is in the Essex Institute, along with some of the manuscript material of his sister, Lydia L. A. Very. The piece is unfinished and is an early draft, as the unconnected, uncompleted parts prove. The developed essay which was presented for the Bowdoin Senior Prize is in *Bowdoin Prize Dissertations*, Vol. VI (1835-1839), in the Archives of the Widener Library at Harvard University. The essay as finally published does show some revision and improvement by the addition of several paragraphs.

[8] Emerson's *Journals*, VI, 290, under date of Oct. 26, 1842.

[9] A letter to the author from Dr. W. Franklin Wood, Director of McLean Hospital, Waverly, Mass., in reply to an inquiry regarding Very's record, reads: ". . . we regret to say that we cannot furnish you the information requested, since these records are private. Mr. Very was admitted to McLean Hospital on September 17, 1838, and discharged from the Hospital on October 17, 1838."

[10] It is a matter of serious regret that the editors of Emerson's *Journals* have failed to index many of the references to Very. Only approximately fifteen references are listed, whereas there are at least thirty-six in the printed *Journals*, many of them so lengthy and important as to deserve particular mention. For a complete index of Very in the *Journals*, see the Bibliography.

[11] *Journals*, V, 98.

statement which proves clearly that Emerson's enthusiasm for the
mystic was carefully tethered and that it would last only so long
as Very's genius proved fresh, inspiring, and helpful to him. For
Emerson, in spite of his own admiration for other transcendentalists, was, after all, sufficiently original and independent in his
thinking to be always free from complete domination by others.
He welcomed new thought and appropriated what he cared to use,
but he never forfeited his own intellectual integrity. His head
might at times float through the romantic clouds of a transcendental
heaven, but his feet gripped the realistic soil of Puritan New England. He was, indeed, as Régis Michaud has called him, "the
Enraptured Yankee."[12] And so one finds the following significant
entry:

Entertain every thought, every character, that goes by with the hos-
pitality of your soul. Give him the freedom of your inner house. He
shall make you wise to the extent of his own uttermost receivings. . . .
For the partial action of his mind in one direction is a telescope for
the objects on which it is pointed. And as we know that every path
we take is but a radius of our sphere, and we may dive as deep in every
other direction as we have in that, a far insight of one evil suggests
instantly the immense extent of that revolution that must be wrought
before He whose right it is shall reign, the all in all.[13]

Therefore, two days later, Emerson made lengthy entries of
Very's expressed ideas, some of which merely amplified the statements made previously. He wrote, in part: "Jones Very says it is
with him a day of hate; that he discerns the bad element in every
person whom he meets, which repels him: he even shrinks a little
to give the hand,—that sign of receiving. The institutions, the
cities which men have built, the world over, look to him like a
huge blot of ink. His own only guard in going to see men is that
he goes to do them good, else they would injure him (spiritually)."[14] Emerson noticed particularly Very's insistence on doing
him "good," and though he was temporarily fascinated by Very's
insistence on will-lessness, he was nevertheless irritated by the young

[12] Régis Michaud, *Emerson the Enraptured Yankee,* trans. from the French by
George Boas (New York and London: Harper & Bros., 1930).
[13] Emerson's *Journals,* V, 98-99.
[14] *Ibid.,* V, 104, under date of Oct. 28, 1838.

enthusiast's deliberate campaign to convert him. In fact, at this time Very's intuitivism was so strong as to make people uncomfortable in his presence. He detected immediately any hostility to his own ideas, and he proceeded to annihilate his opponents so completely that they seldom argued with him again. Emerson thought he sensed the divine afflatus, and he wrote:

He would obey, obey. He is not disposed to attack religions and charities, though false. The bruised reed he would not break; the smoking flax he would not quench. To Lidian he says, "Your thoughts speak there, and not your life." And he is very sensible of *interference* in thought and act. A very accurate discernment of spirits belongs to his state, and he detects at once the presence of an alien element, though he cannot tell whence, how, or where it is. He thinks me covetous in my hold of truth, of seeing truth separate, and of receiving or taking it, instead of merely obeying. The Will is to him all, as to me (after my own showing) Truth. He is sensible in me of a little colder air than that he breathes. He says, "You do not disobey because you do the wrong act; but you do the wrong act because you disobey."[15]

Though Emerson might not agree with Very, he nevertheless admired his sincerity and recorded that "Jones Very charmed us all by telling us he hated us all."[16]

It was on this visit to Concord that Very gave one of his rare demonstrations of pugnacious aggressiveness. Before he entered McLean Asylum he had attempted to correct some of the ministers in Salem, but his efforts aroused such protest that he was thought by many folk to be mentally unbalanced. Now he again—and to Emerson's apparent delight—made a further protest against dogmatic pulpit oratory—a protest so dramatic that Hawthorne and the Peabodys, when the news reached Salem, must have been reminded of a somewhat similar scene in "The Gentle Boy."[17] Emerson's entry concerning the event is significant, not only to a student of Very, but also to one interested primarily in Emerson's prose style:

[15] *Ibid.*, V, 104-105. The substance of this passage is amplified by another entry made Nov. 22, 1841 (VI, 131-132).

[16] *Ibid.*, V, 106, under date of Oct. 29, 1838. See, also, Emerson's letter to Elizabeth Peabody, Oct. 30, 1838, in *The Letters of Ralph Waldo Emerson*, ed. R. L. Rusk, II, 170-171.

[17] *Twice-Told Tales* (Boston: Houghton, Mifflin and Co., 1879), I, 89-91.

I ought not to omit recording the astonishment which seized all the
company when our brave saint the other day, fronted the presiding
preacher. The preacher began to tower and dogmatize with many
words. Instantly I foresaw that his doom was fixed; and as quick as he
ceased speaking, the saint set right and blew away all his words in an
instant,—unhorsed him, I may say, and tumbled him along the ground
in utter dismay, like my angel of Holiodorus. Never was discomfiture
more complete. In tones of genuine pathos he "bid him wonder at the
Love which suffered him to speak there in his chair, of things he knew
nothing of; one might expect to see the book taken from his hands
and him thrust out of the room,—and yet he was allowed to sit and
talk, whilst every word he spoke was a step of departure from the
truth, and of this he commanded himself to bear witness!"[18]

This, apparently, was Very's last public outburst against a society
which he conceived to be so completely disobedient to the will of
God as to be entirely cut off from communion with the Holy
Spirit and to be, therefore, dead. For to Very the only real life
was that of the spirit. Emerson remarked that "He had the man-
ners of a man . . . to whom life was more than meat, the body
than raiment";[19] and added that Very "felt it an honor to wash
his face, being, as it was, the temple of the spirit."[20] Henceforth,
he sought consolation, not from society, but from communion with
God and nature. While walking in the woods with Emerson, he
remarked, "One might forget here that the world was desart and
empty, all the people wicked."[21] And ever after, he was so gentle
and kind in his manner as to impress all who came in contact with
him. Among these was Dr. William Ellery Channing, erstwhile
teacher of Very at Harvard. When Very visited him at the height
of his religious frenzy, Dr. Channing was greatly impressed with
the young man's modesty, and when he later discussed Very's case
with Elizabeth Peabody, he agreed with her that only those lower
activities of the brain, upon which the senses operate, seemed sus-
pended, and that there was an intensity of the intellectual powers
rather than a diminution of them. He commented further: "Yet
there was an iron sequence of thought. . . . Men in general have
lost or never found this higher mind—their insanity is profound—

[18] Emerson's *Journals*, V, 110-111, under date of Oct. 30, 1838.
[19] *Ibid.*, V, 105.   [20] *Ibid.*
[21] *Ibid.*, V, 141, under date of Nov. 17, 1838.

his is only superficial. He has not lost his reason; he has only suppressed his senses."[22] Very's utter unconcern for worldly success made him seem decidedly passive in contrast with nineteenth-century Yankee aggressiveness, set him apart from society, and suggested to most of his fellows his utter loneliness. But Emerson thought he understood Very's obsession with "spiritual communion"; he believed that companionship would be found with the Over-Soul. And after Very had departed for Salem, Emerson in his *Journals* wrote in a tone suggesting reverence: "And he is gone into the multitude as solitary as Jesus. In dismissing him I seem to have discharged an arrow into the heart of society. Wherever that young enthusiast goes he will astonish and disconcert men by divining for them the cloud that covers the profound grief that is in man."[23]

Very left with Emerson both of his Shakespearean essays: the first, it will be recalled, had been sent to Concord two days before his departure for the McLean Hospital; the second, which dealt with "Hamlet," and which had been completed while Very was under Dr. Bell's care, had been taken to Emerson at the time of the recent visit. Emerson was highly pleased with the criticism, and in a letter to Margaret Fuller, dated November 9, 1838, he wrote:

When you come here I will show you Very's two dissertations,—one on the general subject, & the other on Hamlet,—which are pretty great criticism. Very has been here himself lately & staid a few days confounding us all with the question—whether he was insane? At first sight & speech, you would certainly pronounce him so. Talk with him a few hours and you will think all insane but he. Monomania or mono *Sania* he is a very remarkable person & though his mind is not in a natural & probably not in a permanent state, he is a treasure of a companion, & I had with him most memorable conversations.[24]

The concluding sentiment Emerson also undoubtedly expressed in a letter to Very, for the latter replied, "I was glad to hear that my stay with you was improving."[25] But Very was thinking chiefly

---

[22] Wm. P. Andrews, "An Inspired Life," *The Century Magazine,* II (Oct. 1, 1882), 859-862.   [23] V, 106.
[24] *The Letters of Ralph Waldo Emerson,* ed. R. L. Rusk, II, 173.
[25] *Andrews,* p. 20.

of religion and of converting Emerson to his own beliefs; in the
rest of his letter he wrote only of obedience to the Will of God
as a necessity toward oneness with God.[26] Emerson, however, tact-
fully side-stepped the issue of religion, and spurred Very on to the
further creation of verse. The result was gratifying. In the seven
months between Very's dismissal from the McLean Hospital (October 17, 1838) and the final preparation of his manuscripts for
the first edition of his *Essays and Poems* (July 9, 1838), he published 89 poems in the Salem *Observer;* 48 of these were published
in three months (December, 1838, and January and February,
1839), and 20 poems appeared in the month of March, 1839.
Indeed, Very's poetic exaltation seemed to reach its peak during
this period. Soon after he returned from his visit to Emerson,
Very sent to his Concord friend two sonnets published by the
Observer on November 10, 1838—"In Him We Live and Move,
and Have Our Being," and "Enoch"—which, as he stated, he
hardly dared write because he felt they were the message of God
spoken through him, and "were the true letter" as he was "true."[27]
Emerson, though perhaps disagreeing with Very about the source
of his verse, praised it highly, and suggested the publication of a
collection of his works. The following letter proves Emerson's
spontaneous enthusiasm:

[26] See letter from Very to Emerson *(ibid.):* "I was glad to hear that my stay
with you was improving, and that you love that which is spoken by the Word.
If you love it aright, in the spirit of obedience, it shall be unto *you* given to hear
and speak of the Father in Christ. . . . You must pass out of the world in which
you are, naked (that is, willess) as you came in. Then shall you have a *new*
will born of the Spirit, and when this also is submitted to the Father's you shall
be one with Him; that is, be prepared to see Him as a spirit. Every scribe instructed
in the Kingdom shall bring forth, as a householder, new and old; that is, he
himself shall hear the word of the Father, and anew interpret for men the old.
But so far have the false Christs failed in this life, that they do not even claim
to hear of themselves the Word, and vainly attempt to bring forth that once
spoken." Andrews gives the date only as November, 1838.

[27] See an undated letter from Very to Emerson, in *ibid.,* p. 21: "I send you
these by letter that they may come earlier to hand. I hardly dared to write them,
and that will excuse me from a letter. They are the true letter, as I am true.
There is more joy and freedom as I advance, yet still I long to be clothed upon
with my house from heaven. In you, too, may more of the old pass away, and
the new and abiding be more and more felt. This I pray forever, as

    "I am   J. Very."

Concord, Mar. 18, 1838.

My dear Sir,

I have received your two
manuscripts with many thanks.
I have availed myself of your permission to copy them. I shall endeavor
to be directly to use the copies, &
not to prejudice your right of convenience, if you should choose to read the
as lectures. I have perfectly read them
both again with attention in the
transcript of my friend. I am very
sorry that the Mss. should have
been retained by me beyond the allowed
ten days; but no person had gone
from here to Cambridge by whom
I could send them. I hope you have
not wanted them.

Mr Geo. Ripley
Boston

R. Waldo Emerson

Concord, Nov. 18, 1838.

My dear Sir,

I send herewith your two manuscripts with hearty thanks. I have availed myself of your permission to copy them, & shall endeavor so discreetly to use the copies, as not to prejudice your rights & convenience, if you should choose to read them as lectures. I shall presently read them both again, with attention, in the transcript of my friends. I am very sorry that the MSS. should have been detained by me beyond the allowed ten days; but no person has gone from here to Cambridge, by whom I could send them. I trust you have not wanted them.

I have also to thank you for the two sonnets sent me in the Salem Observer. I love them & read them to all who have ears to hear. Do not, I beg you, let a whisper or sigh of the Muse go unattended to or unrecorded. The sentiment which inspires your poetry is so deep & true, & the expression so simple, that I am sure you will find your audience very large as soon as the verses first take air & get abroad. And a man should be very happy & grateful who is the bringer to his fellowmen of a good so excellent as poetry.

As soon as I have the tickets for my lectures printed, I shall send you one, in case you should chance to be in Boston, on a Wednesday Evg. this winter. We all remember you here with great affection & hope. Do not fail to come & visit me, as soon as my lectures are over.— I had intended to have added above—apropos to the poetry—that you must after a little more writing—collect your prose & verse in a volume & make the bookseller give you bread for the same. And let me help you with some of my recent experience in the matter.

Your affectionate servant,

R. Waldo Emerson.

If you write again in the Observer, send me a copy, if you can.—Let me suggest the alternation of the word "Jewish" (patriarch) in the sonnet on Enoch. The country of Enoch I suppose cannot very well be settled though I should think "Syrian" would not be too great a licence. But Jewish is an alibi, and another where.[28]

[28] See letter owned and preserved by the Essex Institute. This letter was acquired from the effects of Miss Lydia L. A. Very after her death, by Miss Harriet I. Wilkins, of Salem, Mass., who, in 1919, presented it to the Essex Institute: see article in the Salem *Evening News* for Thursday, July 24, 1919, headed "Institute Gets Letter Written by Concord Sage."

Professor Rusk lists this letter in *The Letters of Ralph Waldo Emerson*, II, 174, as under the probable date of Nov. 13, 1838; but he refers only to *Andrews* as a source, and apparently has not examined the original letter, which bears the date of Nov. 18, 1838.

Very's "Hamlet" had acted as a spark to kindle anew Emerson's love for Shakespeare, and had stimulated Emerson to further reading, not only in the actual works of the dramatist, but also in Shakespearean criticism. The *Journals* contains numerous references to Shakespeare during November, 1838;[29] thus on November 9, one finds: "Shakespear.—Read Lear yesterday and Hamlet today with new wonder."[30] Three days later he thought so highly of Very's critique that he placed it with those of Coleridge, Lamb, and Goethe.[31]

It was at this time that Emerson was concluding the preparation for his course of ten weekly lectures on "Human Life" to be delivered in Boston, the first of which—"The Over-Soul"—was to be delivered on December 5. Unquestionably Very's relationship with Emerson influenced certain passages of "The Over-Soul," for an entry in the *Journals* for November 25 is almost identical with one in "The Over-Soul," published later (1841) in the *Essays.* The entry reads:

> The great distinction between teachers sacred or literary; between poets like Herbert and poets like Warton; between philosophers like Coleridge and philosophers like Mackintosh; between talkers like Reed and Very and talkers like Walder and Ripley, is, that, one class speak *ab intra,* and the other class, *ab extra.* It is of no use to preach to me *ab extra.* I can do that myself. Jesus preaches always *ab intra,* and so infinitely distinguishes himself from all others. In that is the miracle. That includes the miracle. My soul believes beforehand that it ought so to be. That is what I mean when I say I look for a Teacher, as all men do say. If however you preach *ab extra,* at least confess it.[32]

The passage in the essay omits Very's name and changes some of the others listed, but the thought content is unchanged. The phrase substituted, however, is significantly suggestive of Emerson's vacillating judgment concerning Very's sanity. Here, Emerson regards him as "A fervent mystic, prophesying half-insane under the infinitude of his thought."[33] Emerson's letters to Margaret Fuller[34] had

[29] V, 109, 111, 112, 119, 122, 124-126, 127.

[30] *Ibid.,* V, 124.

[31] *Ibid.,* V, 133: "Shakespear has for the first time in our time found adequate criticism, if indeed ye have yet found it. Coleridge, Lamb, Schlegel, Goethe, Very, Herder."   [32] *Ibid.,* V, 143.

[33] *The Works of Emerson,* Centenary Ed. (1903-1905), II, 287, "The Over-

shown the same concern, and his references in the *Journals* to insanity[35] reflect his strong interest in the subject. He himself had been accused of madness, and in 1828 his brother, Edward Emerson, had been confined in the same asylum where Very had been a patient. Only a few days after the latter's visit to Concord, Emerson had concluded that Very's was a baffling case: he had tested him, but Very had not completely proved himself "a great spirit" with "entire self-command," one never suggesting "the idea of a restless soul bestridden alway by an invisible rider."[36]

When Emerson was lecturing in Boston, and Jones Very, on occasion, attended, Emerson wondered again about the sanity of his Salem friend. For Very repeated his attempt at persuading Emerson to accept his own belief that his mission was divine; and Emerson found the experience annoying. The entry which he made in his *Journals* clearly explains the event:

When I met him . . . one evening at my lecture in Boston, I invited him to go home to Mr. Adams's with me and sleep, which he did. He slept in the chamber adjoining mine. Early the next day, in the grey dawn, he came into my room and talked whilst I dressed. He said, "When I was at Concord I tried to say you were also right; but the spirit said, you were not right. It is just as if I should say, It is not morning; but the morning says, It is the morning."

"Use what language you will," he said, "you can never say anything but what you are."[37]

Soul." The passage reads as follows: "The great distinction between teachers sacred or literary; between poets like Herbert, and poets like Pope; between philosophers like Spinoza, Kant and Coleridge,—and philosophers like Locke, Paley, Mackintosh and Stewart; between men of the world who are reckoned accomplished talkers, and here and there a fervent mystic, prophesying half-insane under the infinitude of his thought, is that one class speak *from within,* or from experience, as parties and possessors of the fact; and the other class *from without,* as spectators merely, or perhaps as acquainted with the fact on the evidence of third persons. It is of no use to preach to me from without. I can do that too easily myself. Jesus speaks always from within, and in a degree that transcends all others. In that is the miracle. That includes the miracle. My soul believes beforehand that it ought so to be. All men stand continually in the expectation of the appearance of such a teacher. But if a man do not speak from within the veil, where the word is one with that it tells of, let him lowly confess it."

[34] *Op. cit.,* n. 22.   [35] *Journals,* V, 117, 120-121, 162.

[36] *Ibid.,* V, 117, under date of Nov. 4, 1838: "One of the tests of sanity is repose. I demand of a great spirit entire self-command. He must be free and detached, and take the world up into him, and not suggest the idea of a restless soul bestridden alway by an invisible rider. He must not be feverish but free."

[37] *Ibid.,* VI, 132.

This seems to have been Very's last attempt toward converting Emerson.

The latter, however, listened with interest to Alcott's account of a meeting with Very during January, 1839, when Alcott gave one of his "Conversations" in Lynn. Alcott's account, as recorded in his *Journal*, is exceedingly helpful to an understanding of Very's mental state at this time, for—with the exception of Emerson's references in his *Journals*—it is one of the few reliable contemporaneous reports available, and is based on an actual interview. The most pertinent statements in Alcott's entry are as follows:

He is a remarkable phenomenon. His look, tones, words, are all sepulchral. He is a voice from the tombs. He speaks of having once lived in the world amongst men and things, but of being now in the spirit; time and space are not, save in the memory. This idea modifies all his thoughts and expressions, and the thoughts and expressions of others also. It is difficult for those who do not apprehend the state of his soul to converse with him. I find it quite possible, by translating his thoughts into my own vocabulary, mentally. By so doing, we talk with ease, and understand each other. His speech is Oriental. He is a psychological phenomenon of rare occurrence. He lives out of his organs; he is dead. Each thought of his soul, when spoken, each act of his body, implies a resurrection of the spiritual life.[38]

Alcott, then, more than Emerson, found himself comparatively at ease with Very. But Alcott, it will be remembered, was one of the most transcendental of the transcendentalists.

Another member of the Transcendental Club sought to become acquainted with Very. This was Margaret Fuller. Her inquiries concerning the mystic led Emerson to express himself further on the subject of his friend's insanity. A request in January for Very's essays induced Emerson to send to her some sonnets instead;[39] the desired prose works on Shakespeare followed in February.[40] Undoubtedly Miss Fuller's criticism of Very's essays[41] did not agree

[38] G. W. Cooke, *An Historical and Biographical Introduction to Accompany The Dial,* II, 138.

[39] *The Letters of Ralph Waldo Emerson,* ed. R. L. Rusk, II, 179: "Concord, January 18, 1839. . . . Very's Dissertations are both wandering in Boston, but here is a roll of his sonnets."

[40] *Ibid.,* II, 184: "Concord, February 15, 1839. . . . I send the Very Dissertations; & the last Blackwoods. . . ."

[41] This criticism undoubtedly was, in substance, what was contained in an

wholly with that of Emerson, who was influenced by his personal relationship with Very and was always trying to judge the work on the basis of Very's mental condition. Emerson's letter written in reply to Miss Fuller's proffered judgment contains the following revealing paragraph:

> I think your estimate of Very's papers very good—just, under the purely literary view; but the man himself is a rare problem, is or was lately a study worthy of all regard for his inspired & prophetic side. But I fear he is dying or becoming hopelessly mad.
>
> I wish Caroline S. had given her own view: Mr. Alcott's opinion of him, I know very well, as we have anatomized him together.[42]

Others also had anatomized Very. Among these was James Freeman Clarke,[43] a Unitarian minister, who, upon graduation from the Harvard Divinity School in 1833, immediately was ordained in Boston and became pastor of a church in Louisville, Kentucky. While in that city he served also as editor of *The Western Messenger*,[44] from April, 1836, until October, 1839. During the latter part of 1838 Clarke was in Boston and heard about Jones Very from Dr. Channing,[45] Emerson, and Elizabeth Peabody. At length—in all probability in the recently opened bookshop of Elizabeth Peabody, located on West Street—Clarke and Very met. The Kentucky editor was deeply impressed with the fervent young mystic, and the result of his analysis was that "Mr. Very's views in regard to religion . . . were not different from those heretofore advocated by many pure and earnest religionists."[46] Clarke spoke

---

article written by Margaret Fuller for *The Boston Quarterly Review* (III, 132-134, Jan., 1840), under "Literary Notices—Chat in Boston Bookstores—No. I." See Chapter V.

[42] *The Letters of Ralph Waldo Emerson,* ed. R. L. Rusk, II, 190-191.

[43] For an account of Clarke's life, see *D. A. B.,* IV, 153.

[44] See Clarence L. F. Gohdes, *The Periodicals of American Transcendentalism* (Durham, N. C.: Duke University Press, 1931). Chapter II is devoted to *The Western Messenger* and *The Dial* and is exceedingly valuable to an understanding of the transcendental movement in America. Another helpful work is R. L. Rusk's *The Literature of the Middle Western Frontier* (2 vols.; New York: Columbia University Press, 1925). *The Western Messenger* is treated in I, 183.

[45] See Clarke's "Biographical Sketch of Jones Very," p. xxv, in *Poems and Essays by Jones Very* (1886); also "Jones Very, the Finest Sonnet Writer in America . . .," Boston *Sunday Herald,* Sunday, May 16, 1880.

[46] *The Western Messenger,* VI (March, 1839), 310.

of him further as "a man in whose intellect all other thoughts have
become merged in the great thought of his connexion with God,"[47]
and he wondered whether Very's case were not one of *Mono-sania*
rather than *Mono-mania*. This judgment was substantially
strengthened in February, 1839, when Very sent to Clarke twenty-
seven sonnets accompanied by the following letter:

Rev. J. F. Clarke, Editor Western Messenger:

Hearing of your want of matter for your Messenger, I was moved
to send you the above sonnets; that they may help those in affliction
for Christ's name is ever the prayer of me his disciple, called to be a
witness of his sufferings and an expectant of his glory. If you should
ask for more as I have them so will they be communicated freely.
Amen.

The hope of Jesus be with you when you are called to be a partaker of his temptations.

Jones Very.[48]

Very undoubtedly had been persuaded by Emerson to communicate
his verse to the editor of *The Western Messenger* for the number
for February, 1839, contained Emerson's "Each and All" and "To
a Humble-Bee," and Clarke had already asked for permission to
use "The Rhodora" and "Good-Bye, Proud World,"[49] which poems
subsequently appeared in the April number.

The Western Messenger for March, 1839, contained nine of
Very's sonnets, the remaining eighteen appearing in the April
number, along with Emerson's two poems. Later numbers[50] contained thirteen additional poems so that *The Western Messenger,*
in publishing forty of Very's poems gave its subscribers an opportunity to read a fairly ample collection of Very's religious verse
and to arrive at a not too hurried judgment of its form and content. This fact is more important than it may seem at first, for
The Western Messenger, in spite of its short life, lasted longer than
The Dial, with which the Western magazine is nearly always compared, and reached a larger number of readers. As a student of

[47] *Ibid.*   [48] *Ibid.*
[49] *James Freeman Clarke: Autobiography, Diary, and Correspondence,* ed. E. D.
Hale (1891); see letter from Clarke to Emerson, pp. 124-125.
[50] VIII (May, 1840), one poem; (Jan., 1841), one poem; (Feb., 1841), five
poems; (March, 1841), six poems.

transcendentalism has pointed out,[51] *The Western Messenger* as early as 1836 had nearly one hundred subscribers in New England alone, while *The Dial* at no time had a list of three hundred subscribers all told. Clarke tried to boost his new contributor by prefacing the first nine sonnets with a three-page personal laudation of Very's verse and a vigorous defense of the poet's sanity.[52] The following selected statements are significant:

. . . They [the sonnets] have been read by ourselves with no uncommon emotions of interest. . . .

We had the pleasure of meeting Mr. Very a few months since, in the city of Boston. We had heard of him before, from various quarters, as a young man of much intelligence and of a remarkably pure character, whose mind had become extremely interested within a few months, upon the subject of religion. He was said to have adopted some peculiar views on this important theme, and to consider himself inspired by God to communicate them. Such pretensions had excited the fears of his friends, and by many he was supposed to be partially deranged. The more intelligent and larger sort of minds, however, who had conversed with him, dissented from this view, and although they might admit a partial derangement of the lower intellectual organs, or perhaps an extravagant pushing of some views to their last results, were disposed to consider his main thoughts deeply important and vital.

With respect to Mr. Very, we have only to say that the intercourse we have ourselves had with him has given no evidence even of such partial derangement. We have heard him converse about his peculiar views of religious truth, and saw only the workings of a mind absorbed in the loftiest contemplations, and which utterly disregarded all which did not come into that high sphere of thought. We leave it to our readers to decide whether there is anything of unsoundness in these sonnets. To us, they seem like wells of thought, clear and pellucid, and coming from profound depths.[53]

The poem which Clarke selected to head his list is, alas! only representative of Very's religious verse at its worst. It shows, however, Very's intense concern to express the message of the Spirit which he believed to be especially revealed to him—the message proclaiming obedience and repentance; it employs Biblical phraseol-

---

[51] Geo. Willis Cooke, *The Journal of Speculative Philosophy*, XIX, 229.

[52] *The Western Messenger,* VI (March, 1839), 310-312. See Appendix III for the entire article, also for the poems published in this periodical and not incorporated in any edition of Very's works. [53] *Ibid.*

ogy, particularly in the use of "thou" and the "st" ending for verbs in the second person singular; and its structural form is that of the Shakespearean sonnet—sometimes purely regular, but in this instance with the addition of an extra foot in the last line. But the poem reflects Very's tendency, which increased with age, to discover spiritual significance in everything and to attach a moral tag even to scientific discoveries or mechanical devices. The result is often merely drab versification. It is exceedingly doubtful, then, that the readers of *The Western Messenger* felt their artistic or poetic natures greatly disturbed by the following initial sonnet:

THE RAIL ROAD

Thou great proclaimer to the outward eye
Of what the spirit too would seek to tell,
Onward thou go'st, appointed from on high
The other warnings of the Lord to swell;
Thou art the voice of one that through the world
Proclaims in startling tones, "Prepare the way;"
The lofty mountain from its seat is hurled,
The flinty rocks thine onward march obey;
The valleys lifted from their lowly bed
O'ertop the hills that on them frowned before,
Thou passest where the living seldom tread,
Through forests dark, where tides beneath thee roar,
And bid'st man's dwelling from thy track remove,
And would with warning voice his crooked paths reprove.[54]

About the same time Very was seeing his verse appear in *The Western Messenger*, Emerson was urging him seriously to publish a volume of his work under his own sponsorship. This idea had been suggested in a letter the previous November,[55] and through Emerson's stimulus had gradually developed into something approaching definite accomplishment. Yet Very was an enigma. Still seated on the heights of spiritual exaltation, he showed only lukewarm enthusiasm for the publication of a book of his own work, and in answer to Emerson's suggestions for altering phrases or lines in his poems or even for careful proofreading, again insisted that his works were not his but those of the Spirit, and

[54] *Clarke*, p. 95; the title is written as one word.
[55] See n. 28.

hesitated to perform an action implying such irreverence. Emerson had little patience with a judgment which confused the Spirit itself with the human expression of it. In reply to Very's insistence upon the infallibility of his literary style because it was the Spirit's, Emerson, as he later did in the case of William Ellery Channing, retorted: "Cannot the spirit parse and spell?"[56] Perhaps it was Very's quiescent demeanor which provoked Emerson's contemporary entry in the *Journals:* "Vanity.—Do not be so troublesome modest, you vain fellow. Real modesty still puts the thing forward and postpones the person, nor worries me with endless apologies."[57] At any rate, Emerson proceeded to edit a volume of Very's prose and verse much to his own liking. He discussed the matter with Elizabeth Peabody, then a guest in Concord, who sent the following report to her sister Sophia:

He (Emerson) says Very forbids all correcting of his verses; but nevertheless he (Emerson) selects and combines with sovereign will, "and shall," he says, "make out a little gem of a volume." "But," says he, "Hawthorne says he (Very) is always vain. I find I cannot forget that dictum which you repeated; but it is continually confirmed by himself, amidst all his sublimities." And then he repeated some of Very's speeches, and told how he dealt with him. . . .[58]

But regardless of how Emerson may have dealt with Very concerning the alteration of his verse—and such alteration was practically negligible, if the manuscripts are reliable—Emerson felt a genuine affection for his twenty-six-year-old friend. This fact is convincingly proved by several entries in the *Journals* for June, 1839. About the middle of the month Very, in order to help in completing the editing of the proposed work, went to Concord for a visit of several days. Emerson's journal entry for June 14 is, therefore, indicative of the relationship between the two men at that time. "Shall I not call God the Beautiful, who daily showeth himself so to me in his gifts?" Emerson asks. Then he records that passage which he later incorporated in "Friendship," a passage unmistakably influenced by Very:

[56] *The Letters of Ralph Waldo Emerson,* ed. R. L. Rusk, II, 331 (letter to Elizabeth Hoar, from Concord, Sept. 12, 1840).

[57] V, 172.

[58] Rose Hawthorne Lathrop, *Memories of Hawthorne* (Boston and New York: Houghton, Mifflin and Co., 1897), pp. 29-30.

I chide society, I embrace solitude, and yet I am not so ungrateful as not to see the wise, the lovely, and the noble-minded, as from time to time they pass my gate. Who hears me, who understands me, becomes mine,—a possession for all time. . . . My friends have come to me unsought. The great God gave them to me. . . . These are not stark and stiffened persons, but the newborn poetry of God,—poetry without stop,—hymn, ode and epic, poetry still flowing and not yet caked in dead books with annotation and grammar. . . .[59]

The last line suggests a comment made about Very and Alcott earlier in the month; when speaking of the languor and complacent ignorance of some young American scholars and contrasting them with the needed geniuses of the age, Emerson records: "This old learning of Bentley and Gibbon was the natural fruit of the Traditional age in philosophy and religion. Ours is the revolutionary age, when man is coming back to consciousness, and from afar this mind begets a dislike for lexicons. Alcott, therefore, and Very, who have this spirit in great exaltation, abhor books."[60] Truly, so Emerson believed, Very was a soul who transcended "to transcendental virtue";[61] he, alone, with the possible exception of Alcott, accepted literally the tenets of transcendentalism and clung to his belief in mysticism with all the tenacity characteristic of zealots. And though Emerson could not accept Very's faith, he nevertheless respected him for his profound devotion to it. He sensed Very's purity of soul, felt the strong current of his deep spiritual life, and rejoiced in his ability to cast off all hypocrisy and social pretense and to face his interrogators frankly and truthfully.

Yet Very baffled Emerson and caused him much anxiety. Certainly the man was good; one sensed immediately his deep spirituality; in fact, Emerson always felt a genuine challenge to a better life when he came in contact with him. Perhaps this led to Emerson's analysis of his guest: was Very's goodness, after all, sufficient to satisfy Emerson's ideal of the perfect life? On the one hand, he tended to represent in spirit and flesh the life Emerson had lectured and written about: his attitude toward nature and books reminded Emerson of much that he himself had stated in "The

[59] *The Complete Works of Ralph Waldo Emerson*, II, *Essays, First Series*, pp. 194-195.
[60] *Journals*, V, 214.   [61] *Ibid.*, V, 223.

American Scholar" and in "Nature"; his brave, independent religion of the immediacy of God was certainly that of nonconformity and suggested that Very was "a new-born bard of the Holy Ghost." Had not Emerson told the divinity students at Cambridge that America needed such? And, finally, Very's partially oriental doctrine of complete reliance on God, of communion with Him through purity of life, obedience, and will-lessness savored strongly of the thoughts which Emerson later expressed in "Self-Reliance," "Compensation," and "The Over-Soul." But to Emerson, all of this was not enough: there must be action; it might be "subordinate," but it was "essential." And here Very failed. His life and his genius were one-sided; he was detached from his fellows, wrapped up in his own unshakable faith in the nearness of God, unconcerned with the "resounding tumult" about him, grimly self-reliant. And yet Very was a Swedenborgian saint whose silent presence spoke more loudly and convincingly than all the shouts of pulpit cant and all the din of "Ann Street oaths" which filled Cambridge and Boston. But the Yankee masculinity of Emerson, in spite of all his admiration for the mysticism of Swedenborg and the feminine quietism of the Hindu, craved active progress, contact with individuals of strong and sharply contrasted personalities. Jones Very was "like the rain plentiful," caring naught for individuals, "annoyed by edge." "I like sharp salts. Strength is wonderful," wrote Emerson.[62]

And so in the summer of 1839, when Emerson and Very were editing the little book of essays and poems soon to be released from the press, Emerson reached a decision which determined the ultimate relationship between the two men. It seemed to him that Very's spiritual exaltation had insulated him, had dwarfed and dulled his personality; his excessive self-effacement and his positive unconcern for worldly affairs made him a monotonous conversationalist and an unstimulating companion. In the midst of the visit Emerson wrote in his *Journals:* "Here is Simeon the Stylite, or John of Patmos in the shape of Jones Very, religion for religion's sake, religion divorced, detached from man, from the world, from science and art; grim, unmarried, insulated, accusing; yet true in

[62] *Ibid.,* VII, 120.

itself, and speaking things in every word. The lie is in the detachment; and when he is in the room with other persons, speech stops
as if there were a corpse in the apartment."[63]

This, then—this detachment from other human beings—was the
price Emerson thought Very paid for his exaltation and his penetrating intuition. To Emerson, it was an unsatisfying freedom and
too dearly bought. Could Very have transferred the full glory of
his ecstasy to others when he had descended the heights after his
communing,[64] Emerson might have felt a greater urge to emulate
his friend; but apparently such mystical rapture was uncommuni-
cable. Very himself had admitted that his literary work was "but
the faint echo" of the Great Voice, and Emerson was not wholly
satisfied with echoes. And yet Very's peaceful and calm spirit
aroused a gnawing envy in Emerson—an envy of the other man's
spiritual happiness which, though it might detach one from common men, Emerson sometimes deeply longed for. When, on
June 17, Very suddenly announced that he must return home immediately, and suggested that he must have seclusion for further
communion with the Holy Spirit, Emerson informed Elizabeth
Peabody: "I cannot persuade Mr. Very to remain with me another
day. He says he is not permitted, & no assurances that his retirement shall be secured, are of any avail. He has been serene, intelligent & true in all the conversation I have had with him, which is
not much. He gives me pleasure, & much relief after all I had
heard concerning him. His case is unique. & I have no guess as to
its issue, which I trust will be the happiest."[65] Emerson added that
he himself should go to Boston and attend to the publication of
Very's book.

By July 9 the manuscript was in the hands of the printers, as

---

[63] *Ibid.*, V, 220-221.

[64] Cf. a passage in the *Journals* for June 18, 1839, V, 223: "The private soul
ascends to transcendental virtue. Like Very, he works hard without moving hand
or foot; like Agathon, he loves the goddess and not the woman; like Alcott, he
refuses to pay a debt without injustice; but this liberty is not transferable to any
disciple, no, nor to the man himself, when he falls out of his trance and comes
down from the tripod."

[65] *Andrews,* p. 19; and *The Letters of Ralph Waldo Emerson,* ed. R. L. Rusk,
II, 204. See also the *Journals,* V, 221: "June 18, 1839. Yesterday Jones Very
departed from my home."

Emerson's letter to Margaret Fuller indicates: "I am editing Very's little book. Three Essays; & Verses. Out of two hundred poems, I have selected sixty-six that really possess rare merit. The book is to cost 75 cents, & I beg you to announce its coming value to all buyers. If it sells, our prophet will get $150 which, little though it be, he wants."[66] The "little book" came from the press early in September.[67]

[66] *The Letters of Ralph Waldo Emerson,* ed. R. L. Rusk, II, 209.

[67] See *The Christian Register* for Sept. 7, 1839. The volume is referred to as a recent publication.

CHAPTER V

ESSAYS AND POEMS, 1839

Essays and Poems by Jones Very was a neat volume of 175 duo-decimo pages, bound in brown paper-covered boards, and published by Charles C. Little and James Brown, of Boston. Very dedicated this, his first edition and the only one published during his life, to Professor Channing, his old teacher at Harvard, with whom he had enjoyed many discussions concerning Shakespeare. The dedication reads: "To Edward Tyrrel [*sic*] Channing, Boylston Professor in Harvard University, This Volume is Inscribed, as a Token of Gratitude, by the Author." The sale price, as Emerson wrote Margaret Fuller, was seventy-five cents, but just how many copies were printed is not known. An effort to secure such information from the firm of Little, Brown and Company met with a response of regret at failure to locate the records for the year 1839.[1] The number printed, however, was certainly not large. The three prose essays—"Epic Poetry," "Shakespeare," and "Hamlet"—comprise 104 pages; the poems, of which there are 65 rather than 66 as Emerson informed Margaret Fuller, fill up the remaining 71 pages. For the sake of coherence, it is convenient to discuss the prose first.

"Epic Poetry," which comprises the first 37 pages of Very's book, was the culmination of considerable study on the author's part. Very's thesis is that, as civilization advances, the production of epic poetry becomes more and more difficult. The early epics—those of

[1] The letter, dated Aug. 30, 1935, reads:

We received last month from you a letter in regard to a little volume of three essays and verses by Very which Charles C. Little and James Brown brought from the press in September, 1839.

We have delayed answering this letter hoping that we might find some information among our records.

The writer has gone back through the old books and is unable to find the records of 1839. We have them in good shape back to 1847 but the records previous to that time seem to be very incomplete and we regret that we cannot give you anything definite or throw any further light on this subject.

Yours very truly,

LITTLE, BROWN & COMPANY
Halladay

Homer, Vergil, and Lucan—exhibited heroic character by means of remote, outward, visible action; but Christianity has shifted interest to the inward, intellectual life, to the conflict within the individual soul. The Greek yearned to project his personality beyond the limits of his earthly existence, but his pagan conception of life led him to believe that the continuance of one's influence could be assured only through physical prowess. Thus he lived only for his country, and his "highest exemplification of morality was patriotism." Hence one finds in the *Iliad* and *Odyssey* that intense epic interest so noticeably absent in later heroic poems. Even Vergil and Lucan found their tasks difficult, because, even by the time they wrote, the human mind had progressed so far towards civilization—had become so introspective—that both writers found it impossible to create successfully the illusion of remoteness and to carry into the past "the heroic spirit of their own day." Thus they failed to give to their characters the heroic dignity of Aeneas.

With the coming of Christianity "a stronger sympathy with the inner man of the heart" was more and more felt; the interest was within rather than without. Dramatic poetry, therefore, tended to succeed the epic. Then, too, Christianity "rendered every finite subject unsuited for an epic poem," for it introduced the conception of man's immortality and thus opened the vista of eternity before the poet's view. To find "a subject, an action to fill those boundless realms of space, and call forth the energies of the spirits that people it" has proved too difficult for most poets; and this very fact presents the reason for not expecting another great epic poem.

Very discusses Tasso, Dante, and Milton as writers of Christian epics, and contends that Tasso, although he followed Dante in point of time, wrote an epic which corresponds fairly closely with Homer's poem, the reason being that the time of action of *Jerusalem Delivered* bore the same relation to Christian civilization that Homer's *Iliad* and *Odyssey* bore to Grecian civilization. It was Dante who transferred interest to the soul of man and exhibited him in conflict with those beings which his own spirit had created and which "his interest and fear shrouded in a sublimity not their own." But Dante's conception of Hell, Purgatory, and Heaven as the separate states into which vice and virtue would meet their fitting reward was only the expression of the material development of Christianity. Science has annihilated Dante's strange world of beings; the more advanced Christian character is concerned less with materiality and more with spirituality. The sublime genius of Milton created the next and highest development of the heroic character yet shown in action. He could not adopt altogether the material or the immaterial system, and he, therefore, raised his structure on the then debatable ground. He placed his action outside time and space, and yet preserved the cardinal element in Christianity by making Adam a free agent. The fact that our minds urge an objection to Milton's characters because of the incongruity between their spiritual properties and their human modes of existence is but further proof that the creation of epic poetry becomes more and more difficult as the mind advances and interest centers on thought rather than action.[2] What made *Paradise Lost* great, "and what can *now* alone make any subject for epic interest great, was the action made *visible* of a superior intellect on an inferior." The increasing inability of the human mind "to represent objectively its own action on another mind" is the greatest proof of the increasing difficulty which poets confront in creating epics. Very rejoices at this inability; to him "it is the high privilege of our age, the greatest proof of the progress of the soul, and of its approach to that state of being where its thought is action, its word power."

The concluding statement is significant, not so much for originality as for proof of Very's preoccupation with things spiritual. Regardless of what subject he might discuss, his viewpoint sooner or later would shift to that of religion. This is obvious even from a casual study of the growth of "Epic Poetry." It had its beginnings in Very's prize-winning Bowdoin dissertation of 1835, when he concerned himself with the influence of the idea of immortality on the

[2] It is interesting to compare Very's thesis with Poe's, as expressed in "The Poetic Principle." Both men regard the day of epics as past; in fact, Poe states: "But the day of these artistic anomalies is over. . . . It is to be hoped that common sense, in the time to come, will prefer deciding upon a work of art rather by the impression it makes, by the effect it produces, than by the time it took to impress the effect, or by the amount of sustained effort which had been found necessary in effecting the impression."

Poe's statement offers excellent proof of the wide contrast between the Massachusetts mystic and the Southerner. The one was obsessed with the ethical, the other with the artistic.

social, political, and literary life of civilized peoples.[3] It developed still further in the Public Exhibition of May 3, 1836, when Very delivered an oration which he called "The Heroic Character."[4] Here, even the opening sentence is strongly suggestive of the plan followed in "Epic Poetry": "The principles of action are ever changing, ever acquiring new strength and purity, and manifesting themselves in new and more noble forms, not seen indeed like those of former days by the outward eye, but which, perceived by the soul, fade not when the faint glimmerings of sense are extinguished, but still live and share in its own eternity." In this oration Homer and Lucan are compared as pagan exhibitors of heroic character, and the palm is given to Lucan's stoic heroes because of their noble "manifestation of the power the soul even then had, of retiring within its own depths unwilling to mingle with the streams of vice —and of the god-like struggles it must have undergone. . . ."

Such ideas, then, were enlarged and incorporated in the essay "Epic Poetry," which, it will be remembered, won for its author the senior Bowdoin prize of fifty dollars in 1836. The essay, as it appeared in the edition of 1839, shows some revision of the manuscript preserved at Harvard. About fifty additional lines have improved and developed the original piece, and a few changes have been made in paragraphing and in sentence structure.[5] These adjustments were probably made in preparation for Very's appearance before the Salem Lyceum in December, 1837, and the essay as printed unquestionably represents the manuscript which Very showed to Emerson on his visit to Concord in the spring of 1838.

Though the work now may not seem so brilliant and original as it did to Elizabeth Peabody, Emerson, and the members of the

[3] See *Bowdoin Prize Dissertations,* Vol. VI (1835-1839), in the Archives of the Widener Library at Harvard University.

[4] See *Exhibitions and Commencement Performances* (1836-1837). Jones Very's oration was No. 12 on the program for May 3, 1836.

[5] A comparison between the Bowdoin prize manuscript and the 1839 edition reveals the following additions to the former: on p. 9 of the 1839 edition, the remaining portion of the paragraph, that part beginning with "When we look back . . ."; on p. 10, the sentences incorporated in line 21 through line 9 on p. 11; on p. 15, the sentence closing the paragraph at the bottom of the page; on p. 23, second paragraph, beginning with "it is in Dante's poem that we find man . . ." and continuing to the close of the paragraph. Furthermore, there are three changes in paragraphing, and five adjustments in sentence structure.

Salem Lyceum, it is nevertheless a scholarly essay, clearly and logically constructed, and written in a style of pleasing maturity. One senses immediately Very's love of the classics, but the flavor of the essay is literary rather than "bookish." Besides the writers of epic poems already mentioned, one discovers Cicero, Aristotle, Plutarch, Sallust, Voltaire, Lamartine (*The Pilgrimage*), Monti, Ariosto, Girandi Cinto, Trissino, Bacon, Shakespeare, Wordsworth, Coleridge, Carlyle (*Sartor Resartus*), Schiller, Lord Kames, Pollok, and Wilkie.

But particularly refreshing is the Greek spirit permeating this essay. Even a casual reader must feel Very's intense love for and sympathy with Greek life—its devotion to nature and to physical beauty, its eager expression of patriotism, its yearning "after a life beyond the narrow limits of its earthly existence." Very's knowledge of the Greek language, his understanding of Greek literature, and his psychological interpretation of the nobility and dignity of Greek heroism offer proof that he was indeed an inspiring teacher at Harvard and a stimulating companion for both Thoreau and Emerson. It is pleasurable for an admirer of Very to reflect that the germ of "Epic Poetry" originated and partly developed before the religious frenzy possessed its creator, and that the work bears unmistakable evidence of a youthful, almost pagan, delight in things Greek. This early joy was like a strong plant; its roots sank deep in the rich soil of Hellenism, drank from its fountains of beauty, and drew forth a sustenance so potent that it was stamped indelibly with the thing that nurtured it. Later fires might wither and sear, strong blasts might twist and gnarl; but always there would remain a bit of green from an early spring, and a suggestion of grace and symmetry from a form once known as beautiful.

The essays "Shakespeare" and "Hamlet" should be considered together, as Very himself suggested. "Shakespeare" is Very's most important prose work; as compared with "Epic Poetry," it is longer, is more intensely unified because of strict adherence to its one central theme, is more felicitous and pungent in its style, and is almost perfectly constructed. Very's object was "to show, by an analysis of the character of Shakespeare, that a desire of action was the ruling impulse of his mind; and consequently, a sense of existence its permanent state. That this condition was natural; not the result felt from a submission of the will to it, but bearing the will along with it; presenting the mind as phenomenal and unconscious, and almost as much a passive instrument as the material world." By skillful phrasing, apt illustration, and varied repetition, Very impresses his thesis upon the mind of his reader. Shakespeare's mind, he contends, was the "unconscious possessor of all things"; it was in a primal state of natural innocence, as spontaneously active as the limbs of a healthy and normal child, identifying itself with everything around it, and thus, like the child, bearing the impress of universal life. For this reason, it could create a Hamlet or a Lear on one hand, or could seemingly revel in the licentious. But this apparent inconsistency is accounted for by the very innocence of Shakespeare's mind; its desire for action had no end in view save that of activity. Very, consequently, can defend Shakespeare's apparent licentiousness, but cannot excuse that of Byron. He says, in part: "But how different is that playful and childlike spirit with which he acted a vicious character, from that which seems to have actuated a Byron. The one represents an abandoned man as he actually exists, with the joys of sense and the anguish of the spirit alternately agitating his troubled breast. . . . But the latter was not innocent, he imparted something of himself to what he describes; he would not and could not, like Shakespeare, put before us a virtuous man with the same pleasure as he does a vicious one." Stressing further the naturalness of Shakespeare, Very states: "What he was and felt he said, he did not strive to build up character, according to his own presumption and preconceived notions, but only described . . . what he himself was and felt in their positions as he severally occupied them." And then Very makes a really quotable statement when he says: "He did not, like Corneille, hold back vice that she might not speak her part, nor did he, like Byron, restrain virtue."

So far, Very's criticism of Shakespeare smacks of much that the Romantic critics—particularly Coleridge,[6] and to a less degree Lamb[7] and Hazlitt—have said. But Very leaves the stamp of his

[6] Cf. Coleridge's "Characteristics of Shakespeare's Dramas," particularly his defense of Shakespeare's morality.

[7] Very quotes from Lamb's criticism; see *Essays and Poems*, by Jones Very, p. 62.

own individuality even on a critique of Shakespeare. This appears
in the form of a condemnation of what he contends is Shakespeare's
marked deficiency: the dramatist had not surrendered his will to
God, had not been baptized with the Holy Ghost. Consequently,
even though Shakespeare's characters are great and natural, they
are only unconsciously so. His mind was a pure and spotless mirror
reflecting nature, but only a nature of pure and spotless innocence—
never of virtue. "Had that love of action which was so peculiarly
the motive of Shakespeare's mind, been followed also as a duty,
it would have added a strength to his characters which we do not
feel them now to possess. Since Shakespeare acted from impulse
rather than principle, he should not be regarded as a man so much
as a phenomenon. "'Twas God's care only that the mind he sent
labored not in vain." This, in short, is Very's explanation of the
peculiar genius of Shakespeare.

"Hamlet" is Very's amplified repetition of his theory of Shakespeare's mind and character. Taking a single play for an example,
Very attempts to demonstrate further that Shakespeare's master
passion was the love of intellectual activity for its own sake, and
that, in consequence, "his continual satisfaction with the simple
pleasure of existence must have made him more than commonly
liable to the fear of death," or at least must have intensified his
interest in the subject of death. *To be or not to be* forever, was a
question which Hamlet yearned to settle; all else faded into noth-
ingness before the all-absorbing importance of the question of existence. Very's belief was that Hamlet's mind was one which "could
never reach that assurance of eternal existence which Christ alone
can give"; in this very fact lay the materials that created the remarkable tragedy of Shakespeare's popular hero. The action, therefore,
was mental, and was so intense as completely to absorb even all
physical energy. Hamlet was not, therefore, as Dr. Johnson has
said, weak and cowardly, but was rather admirably courageous. His
thinking had reached a stage when the ephemeral, earthly life failed
to satisfy; his whole nature suffered the insatiable thirst for per-
petuity. The "dread of something after death"—perhaps even annihilation—tortured him. So, though loving not this life, he endured
it and clung to it because he was uncertain about another, and his

whole existence seemed to an onlooker only as a tragedy of passive indecision. Very naturally finds the "to be or not to be" soliloquy the key to interpretation of the entire play. He rides his theory so hard as almost to exhaust it, and he errs in ignoring the influence of environment and attending circumstances in influencing Hamlet's state of mind. Yet one is impressed with this essay. It is nearly perfect in structure—more so than "Epic Poetry"—and has a pleasing literary flavor. Very disagrees, not only with Dr. Johnson in his interpretation of Hamlet's mind and character, but also with Goethe, with Coleridge, and with Goldsmith.

Both "Shakespeare" and "Hamlet" are characterized by spontaneity and mastery of expression. The reader never gets the impression that Very labored to construct good, sonorous sentences or turn apt phrases; the diction is exact, the sentences are admirable, but both the language and the structural pattern seem effortless. For instance, in "Shakespeare" one finds the following sentence: "Like the ocean, his [Shakespeare's] mind could fill with murmuring waves the strangely indented coast of human existence from the widest bay to the smallest creek; then ebbing, retire within itself, as if form was but a mode of its limitless and independent being." More than fifty-five years ago George Bradford, Jr., declared the word *ebbing* a "master touch."[8]

But perhaps even more prevalent than the element of spontaneity is the genuine ring of conviction in Very's Shakespearean essays. Both are products of that period of his strongest mental exaltation, and both were composed with the same seriousness that marked the creation of his religious sonnets. He clung tenaciously to the belief that he was God's messenger and that what he wrote concerning Shakespeare, therefore, was divinely communicated. Hence, to doubt the truth of his essays or to suggest their lack of divine inspiration was faithlessness on the one hand and sacrilege on the other. He once said very simply to a friend that it was "given him to know" about Shakespeare and that what he wrote was not only "the true word, but the best word that had been spoken on the subject."[9] In a similar frame of mind, he had written Emer-

---

[8] George Bradford, Jr., "Jones Very," *The Unitarian Review,* XXVII (Feb., 1887), 111-118.　　[9] *Ibid.* See Editor's note.

son when mailing him the general essay on Shakespeare: "I am glad at last to be able to transmit what has been told me of Shakespeare. . . . You hear not mine words but the teachings of the Holy Ghost."[10] It will be recalled that Very was led to study Shakespeare because he wished to answer all young men who pointed to Shakespeare as a man who possessed great genius but who was not a saint.[11] To Emerson he also confided that he "thought if he could move Shakespeare he could move the world"; and he had added forcibly, "I begin to see him shake already."[12] Faith in what he believed to be his inspired theory to solve the riddle of Shakespeare's mental greatness led him also to remark to Elizabeth Peabody: "To the preexistent Shakespeare wisdom was offered, but he declined it, and took only genius."[13]

With such an understanding of Very's belief in his divine inspiration, one can turn to the "Poems" with the feeling that he is comfortably prepared to give them just and adequate interpretation.

Emerson wrote Margaret Fuller that he selected from "two hundred poems . . . sixty-six that really possess rare merit."[14] As has been stated, he actually chose sixty-five. Of these, fifty-four had previously appeared in the Salem Observer, and four had been used by James Freeman Clarke in The Western Messenger;[15] seven, however, were being published for the first time.[16] Though Emerson may have erred in his mathematics, he certainly was correct in his criticism of the verse on which he wished the public to base its opinion of Very. An unprejudiced critic may find it somewhat difficult to be enthusiastic about every one of the poems, but he will unquestionably agree with Emerson that each poem is unique and that none is altogether mediocre.

A glance through the collection in search of structural patterns

---

[10] Andrews, p. 20.

[11] Emerson's Journals, V, 105. See also n. 24 in Chapter III.

[12] F. B. Sanborn, Recollections of Seventy Years, II, 438.

[13] Emerson's Journals, X, 108.

[14] See Chapter IV. The letter was dated July 9, 1839.

[15] "He Was Acquainted with Grief," p. 167 (The Western Messenger, VI, March, 1839, 312); "Ye Gave Me No Meat," p. 168 (The Western Messenger, VI, April, 1839, 367); "The Rail Road," p. 170 (The Western Messenger, VI, March, 1839, 311); "The Disciple," p. 171 (The Western Messenger, VI, April, 1839, 369).

[16] "To the Fossil Flower," pp. 114-116; "Nature," p. 118; "The Garden," p. 132; "The Song," p. 133; "To the Pure All Things Are Pure," p. 166; "The Acorn," p. 169; "The Cottage," p. 174.

discloses the fact that only one poem is in blank verse; that nine are in a variety of stanzas, generally the four-line, alternately-rhymed iambic pentameter or iambic tetrameter verse; and that the remaining fifty-five are Shakespearean sonnets, twenty of which employ an extra foot in the concluding line. Approximately five sixths of the poems, then, are sonnets; and the same ratio applies roughly to all of Very's verse. Indeed, the sonnet form seemed best suited to his mature genius, and he, therefore, discarded the heroic couplet of his apprentice years for the more graceful and compact lyric form, and employed the latter chiefly throughout his long but comparatively uneventful poetic career.

Perhaps Emerson had in mind some possible classification of Very's verse according to subject matter, mood, and treatment, for the poems fall conveniently into three groups: (1) those concerned with nature, (2) those concerned primarily with religion, and (3) a small number of poems so personal as to be autobiographic. The initial poem, "To the Humming Bird," belongs to the first group.

Emerson displayed sound judgment and artistic appreciation when he chose this little four-stanza piece as the first poetic offering Very should make to the readers of the 1839 edition. Here one discovers Very in his most pleasant and appealing mood—simple, kind, unaffected, gentle, intensely sympathetic with animal life, and personal in his reaction to nature. In spirit the poem reminds one of Freneau's "The Wild Honey Suckle," and in both mood and structural pattern it suggests Burns's "To a Mouse." Indeed, as one reads the stanzas, one senses the essence of pure nature poetry; and one can easily imagine Wordsworth as responding happily to Very's sincerity of emotion and simplicity of diction:[17]

> I cannot heal thy green gold breast,
> Where deep those cruel teeth have prest,
> Nor bid thee raise thy ruffled crest,
>   And seek thy mate,
> Who sits alone within thy nest,
>   Nor sees thy fate.

[17] Emerson purposed sending Wordsworth a copy of *Essays and Poems,* for in the *Journals* for March 30, 1840, is recorded: "Send Very's Poems to Carlyle and Wordsworth" (V, 377). A year passed, however, before the little book was sent to Carlyle, and it is entirely possible that none was sent to Wordsworth. At least Wordsworth's letters make no mention of the book.

No more with him in summer hours
Thou'lt hum amid the leafy bowers,
Nor hover round the dewy flowers,
            To feed thy young;
Nor seek, when evening darkly lowers,
            Thy nest high hung.

No more thou'lt know a mother's care
Thy honied spoils at eve to share,
Nor teach thy tender brood to dare
            With upward spring,
Their path through fields of sunny air,
            On new fledged wing.

For thy return in vain shall wait
Thy tender young, thy fond fond mate,
Till night's last stars beam forth full late
            On their sad eyes;
Unknown, alas! thy cruel fate,
            Unheard thy cries![18]

Gone, indeed, are the earlier tendencies of Very to use the heroic
couplet and the stilted personification and conventional language
of the Classicists. Pope has been supplanted by Wordsworth and
other Romantics; "nature methodized" has become nature emotion-
alized.

Very's love of birds is represented by two further poems, both
of which are in the Shakespearean sonnet form, with an extra foot
in the last line. "To the Canary Bird"[19] voices artistically an intense
sympathy with a creature imprisoned from its natural habitat.
Speaking to the bird, Very says:

> I cannot hear thy voice with others' ears,
> Who make of thy lost liberty a gain;
> And in thy vale of blighted hopes and fears
> Feel not that every note is born with pain.

In these lines Jones Very expresses that passionate hatred of imprisonment and of tyranny early instilled by his mother's emphasis
of Captain Jones Very's experience in Nova Scotia. Lydia Very
might have chosen a topic from history, but her son Jones found the

[18] *Essays and Poems* (1839), pp. 107-108.
[19] *Ibid.*, p. 117.

simple aspects of nature a more agreeable subject. Byron needed the story of Bonnivard and the prison of Chillon to inflame his pure passion for liberty, but Very needed only a bird to stir his serene nature into a restrained frenzy: the one loved the turbulent; the other, the calm. And as proof of Very's attitude one may consider "The Robin,"[20] the third of the bird poems. Here, Very illustrates a tendency which grew into an unfortunate habit—the wrenching of a sonnet begun with simple observation and pure adoration of the common yet picturesque aspects of nature into stern and ugly moralizing. Thus the poem begins—

> Thou need'st not flutter from thy half-built nest,
> Whene'er thou hear'st man's hurrying feet go by—

and continues through the second quatrain with proof of Very's close observation of the robin's habits. But the third quatrain and the couplet concentrate a sermon:

> All will not hear thy sweet out-pouring joy,
> That with morn's stillness blends the voice of song,
> For over-anxious cares their souls employ,
> That else upon thy music borne along
> And the light wings of heart-ascending prayer
> Had learned that Heaven is pleased thy simple
> joys to share.

Such an obsession with what to some readers is a repellent phase of religion, suggests the poems of Anne Bradstreet almost two hundred years earlier, and, to a greater extent, those of Very's older contemporary, William Cullen Bryant. Indeed, Very's application of the ethical at the close of some of his poems more closely resembles Bryant's "moral tag" than the didactic treatment employed by any other American poet. The nature poetry of the two men is alike in many respects. One has only to compare the poems glorifying American birds and flowers to see that each man is a Puritan, that he passionately loves his subjects, and that he enjoys a deep communion with nature. But Bryant is generally more majestically calm and solemn, more melancholy, more frigid in his association than is Very. The crowning glory of Very is his spirituality; unlike Bryant, he finds a strong mystic meaning in nature, and the realiza-

[20] *Ibid.*, p. 124.

tion of this discovery frequently so permeates his being as to melt his Puritanical reserve and inflame his soul into an intense and passionate interpretation of the spiritual significance of nature. The expression of such spirituality, then, is Very's unique contribution to American literature. His exceedingly simple diction and his almost total lack of conscious rhetoric or of stylistic device are a fitting garment for his sincerity, and accentuate the reverential attitude he bears towards his subject. In truth, Very's poems seem often the essence of spiritual nature transmuted into the language of a devout disciple.

Such are "The Painted Columbine"[21] and "The Columbine,"[22] both of which glorify Very's favorite flower.[23] The latter poem is important, for it expresses Very's belief in the mystical identification of himself with nature. As he lovingly examines the columbine, he loses almost all conscious identification with the flesh, and becomes absorbed in the object of his devotion:

> Still, still my eye will gaze long fixed on thee,
> Till I forget that I am called a man,
> And at thy side fast-rooted seem to be,
> And the breeze comes my cheek with thine to fan.
> Upon this craggy hill our life shall pass,
> A life of summer days and summer joys,
> Nodding our honey-bells mid pliant grass
> In which the bee half hid his time employs;
> And here we'll drink with thirsty pores the rain,
> And turn dew-sprinkled to the rising sun,
> And look when in the flaming west again
> His orb across the heaven its path has run;
> Here left in darkness on the rocky steep,
> My weary eyes shall close like folding flowers
> in sleep.[24]

[21] *Ibid.*, pp. 112-113.   [22] *Ibid.*, p. 125.

[23] In the Essex Institute, at Salem, Mass., is a proposed Christmas booklet prepared by Lydia L. A. Very for Roberts & Co. The book was not published, however, since it was considered by the publishers to be too small for their use. Miss Very designed a cover, using elaborated lettering and columbines, in color, and she selected five of Very's poems on the columbine for the booklet. These poems were: "The Painted Columbine," "The Columbine," "The Return of the Columbine" (*Clarke*, p. 437), "Columbines and Anemones" (*Clarke*, pp. 367-368), and "On Some Blue and Gold Columbines from Pike's Peak, Colorado" (*Clarke*, p. 410).   [24] *Op. cit.*, p. 125.

It is doubtful whether the verse of any other poet in American literature conveys so completely the mystical unity of man with nature, and if one turn to English literature, only the Romantics offer possible comparisons. The lines,

> Nodding our honey-bells mid pliant grass
> In which the bee half hid his time employs,

suggest the sensuous languor of Keats, but the complete absorption with nature is more like Wordsworth or even Shelley.

The columbine poems have companion pieces in "The Wind-Flower" and "The Violet."[25] Though neither of these sonnets represents Very's pure absorption with nature, both glow with a genuine warmth of emotion, and reveal the intimate relationship and deep understanding which exists between Nature and him who loves her. Certainly, one senses in these poems that deep personal feeling Very experienced toward nature, so that to him loneliness was almost impossible. Flowers, birds, and trees were to him companions even as they were to Wordsworth and Thoreau, and his cummunion with nature was just as real as that with men, and was generally more satisfying because less disappointing. That secret Very confided to the violet:

> Thou tellest truths unspoken yet by man
> By this thy lonely home and modest look;
> For he has not the eyes such truths to scan,
> Nor learns to read from such a lowly book;
> With him it is not life firm-fixed to grow
> Beneath the outspreading oaks and rising pines,
> Content this humble lot of thine to know,
> The nearest neighbor of the creeping vines;
> Without fixed root he cannot trust like thee
> The rain will know the appointed hour to fall,
> But fears lest sun or shower may hurtful be,
> And would delay or speed them with his call;
> Nor trust like thee when wintry winds blow cold,
> Whose shrinking form the withered leaves enfold.[26]

Such lines represent Very at his best, for they combine his two dominant traits—love of nature, and love of God. These, blended

[25] *Ibid.*, p. 123 and p. 148, respectively.
[26] *Ibid.*, p. 148.

with an extremely simple diction, unadorned style, and regular
structural pattern, make him, indeed, the unique spiritual inter-
preter of nature in American poetry.

And yet in spite of Very's intense spirituality and his conviction,
as expressed to Emerson and others, that his words were divinely
inspired, he sometimes admitted the inability of language to convey
his feeling. Often, like Wordsworth, with whom he found greatest
joy,[27] he profoundly felt himself to be a part of all he saw and
heard; and so mystical was the union that it broke through the
barriers of rhetoric and illuminated his simple diction until the
reader's imagination and emotions were stirred and he was enabled
to expand and glorify the meager record until he, too, approached
Very's original rapture. Such a poem is the beautiful sonnet, "Nature":

> Nature! my love for thee is deeper far
> Than strength of words though spirit-born can tell;
> For while I gaze they seem my soul to bar,
> That in thy widening streams would onward swell
> Bearing thy mirrored beauty on its breast,—
> Now, through thy lonely haunts unseen to glide,
> A motion that scarce knows itself from rest,
> With pictured flowers and branches on its tide;
> Then, by the noisy city's frowning wall,
> Whose armed heights within its waters gleam,
> To rush with answering voice to ocean's call,
> And mingle with the deep its swollen stream,
> Whose boundless bosom's calm alone can hold,
> That heaven of glory in thy skies unrolled.[28]

Another sonnet bears the same title, but it is far more clearly and
happily religious. Here nature is represented as being in harmony
with God and God's creatures and as being joyously responsive to
him whose life is pure and will-less. Therefore, as Very states,

> The bubbling brook doth leap when I come by,
> Because my feet find measure with its call.[29]

[27] According to the statement of his sister Lydia; see "Jones Very Again," Boston
Sunday Herald, Sunday, June 6, 1880.
[28] *Op. cit.*, p. 118.   [29] *Ibid.*, p. 161.

Morning

The light will never open sightless eyes,
It comes to those who willingly would see;
And every object, hill, and stream, and skies,
Rejoice within th'encircling line to be;
'Tis day—the field is filled with busy hands,
The shop resounds with noisy workmen's din,
The traveller with his staff all ready stands
His yet unmeasured journey to begin;
The light breaks gently too within the breast—
Yet there no eye awaits the crimson morn,
The forge and noisy anvil are at rest,
Nor men nor oxen tread the fields of corn,
Nor pilgrim lifts his staff—it is no day
To those who find on earth their place to stay.

Nature

The bubbling brook doth leap when I come by,
Because my feet find measure with its call;
The birds know when the friend they love is nigh,
For I am known to them both great and small;
The flower that on the lonely hill-side grows,
Expects me there when spring its bloom has given;
And many a tree and bush my wanderings knows,
And e'en the clouds and silent stars of heaven;
For he who with his Maker walks aright,
Shall be their lord, as Adam was before;
His ear shall catch each sound with new delight,
Each object wear the dress that then it wore;
And he, as when erect in soul he stood,
Hear from his Father's lips that all is good.

In somewhat similar vein is "The Tree,"[30] another sonnet in which Very communes with nature and finds the assuring proof of God's eternal cycle of creation and of love. The reader of this poem senses without effort the reverence Very felt for nature and for God; he realizes that Emerson and Alcott rightly saw in this mystical poet a purity of life and an unworldliness which stamped him as a saint. "The Tree" is a tenderly expressed sonnet, simple in style, genuine in emotion, fresh and clean as winter snow. Less spiritual but equally as impressive are the sonnet, "The Latter Rain,"[31] and the blank verse piece, "To the Fossil Flower."[32]

Reference to these poems leads naturally to the consideration of one sonnet, "The Song," unmarked by any touch of the sternly religious or of the didactic. Beginning with an attempt to lyricize his praise of nature, Very quickly admits his inability to achieve his purpose, and at length indulges his remembrance of a past but happy youth, now somewhat idealized:

> When I would sing of crooked streams and fields,
> On, on from me they stretch too far and wide,
> And at their look my song all powerless yields,
> And down the river bears me with its tide;
> Amid the fields I am a child again,
> The spots that then I love I love the more,
> My fingers drop the strangely scrawling pen,
> And I remember naught but nature's lore;
> I plunge me in the river's cooling wave,
> Or on the embroidered bank admiring lean,
> Now some entangled insect life to save,
> Now watch the pictured flowers and grasses green;
> Forever playing where a boy I played,
> By hill and grove, by field and stream delayed.[33]

One regrets that Very did not voice such moods oftener, and one wishes that life might have affected him less seriously, that it might have made him less repellently and sternly Puritanical, less unrelentingly just. But once he was possessed by the religious ecstasy, he gave himself to it wholly and willingly, returning at rare, and then often melancholy, intervals to his first interest—nature.

---

[30] *Ibid.*, p. 119.
[32] *Ibid.*, pp. 114-116.
[31] *Ibid.*, p. 157.
[33] *Ibid.*, p. 133.

Indeed, the poems concerned primarily with religion clearly reflect Very's growing obsession with the spiritual. As one reads on and on through the sonnets, one relives with Very that period of his life which Emerson, more than any other of Very's friends, knew and recorded so well. One sees the intense revelation of a hypersensitive spirit, already predisposed to mystical rapture, in its sympathetic responsiveness to the phases of transcendentalism which stressed love of nature and love of freedom; but one sees more clearly revealed than anything else Very's all-pervading interest in things spiritual—at first only a glow, warming his cool Unitarian reserve, but at length growing into a consuming internal fire, surging through every channel of his soul and escaping outwardly in flaming words of rapt devotion or prophetic warning. It is not strange that such an experience should have seared the body, leaving it racked and torn, that Jones Very in his old age should have reminded one of an extinct volcano.

Perhaps no sonnet better illustrates Very's early attitude toward the spiritual than the poem, "Life." Herein he expresses his hunger for a stronger, firmer faith, his thirst for the very Fountain Head, his passion for actual absorption with God, and a life rich in its fruitage. Nature furnishes the imagery, but religion supplies the treatment; the tree is Very, but the earth, sky, sun—all elements that give life—are God:

> It is not life upon Thy gifts to live,
> But, to grow fixed with deeper roots in Thee;
> And when the sun and shower their bounties give,
> To send out thick-leaved limbs; a fruitful tree,
> Whose green head meets the eye for many a mile,
> Whose moss-grown arms their rigid branches rear,
> And full-faced fruits their blushing welcome smile
> As to its goodly shade our feet draw near;
> Who tastes its gifts shall never hunger more,
> For 'tis the Father spreads the pure repast,
> Who, while we eat, renews the ready store,
> Which at his bounteous board must ever last;
> For none the bridegroom's supper shall attend,
> Who will not hear and make his word their friend.[34]

[34] *Ibid.*, p. 151.

Such a poem demonstrates no great spiritual struggle and suggests no turmoil of doubt; it merely expresses definitely that humble, unostentatious, complete devotion to God which characterized Very's life from youth to death.

This early devotion brought a richer spiritual experience. Very gradually felt that his life was becoming absorbed with that of the Spirit; and he became firmly convinced that the more will-less he grew, the more abundantly the streams of God-love might flow through his being. Grateful for the revelation of divine presence and now unshakably certain of the value of will-lessness, he grew more eager for self-effacement and yearned for an absorption so complete as to suggest the Mysticism of the Orient.[35] The sonnet, "In Him We Live," splendidly represents such a mental attitude:

> Father! I bless thy name that I do live,
> And in each motion am made rich with thee,
> And when a glance is all that I can give,
> It is a kingdom's wealth if I but see;
> This stately body cannot move, save I
> Will to its nobleness my little bring;
> My voice its measured cadence will not try,
> Save I with every note consent to sing;
> I cannot raise my hands to hurt or bless,
> But I with every action must conspire;
> To show me there how little I possess,
> And yet that little more than I desire;
> May each new act my new allegiance prove,
> Till in thy perfect love I ever live and move.[36]

[35] Arthur Christy, *The Orient in American Transcendentalism* (New York: Columbia University Press, 1932), makes no mention of Very. His study, however, concerns only the Concord group—Emerson, Thoreau, and Alcott. Any complete study of the Orient in American transcendentalism would devote a considerable space to Jones Very. Had Mr. Christy chosen to do so, he could have greatly enriched his book by quotations from the Salem mystic.

[36] *Op. cit.*, p. 128. This sonnet, which first appeared in the Salem *Observer* for Nov. 10, 1838, was one of two which Very sent to Emerson, and the receipt of which Emerson acknowledged in his letter of Nov. 18 to Very (see Chapter IV). The second sonnet was "Enoch," in the 1839 edition, p. 129. Emerson's enthusiasm had led him to write, "I love and read them to all who have ears to hear."

The reader will note Very's inconsistencies in capitalization and punctuation. Sometimes the pronominal adjective *thy,* referring to the Deity, is capitalized and sometimes it is not; pronouns referring to the Deity are similarly treated. The

This sonnet offers proof for the statements made by James Freeman
Clarke and by Dr. Channing as to Very's behavior when the young
mystic once visited Dr. Channing in response to the latter's invitation to express his views concerning his absolute will-lessness. Dr.
Channing, as a test, had stated: "I observed that during your conversation you left your chair and went while speaking to the fireplace, and rested your arm on the mantel. Did you do this of your
own accord or in obedience to the Spirit?" Very's immediate answer had been, "In obedience to the Spirit."[37]

The result of such complete annihilation of the willful self was
that the zealous mystic felt reborn to a new life. In ringing verse
he chanted his praise and thanksgiving for the vibrant intellectual
and spiritual experiences which now seemed constant with him:

> 'Tis a new life;—thoughts move not as they did
> With slow uncertain steps across my mind,
> In thronging haste fast pressing on they bid
> The portals open to the viewless wind
> That comes not save when in the dust is laid
> The crown of pride. . . .[38]

But Very's "crown of pride" had been removed long since. He, like
the sun, the cloud, and the bird, awaited the command to sing the
Father's praise. "The Son" is one of many poems expressing such
a mood; the first ten lines suggest the figures of comparison, and
the last four lines conclude the simile, as follows:

> So does my spirit wait thy presence now
> To pour thy praise in quickening life along,
> Chiding with voice divine man's lengthening sleep,
> While round the Unuttered Word and Love their
> vigils keep.[39]

The phrase, "chiding with voice divine," is significant, for it definitely expresses Very's conviction that his was the voice of God.

poems quoted in this chapter have been reproduced as they were printed in the
1839 edition.
   Cf. Emerson's entry in the *Journals*, Vol. VIII, under date of May, 1851, referring to Very's attitude toward altering his sonnets.
   [37] See Chapter III for a fuller discussion of this event; also Clarke's biographical
sketch of Very in the edition of 1886: *Poems and Essays*, by Jones Very.
   [38] *Op. cit.*, p. 126.   [39] *Ibid.*, p. 127.

The same thought is repeated often in the religious sonnets. In "The Disciple" he emphasizes this idea, together with that of his constant communion with God and his joy in service. One can even sense that Very, like his Calvinist forbears, felt himself one of the "elect"; but it is a realization void of all arrogance. With abject humility and simple trust, he says:

> Thou wilt my hands employ, though others find
> No work for those who praise thy name aright;
> And in their worldly wisdom call them blind,
> Whom thou has[t] blest with thine own spirit's sight.[40]

As Very's mysticism deepened, he became more physically passive, more spiritually active. So intense was his feeling of communion with God that he saw the Divine Presence in every material object, and thought of matter, not in terms of science, but in terms of religion. Perhaps in "The Presence" one discovers the very quintessence of mysticism in American literature:

> I sit within my room, and joy to find
> That Thou who always lov'st, art with me here,
> That I am never left by Thee behind,
> But by thyself Thou keep'st me ever near:
> The fire burns brighter when with Thee I look,
> And seems a kinder servant sent to me;
> With gladder heart I read thy holy book,
> Because thou art the eyes by which I see;
> This aged chair, that table, watch and door
> Around in ready service ever wait;
> Nor can I ask of Thee a menial more
> To fill the measure of my large estate,
> For Thou thyself, with all a father's care,
> Where'er I turn, art ever with me there.[41]

Naturally, a man whose processes of thinking and feeling had reached a stage of such unearthly rapture could find little to interest him in the practical lives of his fellows. He lived only in "The Spirit Land," chanting with unfeigned praise the ineffable joys of his own mystical world:

> Father! thy wonders do not singly stand,
> Nor far removed where feet have seldom strayed;

[40] Ibid., p. 171.   [41] Ibid., p. 145.

> Around us ever lies the enchanted land
> In marvels rich to thine own sons displayed.[42]

In a reverie he became Adam in the Garden of Eden, and thrilled with the sense of sinlessness, with the primal innocence of God's newly created one. The experience was recorded in the sonnet, "The Garden," opening with the lines:

> I saw a spot where our first parents dwelt;
> And yet it wore to me no face of change,
> For while amid its fields and groves I felt
> As if I had not sinned, nor thought it strange.[43]

Life teemed; death seemed annihilated. The physical body hastened to express its joy at being created by the Spirit; and Very sang exultantly:

> There is no death with Thee! each plant and tree
> In living haste their stems push onward still,
> The pointed blade, each rooted trunk we see
> In various movement all attest thy will.[44]

As so often happens with enthusiasts, Very grew anxious about having others share his rapture. But the physically aggressive, practical New Englanders showed little interest in their poet's mysticism. To Very, they seemed alive only in the body: they responded only outwardly, and then only to the world and its interests. The inner life of the spirit was dormant; the eyes of the soul seemed blind. Thus the physical light of the morning brought interest and activity in the field and the shop, but the light of the spirit met with no responsiveness. Very lamented this, and said:

> The light breaks gently too within the breast,—
> Yet there no eye awaits the crimson morn,
> The forge and noisy anvil are at rest,
> Nor men nor oxen tread the fields of corn,
> Nor pilgrim lifts his staff,—it is no day
> To those who find on earth their place to stay.[45]

[42] Ibid., p. 140.
[43] Ibid., p. 132.   [44] Ibid., "The Living God," p. 131.
[45] Ibid., "Morning," p. 160. A similar idea occurs in "The Morning Watch" (p. 130), though in this sonnet people are represented as sleeping long after "the light" has arrived.

As Very brooded over the state of society, he at length concluded that men had no faith,[46] that their prayers were empty, and that their worship was pure vanity.[47] They reminded him of dead trees. "I see them," he shouted,

> crowd on crowd they walk the earth
> Dry leafless trees to autumn wind laid bare.[48]

The earth became a graveyard peopled with these spiritually dead folk. In his loneliness he said, "I have no Brother."[49] Yet he felt himself to be a prophet, and he fervently but vainly exhorted those around him to repent and accept salvation. In anguish he wailed:

> My heart grows sick before the wide-spread death,
> That walks and speaks in seeming life around;
> And I would love the corse without a breath,
> That sleeps forgotten 'neath the cold, cold ground.[50]

The cry of bitterness went unheeded. He, too, was one who "came unto his own, and his own received him not." Men chose to be willful, to "live upon the husks of corn,"[51] instead of the kernels underneath; they chose freedom of the will, and in their disobedience forged for themselves chains which bound them in eternal slavery.[52] Even nature offered proof of God's love, but men heard and saw not. In the opening lines of "Enoch" Very recorded his experience at this state of his religious excitation:

> I looked to find a man who walked with God,
> Like the transplanted patriarch of old;—
> Though gladdened millions on his footstool trod
> Yet none with him did such sweet converse hold;
> I heard the wind in low complaint go by
> That none its melodies like him could hear;
> Day unto day spoke wisdom from on high,
> Yet none like David turned a willing ear;
> God walked alone unhonored through the earth;
> For him no heart-built temple open stood,
> The soul forgetful of her nobler birth
> Had hewn him lofty shrines of stone and wood,

[46] *Ibid.*, "Faith," p. 156.
[47] *Ibid.*, "Worship," p. 141.
[48] *Ibid.*, "The Dead," p. 146.
[49] *Ibid.*, "Thy Brother's Blood," p. 154.
[50] *Ibid.*, "The Grave Yard," p. 153.
[51] *Ibid.*, "Bread," p. 139.
[52] *Ibid.*, "The Slave," p. 138.

And left unfinished and in ruins still
The only temple he delights to fill.[53]

Apparently one of those ministers who presided in the "lofty shrines of stone and wood" dared to argue with Very, and perhaps to intimate that his message was not divinely inspired. He might have been the minister in Concord whom, in the words of Emerson, Very "unhorsed." Whoever he was, Very answered him in a sonnet more dramatic than lyric, more sternly just than completely annihilating:

Thou art more deadly than the Jew of old,
Thou hast his weapons hidden in thy speech;
And though thy hand from me thou dost withhold,
They pierce where sword and spear could never reach.
Thou hast me fenced about with thorny talk,
To pierce my soul with anguish while I hear;
And while amid thy populous streets I walk,
I feel at every step the entering spear;
Go, cleanse thy lying mouth of all its guile
That from the will within thee ever flows;
Go, cleanse the temple thou dost now defile,
Then shall I cease to feel thy heavy blows;
And come and tread with me the patch of peace,
And from thy brother's harm forever cease.[54]

It is fortunate that Very's indignation waned and that he again grew serene, for the role of Isaiah did not suit him. The inherent traits of modesty and reserve in his personality appeared at their best only when in company with the calm gentleness and the unworldly rapture which provoked his communings with nature and with God. Growing out of such a mood is the sonnet "Night," saturated with the humility of spirit and the weariness of mind and body which followed Very's few exertions to be dramatically prophetic or oratorically evangelistic:

I thank thee, Father, that the night is near
When I this conscious being may resign;
Whose only task thy words of love to hear,
And in thy acts to find each act of mine;
A task too great to give a child like me,
The myriad-handed labors of the day,

---

[53] *Ibid.*, p. 129.   [54] *Ibid.*, "The Jew," p. 155.

Too many for my closing eyes to see,
Thy words too frequent for my tongue to say;
Yet when thou see'st me burdened by thy love,
Each other gift more lovely then appears,
For dark-robed night comes hovering from above,
And all thine other gifts to me endears;
And while within her darkened couch I sleep,
Thine eyes untired above will constant vigils keep.[55]

No ascetic of the Middle Ages prostrated himself more fervently or more completely before his God; no disciple of St. Francis knew better the joy of poverty and humility, the peace of quiet seclusion.

In later years Very's poetry was to be compared to that of Donne, of Herbert, of Herrick, of Vaughan, and even of Blake; but in no case is the comparison very apt. Perhaps any religious poem, because of its mood if for nothing else, will remind one of other religious poems; but Very's verse is unlike that of any other poet, English or American. His piety may suggest Herbert; his simple diction and childlike faith may remind a Blake enthusiast of Blake; his intense fervor and his mysticism may faintly suggest Herrick's "His Litany, to the Holy Spirit," Vaughan's "The World," or Donne's "A Hymn to God the Father" or "Holy Sonnets": but Very's sonnets display none of Donne's fondness for literary conceits; none of Vaughan's cogitations over metaphysics; no lament over the loss of primal innocence, such as Herrick expressed; none of the intricacy and subtlety of thought which are found in Blake; and certainly nothing of the elaborate and conscious workmanship and the literary brilliance which dominate "The Temple" of Herbert. What uniqueness Very possesses lies in his humility, his complete simplicity of expression, and his rich, mystical communion with God. Others have possessed these virtues, but no other has owned them in exactly the same proportion. Perhaps every one of the English poets with whom Very has been compared is a greater poet than the New Englander; but no one of them has lived more humbly, or has written with less thought of literary effect, and no one of them has revealed so close, so constant, or so strong a communion with God.

This communion had reached a temporarily devastating inten-

[55] *Ibid.*, p. 136.

sity in September, 1839, when Very was twenty-six years old, and it had resulted in a month's hospitalization under the care of Dr. McLean, in Somerville. The consequent controversy regarding his sanity had convinced Very that he could be happiest only when he retired from men and lost himself in nature and in God. This decision undoubtedly accounted for such a poem as "The Spirit,"[56] in which Very seems to have severed all human connection with the world and to have become lost in a pure and passionate absorption with his chosen companions. In this sonnet he expresses a state of mysticism so complete as to enable him to suspend the normal functions of a bodily organ; "I would not breathe, when blows thy mighty wind," says Very. Nevertheless, he still felt that he was God's messenger, and he was eager that men know it. But he chose to prove his representation of divinity, not by a verbal crusade, but by unmistakable example; his life should be so pure and holy that men would recognize him as God's spokesman. They should be inspired, first to true will-lessness, and secondly to passionate unity with the spiritual. In "The Earth" he voices his willingness to be an instrument used by God for spreading the Message. Shelley, in his "Ode to the West Wind" had passionately pleaded to be a "dead leaf," a "swift cloud," a "wave" to respond to the wind; but Very—entirely unlike the "tameless, and swift, and proud" Shelley—bowed in meek submission and said:

> I would lie low, the ground on which men tread,
> Swept by Thy spirit like the wind of heaven;
> An earth where gushing springs and corn for bread,
> By me at every season should be given;
> Yet not the water or the bread that now
> Supplies their tables with its daily food,
> But thou wouldst give me fruit for every bough,
> Such as Thou givest me, and call'st it good;
> And water from the stream of life should flow,
> By every dwelling that thy love has built,
> Whose taste the ransomed of thy Son shall know,
> Whose robes are washed from every stain of guilt;
> And men would own it was thy hand that blest,
> And from my bosom find a surer rest.[57]

[56] *Ibid.*, p. 144.　　　　　　[57] *Ibid.*, p. 158.

The idea of willing instrumentality is expressed also in a different type of figure. Very would be a mere holder of the pen,
through which God's message might flow into words for men to
read and hear. In "Who Hath Ears to Hear Let Him Hear,"[58] he
compares his songs to those of a bird, and he imagines the joy
which they may bring to the "willing heart." The pertinent lines
are the second and third octave and the couplet, reading,

> The bird does not betray the secret springs,
> Whence note on note her music sweetly pours;
> Yet turns the ear attentive while she sings,
> The willing heart while falls the strain adores;
> So shall the spirit tell not whence its birth,
> But in its light thine untold deeds lay bare;
> And while it walks with thee flesh-clothed the earth,
> Its words shall of the Father's love declare;
> And happy those whose ears shall hail its voice,
> And clean within the day it gives rejoice.

Very found this mystical union to be constantly and increasingly
satisfying, and he gave himself completely to it. He was the willing and pliable clay in the hands of God the potter, chanting rap-
turously:

> Thou shalt do what Thou wilt with thine own hand,
> Thou form'st the spirit like the moulded clay.[59]

The theme occurs often in Very's later poems, indeed so often
as to become monotonous, but it is highly important because it
offers some explanation of the four poems of autobiographic significance in Very's first edition. Each of these poems concerns
love, and since Very never married, they interest the biographer
exceedingly. Certainly Very was susceptible to feminine charm,
and in his early twenties seemed thoroughly responsive. On January 10, 1835, his poem, "Sleigh Ride,"[60] had appeared in the Salem
Observer, and in one of the stanzas he had referred enthusiastically
to eyes that "kindle the heart with soft delight." By August he
had vowed eternal love and had defied Time to destroy his faith-
fulness. This declaration served as the motif for the first of those

[58] *Ibid.*, p. 165.
[59] *Ibid.*, "The Clay," p. 164.   [60] See Appendix II, p. 189.

autobiographic poems selected by Emerson for publication. The
poem had already appeared in the *Observer* for August 1, 1835.
Speaking to Time, Very said:

> Thou may'st touch with blighting finger
> All that senses can here enjoy;
> Yet within my soul shall linger
> That which thou canst not destroy.
>
> Love's sweet voice shall there awaken
> Joys that earth cannot impart;
> Joys that live when thou hast taken
> All that here can charm the heart.
>
> As the years come gliding by me,
> Fancy's pleasing visions rise;
> Beauty's cheek, ah! still I see thee,
> Still your glances, soft blue eyes![61]

George Batchelor, writing in *The Dial* (Chicago) for July, 1883,
commented concerning this poem: "One would like to know
whether he wrote this 'by permission, not by commandment.' "[62]
The answer is obviously "no," for Very wrote the piece before he
had arrived at the stage of thinking suggested by Mr. Batchelor.

The sonnet, "Beauty,"[63] however, does belong to the period
which marked Very's religious excitation. Published in the *Observer* on December 30, 1837, and again in slightly corrected form
on January 6, 1838, it represents that great emotional upheaval in
the poet's life and clearly represents a struggle between natural
human passion and divine, spiritual love. In the first two quat-
rains his lyric beauty and intensity remind one of the Elizabethans:

> I gazed into thy face,—and beating life
> Once stilled its sleepless pulses in my breast,
> And every thought whose being was a strife
> Each in its silent chamber sank to rest;
> I was not, save it were a thought of thee,
> The world was but a spot where thou hadst trod,
> From every star thy glance seemed fixed on me,
> Almost I loved thee better than my God.

[61] *Op. cit.,* "Eheu! Fugaces, Posthume, Posthume, Labuntur Anni," p. 109.
[62] George Batchelor, "A Poet of Transcendentalism," *The Dial* (Chicago), IV,
(July, 1883).   [63] *Op. cit.,* p. 122.

Perhaps we shall never know the identity of the woman who stirred Very to such depths. That she had inspired a love so great is ample proof of her beauty; and that she never married her sonneteer is accounted for by the tremendous power of the religious ecstasy which possessed him.[64] The concluding lines of the poem offer sufficient explanation:

> And still I gaze,—but 'tis a holier thought
> Than that in which my spirit lived before,
> Each star a purer ray of love has caught,
> Earth wears a lovelier robe than then it wore,
> And every lamp that burns around thy shrine
> Is fed with fire whose fountain is Divine.

One who had so thoroughly mastered human passion could sincerely write the other two autobiographic poems, "Thy Beauty Fades"[65] and "Love,"[66] in both of which the ephemeral quality of earthly love is contrasted with the soul-satisfying, everlasting quality of divine love. For to Very only the spiritual life was a vital reality; the body and its fleshly hungerings must be conquered by a supreme will-lessness that annihilated the barriers to communion with the Father. To this state Very the mystic had attained at the time his *Essays and Poems* was published.

The little book certainly was not immediately known to a wide circle of readers, but gradually copies were sold and circulated in sufficient numbers to create a small group of loyal admirers. Though evidence is not abundant, enough exists to prove that Very's book created considerable interest among the New England transcendentalists and their friends.

In the Antiquarian House at Concord are Emerson's copy[67] and another presented by Samuel May, brother of Mrs. Alcott, to Charles Lane, the Englishman, who, with Alcott, attempted the experiment at "Fruitlands."[68] Neither of these copies is annotated,

[64] Mrs. Edmund R. Brown, of 10 Viaduct St., Sharon, Mass., grandniece of Very, told the author in August, 1935, that she had heard from her father (Frank Washington Very) something of Jones Very's love for and engagement to a young woman of Salem. The engagement was broken because of Very's illness and the consequent stamina of insanity.

[65] *Op. cit.,* p. 121.   [66] *Op. cit.,* p. 134.

[67] Number 1175, in the "Emerson Library" collection.

[68] Number 2127, in the "Emerson Library" collection.

but James Russell Lowell's copy[69]—now preserved in the Treasure Room of the Widener Library, at Cambridge, Massachusetts—is rich in critical comments. On the first page of the volume is Lowell's signature in ink, "J. R. Lowell," followed by the date of purchase, "1840." Just above the name Lowell has written in pencil this statement: "Some of the sonnets printed in this volume are better poetry than has yet been published in America.—"

Lowell read the poems carefully, for the titles of twenty-three of them are checked (an "X" is used) once, and six are checked twice. Numerous lines are also underscored, and in some instances portions of the poems are marked perpendicularly. Apparently he admired most the sonnet "Beauty" (p. 122), but he indicated by his markings that he had other favorites, such as "The New Birth" (p. 126), "Enoch" (p. 129), "Love" (p. 134), "The Rose" (p. 159), "The Poor" (p. 169), "The Stranger's Gift" (p. 120), and "Thy Beauty Fades" (p. 121).[70]

In reading the prose essays, Lowell seems to have been most interested in "Shakespeare," for several pages of this piece are annotated. On page 62, Lowell has put an interrogation mark by Very's quotation from Lamb, reading—". . . he (Shakespeare) fetched those images of virtue and of knowledge, of which every one of us recognising a part, think we comprehend in our natures the whole, and oftentimes mistake the powers which he positively creates in us for nothing more than indigenous faculties of our own minds, which only wanted the application of corresponding virtue in him to return a full and clear echo of the same"—and in the margin has written in pencil the following: "He creates no power in us, but only gives us to see those which we unwittingly possess. We call the poet *vates,* seer, thereby intimating that they can only write that which they have seen. So are all of us readers seers also, in as far as we feel what we read. The silent strings are in our souls, & whenever the poet strikes the keynote the string will answer. I think we rather create in the poet, than he in us."[71]

---

[69] This book was acquired through the Howe Fund, Dec. 14, 1934.

[70] It is interesting to note that Lowell was particularly impressed with Very's love poems. This reaction may have been due to his engagement in 1840 to Miss Maria White, who read contemporary poetry and inclined to mysticism. Lowell, in referring to her, stated: "They say that she is 'transcendental.' "

[71] In Lowell's essay, "Shakespeare Once More" (published in 1870 as a part of

Some of the domestic poetry
this volume are better poetry
than does not been published
in America —

J. R. Lowell —

1849 —

with annotations by J.R.L.

see pp 62-69 72-6-7-9- 81-

ESSAYS AND POEMS:

BY

JONES VERY.

———

BOSTON:
CHARLES C. LITTLE AND JAMES BROWN.
———
MDCCCXXXIX.

On page 69 by Very's sentence, reading—"We look in vain therefore in Shakespeare for that consciousness of the unconquerable will that we find in Milton"—Lowell has written "Coriolanus." Again, on page 72, as a comment on Very's statement that Shakespeare's mind is one of those which "seem to be exceptions, for wise purposes, to the rest of our race," Lowell has underlined the phrase *for wise purposes,* and has written in the margin: "exceptions for unnatural state."

Lowell's fullest comment concerns Very's statement, on page 76, that "He (Shakespeare) could but give to them (his characters) his own life, which was one of impulse and not of principle." Using both the side margin and the space at the bottom of the page, Lowell has written:

This is just what makes the difference between the characters of Shakespeare & that of Wordsworth. All nature *must* be unconscious. The doing of a good deed or the writing of a good poem should be to us like the act of breathing. Life is thereby supported, but we feel it not.

We may indeed have one continual impulse like that of the spheres, but it must not degenerate into a principle. As soon as we begin to see how & why we do anything good, we have lost our naturalness. Pyrites grow in a perfect cube, but no square or cube has aught to do with it. We only feel life when we are sick.[72]

Very, it will be recalled, considered Shakespeare's dominant weakness to be his lack of Christianity; he was "natural from an unconscious obedience to the will of God" rather than "by a conscious obedience to it. . . . Had that love of action which was so peculiarly the motive of Shakespeare's mind been followed also as a

Among My Books), he states the identical thought in these words: "Shakespeare understood perfectly the charm of indirectness, of making his readers seem to discover for themselves what he means to show them." See *Among My Books* (Boston: Houghton, Mifflin and Co., 1870), p. 185.

[72] For the expression of a similar idea regarding Wordsworth and his verse, see Lowell's "Wordsworth" (in *Among My Books, Second Series,* Boston: Houghton, Mifflin and Co., 1876, pp. 236-237): "He forced his readers to come to his poetry with a certain amount of conscious preparation, and thus gave them beforehand the impression of something like mechanical artifice, and deprived them of the contented repose of implicit faith . . . to a tree that has grown as God willed we come without a theory and with no botanical predilections, enjoying it simply and thankfully; or the Imagination recreates for us its past summers and winters, the birds that have nested and sung in it, the sheep that have clustered in its shade, the winds that have visited it, the cloud-bergs that have drifted over it, and the snows that have ermined it in winter."

duty, it would have added strength to his characters which we do not feel them now to possess."[73] The word *duty* Very stressed further; and at length when he stated, on page 77, that "our feelings ... are weak as flaxen cords in the giant hands of selfishness, unless strengthened by duty,"[74] Lowell heavily underlined *duty,* and noted in the margin: "What we now call duty, in a natural state would be nature. We have left that state & so we see it as a want. Were we fully natural & as God would have us we could conceive of no rules, as far as we ourselves were concerned."

Lowell also disagreed with Very's interpretation of the word *conscience.* Speaking of Adam and his primal naturalness, Very stated: "But even from the first moment of his existence, when he dared disobedience to his conscience, he became unnatural."[75] Lowell underlined *conscience,* and penciled in the right-hand margin the comment: "Adam had no conscience till he had sinned. We all create our consciences for ourselves. If we twist our bodies unnaturally, it pains us & so it is with our souls. So that there can be no such thing as 'conscious nature.' It is an absurdity."

Lowell, then, found Very's prose sufficiently stimulating to provoke a number of comments, and he found some of the sonnets to be better poetry than had previously appeared in America.

The first periodical to mention Very's book was *The North American Review.* In the number for October, 1839, under the caption "New Publications," is this item: "Essays and Poems. By Jones Very. Boston: C. C. Little & Co. 16 mo. pp. 75."[76] No critical review of the book, however, ever appeared in that magazine. It is to the aggressive Margaret Fuller that Very owes the first published criticism of his work. In *The Boston Quarterly Review* for January, 1840, under "Chat in Boston Bookstores—No. I," is a conversation between "Professor Partridge" and the "Reverend Mr. Nightshade." In this attempt to present a novel book review, Margaret Fuller, in the guise of "Professor Partridge," offers her judgment of Very's prose and poetry, as follows:

[73] *Op. cit.,* pp. 76-77.
[74] *Op. cit.,* p. 77, three lines from the bottom of the page.
[75] *Op. cit.,* p. 79.
[76] XLIX, 507. The number of pages given is incorrect, the "75" undoubtedly referring to the sale price of the book.

Prof. P.—Here is another little volume for you.

Rev. Mr. N.—"Poems and Essays by Jones Very"—I do not remember ever to have heard of it.

Prof. P.—Its circulation is limited, its merits unobtrusive. But in these little poems, though unfinished in style, and homely of mien, you will find an elasticity of spirit, a genuine flow of thought, and an unsought nobleness and purity almost unknown amid the self-seeking, factitious sentiment, and weak movement of our overtaught, and over-ambitious literature, if indeed we can say we have one. The essays, also, are full of genuine thought, but not, I think, of just criticism. The author seeks too resolutely for unity, and loses sight of condition. Especially is this the case in the Essays on Shakespeare and Hamlet. He has not found the center of the Shakespearean circle, and he has strained many points in the attempt.

Rev. Mr. N.—Singular! how little worthy criticism exists on Shakespeare.

Prof. P.—Surely, a dozen or more fineries by Schlegel, two or three just reviews by Goethe, and some invaluable hints by Coleridge, are all I know of. Amid such destitution, Mr. Very's observations seem well worth considering. His view, whether you agree with it or not, boasts a height and breadth not unworthy of his subject; and in details he is delicate and penetrating.

. . . .

Rev. Mr. N.—Well, I must go now.

Prof. P.—Write me what you think of Very; whether he does not carry out the promise of these lines of his:—

> "There is no moment but whose flight doth bring
> Bright clouds and fluttering leaves to deck my bower;
> And I within like some sweet bird must sing
> To tell the story of the passing hour;
> For time has secrets that no bird has sung,
> Nor changing leaf with changing season told;
> They wait the utterance of some nobler tongue
> Like that which spoke in prophet tones of old."[77]

But what of Emerson during this time? Was he neglecting his protégé? On September 4, 1839, he returned from a short vacation in the hills of New Hampshire. By the end of the month Jones Very's book was offered for sale in the shops of Boston; and under date of September 28 Emerson wrote in his *Journals:* ". . . I hate

[77] III, 127-134. The article is signed *Dahlia*. The lines quoted from Very are the opening ones in the sonnet "Time," found on page 172 of the 1839 edition.

Early Poems.''[78] Was he referring to Very's poems? At any rate, he seems to have done nothing to increase Very's immediate, general popularity. Perhaps his critical acumen convinced him that Very's appeal would always be to a few kindred souls, that he would never be popular with the masses. When Emerson was on a lecture tour in the spring of 1840, he wrote to Mrs. Lidian Emerson from New York, requesting a copy of "Very's Poems."[79] It is likely that he wished to show the book to Bryant and others. At any rate, the young mystic was not forgotten, for on March 28, when the lecture itinerary had taken Emerson to Providence, Rhode Island, he wrote to Mrs. Emerson: "Your letters are a great joy & comfort to me; as Very said of his Angels,—'they make one wish to be good.' "[80] Two days later, while still in Providence, Emerson wrote in his *Journals:* "Send Very's Poems to Carlyle and Wordsworth."[81]

Why Emerson should have waited a year before sending the volume to Carlyle is difficult to decide. Carlos Baker, writing in *The New England Quarterly,* for March, 1934, attempts to prove that Emerson was disgusted with Very's poems and tired of Very, and that he was seeking "to evict the germ of Orientalism" from his circle of friends.[82] Mr. Baker, however, is unconvincing, for he narrows his thesis so much as to find it necessary to ignore much of the available evidence. Certainly, in 1840 Emerson found Very's friendship deficient and at times boring,[83] but subsequent entries in the *Journals* prove unmistakably that Emerson's high opinion of Very as a man and as a poet increased with the passing of the years.

On May 30, 1840, Emerson finally sent Very's book to Carlyle. The letter accompanying the package reads, in part:

---

[78] V, 266.

[79] The letter, dated March 8, reads in part: "If you want it before I come send Adams, Stagedriver, to fetch it & also a Very's Poems which is there" (*The Letters of Ralph Waldo Emerson,* ed. R. L. Rusk, II, 261).

[80] *Ibid.,* II, 265.   [81] *Op. cit.,* V, 377.

[82] "Emerson and Jones Very," VII, 90-99.

[83] Cf. the *Journal* entry for July 6, 1840, which Edward Emerson considers a possible "reflection on a recent walk with the sad and austere Jones Very":—"As for walking with Heraclitus, said Theanor, I know nothing less interesting; I had as lief talk with my own conscience" (V, 436).

I believe I shall also make Brown the bearer of a little book written some time since by a young friend of mine in a very peculiar frame of mind,—thought by most persons to be mad,—and of the publication of which I took the charge. Mr. Very requested me to send you a copy.— I had a letter from Sterling, lately, which rejoiced me in all but the dark picture it gave of his health. I earnestly wish good news of him. When you see him, show him these poems, and ask him if they have not a grandeur.[84]

Carlyle's opinion of Very's work is not known, but doubtless he found it to be—like much that appeared in *The Dial*—"too spirit-like."

Finally, after almost two years had passed since the publication of Very's little volume, Emerson wrote an excellent review for *The Dial*. Margaret Fuller had "demanded" that it be delivered to her by June 16, 1841, as Emerson's letter to her indicates.[85] The criticism was sufficiently laudatory to amend any earlier procrastination:[86]

This little volume would have received an earlier notice if we had been at all careful to proclaim our favorite books. The genius of this little book is religious, and reaches an extraordinary depth of sentiment. The author, plainly a man of pure and kindly temper, casts himself into the state of the high and transcendental obedience to the inward Spirit. He has apparently made up his mind to follow all its leadings, though he should be taxed with the absurdity or even with insanity. In this enthusiasm he writes most of these verses, which rather flow through him than from him. There is no composition, no elaboration,

[84] *The Correspondence of Thomas Carlyle and Ralph Waldo Emerson—1843-1872*, ed. Charles Eliot Norton (Boston: James R. Osgood and Co., 1883), I, 333-334.

[85] "Concord, June 15, 1841. Here is a notice of Very's Poems which you demanded for the 16th" (*The Letters of Ralph Waldo Emerson*, ed. R. L. Rusk, II, 405).

[86] Carlos Baker (*op. cit.*, p. 97) states regarding this review: "A year of *The Dial* went by without any review of these supremely transcendental poems; and only in the second year of the periodical did Emerson publish his faintly laudatory anonymous critique."

The answer to Mr. Baker's latter insinuation is, quite obviously, that practically all readers of *The Dial* knew Emerson to be Very's editor; that he certainly had written and talked to his friends (Margaret Fuller, Elizabeth Peabody, Carlyle, and others) of his part in the publication of the book; and that it was the general custom of periodicals at that time, as examination of *The North American Review, The Dial*, and *The Boston Quarterly Review* will prove, to publish reviews without the names of the reviewers.

no artifice in the structure of the rhyme, no variety in the imagery; in short, no pretense to literary merit, for this would be departure from his singleness, and followed by loss of insight. He is not at liberty to correct these unpremeditated poems for the press; but if another will publish them, he offers no objection. In this way they have come into the world, and as yet have hardly begun to be known. With the exception of the few first poems, which appear to be of an earlier date, all these verses bear the unquestionable stamp of grandeur. They are the breathings of a certain entranced devotion, which one would say, should be received with affectionate and sympathizing curiosity by all men, as if no recent writer had so much to show them of what is most their own. They are as sincere a literature as the Songs of David or Isaiah, and only less than they, because indebted to the Hebrew muse for their tone and genius. This makes the singularity of the book, namely, that so pure an utterance of the most domestic and primitive of all sentiments should in this age of revolt and experiment use once more the popular religious language, and so show itself secondary and morbid. These sonnets have little range of topics, no extent of observation, no playfulness; there is even a certain torpidity in the concluding lines of some of them, which reminds one of church hymns; but, whilst they flow with great sweetness, they have the sublime unity of the Decalogue or the Code of Manu and if as monotonous, yet are they almost as pure as the sounds of surrounding Nature. We gladly insert from a newspaper the following sonnet, which appeared since the volume was printed:

> "The bush that has most briars and bitter fruit,—
> Wait till the frost has turned its green leaves red,
> Its sweetened berries will thy palate suit,
> And thou may'st find e'en there a homely bread.
> Upon the hills of Salem, scattered wide,
> Their yellow blossoms gain the eye in Spring;
> And straggling e'en upon the turnpike's side,
> Their ripened branches to your hand they bring.
> I've plucked them oft in boyhood's early hour,
> That then I gave such name and thought it true;
> But now I know that other fruit as sour
> Grows on what now thou callest *Me* and *You;*
> Yet, wilt thou wait the Autumn that I see,
> Will sweeter taste than these red berries be."[87]

[87] II (July, 1841), 130-131. "The Barberry Bush" was first published in the Salem *Observer,* Nov. 16, 1839; later it was included in *Andrews,* p. 103, and in *Clarke,* p. 119.

The Barberry Bush.

The bush ~~that has~~ which bears most briars, and bitter fruit,
Wait till the ^frost has turned its green leaves red,
Its sweetened berries will thy palate suit,
And thou may'st find, ~~ere there~~ een there a homely bread.
Upon the hills of Salem, scattered wide,
Their yellow blossoms gain the eye in Spring;
And straggling ~~down~~ upon the turnpike's side,
Their ripened bunches to your hand they bring.
I've plucked them oft in boyhoods early hour,
What then I gave such name and thought it true,
But now I know, that other fruit, as sour,
Grows on what now thou callest Me and You;
Yet, wilt thou wait the Autumn that I see,
~~Will~~ 'Twill sweeter taste than these red berries be.

Perhaps even before Emerson's review appeared, Richard Henry Dana was attracted to Very's poetry, and, in the words of Andrews, "sent a copy of this little book, warmly commending it, to Mr. Bryant, and he in reply cordially agreed with his friend that the sonnets stood 'quite *apart* here' in poetical merit, and spoke of them as exhibiting 'extraordinary grace and originality.' "[88]

Meanwhile, the author of *Essays and Poems,* little heeding the comments of his literary well-wishers, was living a life in Salem "quite apart" from that of his contemporaries.

[88] "Jones Very," *Harvard Register,* March, 1881, pp. 131-136. Andrews also speaks of letters from Dana and Bryant concerning Very. These were undoubtedly among the many letters which were burned by Mrs. Cooper, caretaker and housekeeper, following the death of Miss Lydia L. A. Very in 1901. See Epilogue, p. 176.

CHAPTER VI

LAST YEARS

JONES VERY, in the meantime, was living quietly in Salem with his mother, his sisters Lydia and Frances, and his brother Washington. The publication of a book of verse and prose essays under the sponsorship of Emerson had quelled most of the gossip concerning the man's sanity, but there were still curious and unconvinced busybodies who shook their heads dubiously and peered inquisitively over the high board fence around the gambrel-roof house at 154 Federal Street. Jones's mother and sisters, however, guarded the man carefully from idle saunterers, treated him with extreme gentleness, and bestowed on him the genuine reverence which they felt their saint to deserve. Indeed, as older residents of Salem now recall,[1] Mrs. Very and her daughters believed strongly in the godliness of Jones, and made him realize that they regarded him as a very precious being, for whom they gladly and dutifully made sacrifices. This attitude of his family, combined with the man's own conduct, eventually impressed all who knew or heard of Jones Very, and at length resulted in his acceptance by the Salem residents as a very saint of God.

Such an opinion had been held by Sophia Peabody ever since she had met Very, and his nervous collapse in September, 1838, had merely strengthened her belief in him. In the late autumn of 1838, in a letter to Elizabeth Peabody, who had left Salem and was then living in Boston, Sophia Peabody had written: "I do not think I am subject to my imagination; I can let an idea go to the grave that I see is false. When I am altogether true to the light I have, I shall be in the heaven where the angelic Very is now."[2] At that time George Peabody, brother of Sophia and Elizabeth, was very ill. Very's visits cheered and comforted the invalid exceedingly, as Sophia's letter to Elizabeth proves:

[1] Miss Harriet Wilkins, Miss Carrie Martin, and Miss Jennie Dale Fuller.
[2] Rose Hawthorne Lathrop, *Memories of Hawthorne*, p. 23.

Jones Very came to tea that afternoon. He was troubled at first, but we comforted him with sympathy. His conversation with George was divine, and such level rays of celestial light as beamed from his face upon George every time he looked up at him, were lovely to behold. We told him of our enjoyment of his sonnets. He smiled, and said that, unless we thought them beautiful because we also heard the Voice in reading them, they would be of no avail. "Since I have shown you my sonnets," said he to me, "I think you should show me your paintings." Mary brought my drawing-book and "Aeschylus." He deeply enjoyed all. I told him of my Ilbrahim. He said he delighted in the "Twice-Told Tales."[3]

Hawthorne, it seems, sometimes met Very at the Peabody home, for Sophia, further on in her letter, states: "He [Hawthorne] said he should not be able to come this evening to meet Very, because he had something to read, for he was engaged Monday and Tuesday evening, and could not read then. I am so sorry." It is doubtful, however, that Hawthorne regretted his absence. He told Emerson he found Very "always vain,"[4] and he found that the poet's lack of humor made him a dull and monotonous conversationalist. But Sophia Peabody's admiration remained unshaken. She welcomed each letter from Elizabeth, informing her of Emerson's opinion of Very, and on June 29, 1839, she wrote to Elizabeth: "I am rejoiced that Mr. Emerson has uttered no heresies about our High Priest of Nature."[5]

The "High Priest" visited Emerson shortly after *Essays and Poems* came from the press, but Emerson found his visitor's conversation lacking in stimulation. Under date of October 18, 1839, one finds in the *Journals:* "Jones Very only repeated, in a form not agreeable, the thought which agitated me in earlier years, when he said, 'The same spirit which brings me to your door prepares my welcome.' "[6] Another visit early in April, 1840, was more agreeable to Emerson. He and Very chose a pleasant afternoon to walk out to "Edmund Hosmer's and Walden Pond," and the ideas exchanged were recorded in the *Journals* for April 9:

We walked this afternoon to Edmund Hosmer's and Walden Pond. The South wind blew and filled with bland and warm light the dry

---

[3] *Ibid.,* p. 25.
[4] *Ibid.,* p. 29. (Elizabeth Peabody quotes Emerson.)
[5] *Ibid.,* p. 30. [6] V. 289.

sunny woods. The last year's leaves flew like birds through the air. As I sat on the bank of the Drop, or God's Pond, and saw the amplitude of the little water, what space, what verge, the little scudding fleets of ripples found to scatter and spread from side to side and take so much time to cross the pond, and saw how the water seemed made for the wind, and the wind for the water, dear playfellows for each other,—I said to my companion, I declare this world is so beautiful that I can hardly believe it exists. At Walden Pond the waves were larger and the whole lake in pretty uproar. Jones Very said, "See how each wave rises from the midst with an original force, at the same time that it partakes the general movement."[7]

On the way out to Concord, Very had visited his brother Washington, now a student at Harvard. The account of the visit delighted Emerson, and he recorded with gusto an episode that further warranted his expression of ideas previously stated in "The American Scholar":

He said that he went to Cambridge, and found his brother reading Livy. "I asked him if the Romans were masters of the world? My brother said they had been: I told him they were still. Then I went into the room of a senior who lived opposite, and found him writing a theme. I asked him what was his subject? And he said, Cicero's Vanity. I asked him if the Romans were masters of the world? He replied they had been; I told him they were still. This was in the garret of Mr. Ware's house. Then I went down into Mr. Ware's study, and found him reading Bishop Butler, and I asked him if the Romans were masters of the world? He said they had been: I told him they were still."[8]

This particular visit proved unusually fruitful to Emerson, for it occasioned, among other results, an entry in the *Journals* which served later as one of the most significant parts of the essay on "Friendship." Referring to Very's bold truthfulness and absolute sincerity under all circumstances, Emerson wrote:

Very obvious is the one advantage which this singular man has attained unto, that of bringing every man to true relations with him. No man

[7] *Ibid.*, V, 381.

[8] *Ibid.*, V, 382.

See also in "The American Scholar" the following: "II. The next great influence into the spirit of the scholar is the mind of the Past. . . . Yet hence arises a grave mischief. . . . Meek young men grow up in libraries, believing it their duty to accept the views which Cicero, which Locke, which Bacon, have given; forgetful that Cicero, Locke, and Bacon were only young men in libraries when they wrote these books."

would think of speaking falsely to him. But every man will face him, and what love of nature or what symbol of truth he has, he will certainly show him. But to most of us the society shows not its face and eye, but its side and its back. To stand in true relations with men in a false age is worth a fit of insanity, is it not?[9]

The paragraph, slightly modified and enlarged, was included in that part of "Friendship" in which Emerson discusses the necessity of Truth, and reads as follows:

I knew a man who under a certain religious frenzy cast off this drapery (hypocrisy), and omitting all compliment and commonplace, spoke to the conscience of every person he encountered, and that with great insight and beauty. At first he was resisted, and all men agreed he was mad. But persisting as indeed he could not help doing for some time in this course, he attained to the advantage of bringing every man of his acquintance into true relations with him. No man would think of speaking falsely with him, or of putting him off with any chat of markets or reading-rooms. But every man was constrained by so much sincerity to face him, and what love of nature, what poetry, what symbol of truth he had, he did certainly show him. But to most of us society shows not its face and eye, but its side and its back. To stand in true relations with men in a false age is worth a fit of insanity, is it not?[10]

Since Emerson wrote to S. G. Ward on June 22, 1840, that he was just "finishing a Chapter on Friendship" and that he had "written nothing with more pleasure,"[11] it is apparent that his relationship with Very was highly significant and often both enjoyable and fruitful in literary attainments.

Very waited scarcely a month after his satisfactory visit to Emerson in April before he returned to Concord, this time to attend the May meeting of the Transcendental Club, for which Emerson was serving as host. The discussion centered on "the inspiration of the Prophet, and Bard, the Nature of Poetry, and the causes of the sterility of Poetic Inspiration in our age and country."[12] Sometimes, too, Very journeyed to Boston, where he visited Elizabeth Peabody in her bookstore, or called on Hawthorne, then established in the

[9] *Journals*, V, 383.
[10] *Essays, First Series*, II, 203; also editor's note, II, 415.
[11] *Journals*, V, 415.
[12] Franklin Benjamin Sanborn, *Henry D. Thoreau*, p. 190.

customhouse. A visit to the latter on the evening of July 8 seems to have interfered with Hawthorne's more pleasurable duty of writing to Sophia Peabody in Salem, for on July 10, he sent the following excuse:

Dearest,—My days have been so busy and my evenings so invaded with visitants, that I have not had a moment's time to talk with you. Scarcely till this morning have I been able to read your letter quietly. Night before last came Mr. Jones Very; and you know he is somewhat unconscionable as to the length of his calls.[13]

Nevertheless, in May, 1842, when Hawthorne published "A Virtuoso's Collection" in *The Boston Miscellany of Literature,* he paid his fellow townsman a high tribute by listing his poems among the objects worthy of preserving. The criticism of Very's work has proved prophetic: "From Jones Very, a poet whose voice is scarcely heard among us by reason of its depth, there was a Wind Flower and a Columbine."

Whether Very visited Emerson again in October is not certain, but for some reason the latter made a record in his *Journals* of Very's apparent spiritual happiness. He seemed to Emerson to be "at rest and blessed." His words, wrote Emerson, "were loaded with this fact. What he said, held; was not personal to him; was no more disputable than the shining of yonder sun or the blowing of this south wind."[14] In fact, Very's presence in almost any assembly seemed to indicate spiritual power and to occasion reverence. Only once did Emerson find himself amused when he watched the man, and that was at the meeting, in Boston, of the Convention of Friends of Universal Reform, held in the Chardon Street Chapel in November, 1840.[15]

After the spring of 1841, when Thoreau came to live with Emerson, the *Journals* mentions Very less often than before. Apparently Emerson found in his new friend much that he had expected in Very, but had not received. And yet, Very's power always attracted him. In March, 1842, when Alcott was leaving for England and

---

[13] Julian Hawthorne, *Nathaniel Hawthorne and His Wife,* I, 221.

[14] *Journals,* V, 482, under date of Oct. 24, 1840.

[15] See Emerson's article, "Chardon Street and Bible Conventions," *The Dial,* III (July, 1842), 100-102.

Emerson was preparing a letter of introduction for him to Carlyle, Emerson found it convenient to compare the two mystics, particularly with regard to conversational powers. Alcott, he wrote in the *Journals,* "so swiftly and naturally plants himself on the moral sentiment in any conversation that no man will ever get any advantage of him, unless he be a saint, as Jones Very was."[16] And yet, as Emerson recognized, this advantage was often the result of a "certain trick . . . which may be soon learned by an acute person, and then that particular style be continued indefinitely."[17] This was particularly true, Emerson felt, of such mystics as Very, Alcott, and Lane.

But though Very now visited Emerson less often than formerly, he continued his correspondence and also sent him new poems. One such reached Concord on May 9, 1842, but, as Emerson informed Margaret Fuller, it was "indifferent."[18] Nevertheless, two poems which Very sent, Emerson used in *The Dial* for July, 1842. These were "The Evening Choir"[19]—a blank verse piece proclaiming the eternal warfare between the willful and the will-less—and "The World"—a five-stanza piece in which Very interrogates concerning the spiritual darkness of the world in somewhat the manner employed by Emerson in "The Sphinx." This second poem seems to have been popular among the Unitarians and the transcendentalists, for *The Christian Register* soon reprinted it; and *The Harbinger,* published by the Brook Farm Phalanx, reprinted it in turn from *The Christian Register.*[20] For, contrary to the opinion expressed by many commentators, the man was not idle during the forty-odd years following his nervous collapse. Many poems went to the Salem *Gazette* and *The Christian Register* during those years,[21] and hymns or special songs were written for many celebra-

---

[16] VI, 172, under date of March 23, 1842.

[17] *Ibid.,* VI, 257-258, under date of Sept., 1842.

[18] *The Letters of Ralph Waldo Emerson,* ed. R. L. Rusk, III, 54: ". . . Jones Very wrote me today a letter with an indifferent poem."

[19] III (July, 1842), 97-98. This poem is not included in any edition of Very's works. See Appendix, IV, p. 206.

[20] *The Harbinger,* II (Saturday, June 6, 1846), 204.

[21] *Bulletin of the Essex Institute,* XII (Jan.-June, 1880), 74-75. Because copies of these newspapers have been unavailable, no examination of them has been possible.

tions in Salem. The great number of manuscripts left at his death
offer ample proof that the creative impulse, though often uninspired
and generally narrow in its range, was still alive and sometimes
became so intense as to express itself admirably. Then, too, he
studied diligently, usually in the morning, and in the afternoons he
walked in the woods and fields near Salem.

Meantime Very's religious fervor remained constant. In the
autumn of 1842 he began preaching. Emerson, one of the first
persons who learned of this venture, communicated the news to
Frederic Henry Hedge on November 25, his letter reading in part:
"Jones Very, as I learn by a letter from him yesterday, has begun
to preach, has preached at New Bedford."[22] The following year
the Cambridge Association licensed Very to preach, but he was
never officially ordained. He always spoke of himself as a "Channing Unitarian." Though offered several pastorates, he never accepted them, because, as his sister Lydia said, "he did not wish
to leave his home";[23] and he preached frequently in many towns
throughout New England, but principally in Eastport, Maine,
North Beverly, East Bridgewater, Danvers, Plymouth, Marblehead,
and Salem, Massachusetts. Very's sermons have never been published, but in the Harris Collection of American Poetry in the
library of Brown University, at Providence, Rhode Island, are letters
concerning Very's preaching,[24] and also the manuscripts of 28 of
his sermons;[25] and in the library of the Andover Theological Seminary, at Cambridge, Massachusetts, are manuscripts for 105 additional sermons, all of which are neatly and legibly written and
sturdily bound in one volume—a gift made by Very's sisters on
March 22, 1895. Allowing for four duplications among the manu-

[22] *The Letters of Ralph Waldo Emerson*, ed. R. L. Rusk, III, 99.
[23] "Jones Very Again," Boston *Sunday Herald*, June 6, 1880.
[24] Among these is one from William Allen, of East Bridgewater, dated July 16,
1855, inviting Very to supply the pulpit of Mr. Phipps, who was ill. Very's reply
reads: "I am very glad to hear from you, and to have the opportunity of a visit
on the next Sabbath. Did my circumstances permit I would gladly preach to your
people gratuitously. They can pay whatever they can afford. I am sorry to hear
of Mr. Phipps' sickness. You will please to remember me to him. Give my love
to all your family. You can expect me on Saturday afternoon, 21st. Your friend."
[25] The records of Brown University reveal that the University purchased these
MSS from Goodspeed's, in Boston, in 1903. When or how the latter acquired
them is not recorded.

scripts at Cambridge,[26] one calculates that Very left manuscripts
for 129 sermons. Some of these were delivered from two to eleven
times in different churches, as the notations on the manuscripts
indicate, so that during Very's ministerial career of approximately
thirty years,[27] he preached hundreds of times. The contents of the
sermons are in strict harmony with the deep spirituality and reverent devotion which saturate the poems. Always Very pleads for
will-lessness, elevated thoughts, sinless living, prayer, worldlessness,
communion with the Great Spirit, and love of nature. Frequently
one detects the doctrine of the transcendentalists, particularly of
Emerson and Alcott; for example, in speaking of the necessity of
faith and intuition and the superiority of these to knowledge gained
through the senses, Very says: "We need an inward knowledge,
kindred with our own nature that we may personally know the
Creator of all things and the Father of all men. We need an intellectual and spiritual communication with the Father of light, else
even the very stars would be to us but glittering tinsel."[28] And,
again, he stresses the doctrine of self-reliance, using language of
such strength and realism as to suggest the words of Emerson
himself: "Men lose their self-confidence by the dependence they
put upon things and upon the works of their hands. They are not
only surrounded at their birth but they pass their lives in surrounding themselves with objects on which they can depend and to which
they give their confidence. They trust in the fair day, in the smooth
river, in the firm earth; they rely upon the swift ship, the strong-
built house, the Press, the Steam Engine, and the Power of Ma-
chinery."[29]

One of the most convincing of the sermons is that which de-
velops the text: "The Kingdom of God is not in word, but in
power."[30] Herein Very discourses concerning books in much the

[26] These are numbers 3 and 64, 37 and 66, 86 and 100, and 89 and 96. All
the sermons in this volume are numbered.

[27] The earliest date recorded on the MSS is March 26, 1843 (Sermon 16 of
the Brown University MSS); the latest date recorded is March 30, 1873 (Sermon 3
of the Andover Theological MSS, delivered in the First Church, Salem).

[28] See Sermon 11 in the Andover Theological MSS.

[29] See Sermon 48 in the Andover Theological MSS.

[30] See Sermon 57 in the Andover Theological MSS. The scriptural passage
read for a text is I Corinthians 4:20.

way Emerson spoke of the "grave mischief"[31] arising from too
much reading. The pertinent passages are the following:

As too much food renders the body inactive and dull, and at last injures
it, so the reading of too many books, or the hearing of too many sermons, when it degenerates into a mere habit of skimming over words
or listening to their sound, injures the mind. In the first place the
mind is deceived by taking words for ideas, sounds for knowledge.
Men know the worth of the coin that they pass from hand to hand,
and will not take even the smallest piece beneath its true value, but
how many are continually using words and hearing them without
attaching any definite ideas to them, deceiving themselves with the
thought that they have been imparting or receiving knowledge when
they have only been abusing its medium.

In at least one of his sermons Very strongly expressed his sen-
sibility to the importance of nature in modern, as contrasted with
antique, poetry. "There is," he stated, "a depth of meaning, and a
spiritual beauty and grandeur in the outward world, which can be
found reflected only from the pages of modern poetry."[32] The same
idea is emphasized again, though less strongly, by quoting Shakespeare's lines from As You Like It:

> Finds tongues in trees, books in the running brooks,
> Sermons in stones and good in everything.[33]

The Reverend Charles T. Brooks, himself a poet and a lifelong
friend of Jones Very, writing of the nature element in the sermons,
stated: ". . . among all the numerous sermons I have heard from
my boyhood in Salem, that was the only one in which I ever heard
any reference to the beauty and glory of our old town pastures,
upon which Jones dwelt with a great enthusiasm."[34]

The sermons clearly reveal Very's attitude toward slavery. There
is often an appeal for national unity, for purity of politics, for spiritual strength among American citizens—all of which he believed
would be effective in combating the evil of slavery. Like Carlyle
and Emerson, he considered evil by its very nature to be negative;

[31] In "The American Scholar."
[32] See Sermon 95 in the Andover Theological MSS.
[33] See Sermon 101 in the Andover Theological MSS.
[34] "The Life and Services to Literature of Jones Very," Bulletin of the Essex
Institute, XIII (Jan.-June, 1881), 30.

good, to be positive: and he stressed the importance of settling the problem of slavery peaceably.[35] Modern society, he insisted, needed a spiritual reformation.[36] Shortly after the Civil War broke out, Very delivered his sermon on the text: "From whence then hath it tares?"[37] His answer, emphasized through varied repetition, was given in his opening sentence: "Slavery has again involved our Government in War. War is never, I believe, *absolutely* necessary. It is from the neglect and want of faith in other means of remedying evils that it may be said, in any sense, to be necessary." After the war had closed, Very warned against spiritual slavery, which he believed a far greater evil than negro slavery. His attitude never suggests the militant zeal of Whittier, but reminds one strongly of that of Emerson, as expressed in his "Ode—Inscribed to W. H. Channing." Very warned his hearers thus: "As a nation we abound in wealth and every luxury. As slavery proved a trial to us, so also may our wealth and power. . . . But if our material prosperity prove too great a trial for our virtue . . . then will the flood of Ignorance and the desolation of war again sweep over and destroy our land."[38]

Since Very loved peace, he was most himself when he chose a subject less controversial than that of slavery. For this reason, his sermon on "Miracles" is perhaps more readable than any other of his manuscripts. Particularly pleasing are his comments on the language of the New Testament; and one who has already read Very's poems thoroughly feels, as he scans the sermon, that the simple diction and the dignified style of Very's sonnets, are due in large measure to the inspiration of the Bible. For example, Very states:

The simplicity and dignity of the language in which the miracles of the New Testament are recorded are as wonderful as the events which they describe. The words correspond with the works, as proceeding from one and the same source. They are the words, not of men recording or inventing myths, but of men who have actually *seen* supernatural events. They write as those whose minds have been raised to a

[35] See Sermon 17 in the Andover Theological MSS.
[36] See Sermons 14 and 31 in the Andover Theological MSS.
[37] See Sermon 52 in the Andover Theological MSS. It was delivered at the evening service on June 9, 1861, in Salem.
[38] See Sermon 80 in the Andover Theological MSS.

level with the things they describe. It is this which gives their narrative a simplicity, dignity and power which is unequaled and which cannot be accounted for in any other way.[39]

Again, in Sermon 28 one finds a similar expression: "With what calmness and simplicity do the Evangelists write; and yet what scenes of wonder and power do they record!"[40]

Though favoring the Biblical writers, Very does not slight the secular; in fact, the sermons reveal his remarkable acquaintance with books and authors, both classical and modern. In their order of reference, they are: Coleridge, Milton, Waller, Wyclif, Tyndale, Luther, Plato, "the ancient Greek tragedies," Ovid, Cicero, Mitford, Homer, Persius, Horace, Dr. Samuel Johnson, Sterling, Burns, Wordsworth, and Shakespeare. There are also many references to science, history, government, and economics.

Most of the sermons are exceedingly well constructed, and only a few are of great length. Some of the manuscripts show revision, and all reveal careful planning, sound reasoning, and deep spirituality. But Very was never greatly successful as a preacher, for his pulpit manner was entirely against him. He had no strong, arresting voice, no dramatic presence: in fact, his voice was so low as to be at times indistinct or even inaudible; and his extreme humility and excessive modesty prevented a convincing delivery of even a carefully prepared sermon. And yet Jones Very's hearers were impressed when he stood before them. In personal appearance, he was not unusual: he was tall and exceedingly slender; and he kept his thin but healthy-colored face clean shaven, parted his glossy black hair on the left of his high forehead, and combed it straight back from his kind yet serious eyes. But there was about the man a spiritual quality which every one recognized, and in his very presence men felt a nearness to divinity. Emerson referred to "the poetic way" in which Very quoted scripture,[41] and in April, 1843, he again emphasized his belief that Jones Very's center of life was "coincident with the Center of Life" and that for this reason "our saint had affected us with what was best in him."[42]

[39] See Sermon 12 in the Andover Theological MSS.
[40] In the Andover Theological MSS.
[41] *Journals*, VI, 198, under date of April 13, 1842.
[42] *Ibid.*, VI, 385.

Five years later Emerson's high regard had been somewhat modified; Very, he admitted, was godly, but he was too narrowly so—
like Swedenborg. And, considering the latter, Emerson wrote:
"*Swedenborg.* He reminds me again and again of our Jones Very,
who had an illumination that enabled him to excel everybody in
wit and to see farthest in every company; and yet he could never
get out of his Hebraistic phraseology and mythology, and, when
all was over, still remained in the thin porridge or cold tea of
Unitarianism."[43]

Here, then, at least for Emerson, was one weakness in Very's
preaching, in his verse, and in his life. He had once been so pow-
erfully excited, and under that excitation had uttered a message of
such tremendous purport, that his subsequent quietism was too
definitely an anticlimax. Emerson had expected the light to sustain
its brilliance, and he had been disappointed. A reader of the *Journals* notices particularly that after 1843 Emerson always writes of
Very in the past tense, as a man whose friendship in the past had
illuminated even the darkest recesses of his thought, but whose
light had flickered and, for Emerson, had died. And yet, as the
years passed, the Concord sage again and again thought of Very,
refreshed his tired spirits by recalling the preceding visits from his
disciple in Salem, and lamented that his kind had passed. "I seem
to meet no more such. Very and Rebecca Black were the last,"
he wrote.[44]

But Jones Very all the while lived peaceably in Salem. Travel
held no attraction for him, for he felt that one could find the
Spirit at home as well as abroad.[45] In the attitude of Thoreau, he
might have said, "I have travelled much in Salem." After his death,
his sister Lydia wrote that she believed Very's extreme simplicity
of style, as exemplified in his later verse, was partly accounted for
by his "having lived in the daily routine of home life, not having
passed a night from home in more than 30 years."[46] And he never

[43] *Ibid.*, VII, 136-137.
[44] *Ibid.*, VII, 555; the date is Nov. 9, 1848. See also VIII, 62 (1849), 293
(June 1, 1852); IX, 504 (April 20, 1863), 524 (Very—important as a minority);
X, 77 (Oct. 20, 1864); 108 (July 23, 1865).
[45] Cf. his sonnets—"Nature Pleads with the Traveler" (*Clarke,* p. 142), and
"The Traveler at the Depot" (*ibid.,* p. 248).
[46] "Jones Very Again," Boston *Sunday Herald,* June 6, 188c

regretted his failure to achieve material success; the life of the spirit was, as always to him, paramount.

And the home life was, for the most part, exceedingly happy. After Washington graduated with honors from Harvard in 1843, he, too, studied for the ministry; he was ordained, and preached for a year, but at length returned to his mother's home in Salem and taught a private school.[47] When, in 1851, he married Miss Martha N. Leach, a member of the socially prominent and wealthy Nichols family, he brought his bride to the Federal Street home, where his son and daughter were born. The latter lived only two years, but the boy Franklin became a robust youngster whom Jones Very loved greatly, and whose career as a famous scientist he truthfully predicted.[48] When Washington Very died in 1853, a dispute, followed by a violent quarrel, arose between his widow and her mother-in-law. Mrs. Washington Very subsequently removed to 78 Federal Street,[49] leaving Mrs. Lydia Very, Jones, and the two girls to occupy the house alone. But Jones Very entered into none of the squabbles so vigorously pursued by his aggressive mother and his sister Lydia; he visited his sister-in-law and his nephew as long as they lived in Salem, and after their removal he wrote to them, though infrequently.[50] For Jones Very's gentle, modest life was too thoroughly saturated with human love and sympathy to know the passion of hate; then, too, his annihilation of the will had made him passive, unaggressive, patient, and of course peaceable.

[47] See advertisement, "School for Young Ladies," in the Salem Gazette, April 13, 1847.

[48] For an account of the life and achievements of Frank Washington Very, see Who's Who in America, XIV (1926-27); for a record of his numerous pamphlets, magazines, and books, see the Catalogue in the Library of Congress, Washington, D. C.

[49] Here for a number of years she successfully continued the school organized by her husband; and here scores of girls from the more cultivated families of Salem were educated.

[50] This information was furnished the author in August, 1934, by Miss Charlotte Nichols, now deceased, a relative of Mrs. Washington Very; and in September, 1935, by Mrs. Edmund R. Brown, 10 Viaduct St., Sharon, Mass., one of the five children of Frank Washington Very, and a grandniece of Jones Very, the poet. The other children are: Miss Marjorie Very, an artist, living in her father's old home, Westwood, Mass.; Mrs. Arthur Bartlett, 60 Grammercy Park, New York City; Arthur O. Very, Richardson, Tex.; and Ronald W. Very, 636 Westminster Road, Brooklyn, N. Y.

HOME OF JONES VERY
154 Federal Street, Salem, Massachusetts

The Very women, on the other hand, were fiery souls, persistent in their household management, their nature study, and their humanitarian interests. They were so individualistic as to gain early the reputation of eccentrics. The mother's ample resourcefulness and practical common sense combined with her frugality and industry to assure her family a marked financial independence; her capacity for love expressed itself in the almost worshipful care she bestowed on all her children, especially Jones, and upon plants, birds, and dumb animals. Both the girls developed into capable teachers, following their profession for over thirty years in the public and private schools of Salem. Lydia Louisa resembled her mother in both appearance and personality. She possessed a vigorous mind, a keen sensitiveness to music and all forms of natural beauty, and an apparently inexhaustible industry in the pursuit of her strong ambitions. Though inheriting her mother's love of nature, she was not satisfied with only the quiet enjoyment of plant cultivation in the large garden back of the Very home, but she organized field trips to near-by places of interest, collected plant specimens, led discussions at the Essex Institute, and wrote fairy tales and fables for children, novels, and nature poems, which she published both in America and in Europe.[51] Though having some talent in clay modeling, she was more gifted as an artist, and she made pencil sketches and water colors of scenes and plant life in the neighborhood of Salem.[52] In her later years she was an outstanding leader in the Society for Prevention of Cruelty to Animals, and the court records of Essex County and the newspaper files of Salem prove the zeal with which she pursued her interests. Always, she carried in her pockets lumps of sugar with which to feed overloaded horses, and frequently her tirades against the drivers were noticeably effective.[53] Frances Very was more gentle and

[51] Some of her published works are: (1) *Poems* (Andover: W. F. Draper, 1856); (2) *Sylph, or the Organ-Grinder's Daughter,* with illustrations by the author (Boston: James H. Earle, n.d.); (3) *A Strange Recluse* (Salem: The Salem Press, 1899); (4) *An Old-Fashioned Garden* (Salem: The Salem Press, 1900).

[52] See the Essex Institute collection of approximately fifty sketches by Lydia L. A. Very.

[53] Miss Jennie Dale Fuller, 27 Barr St., Salem, Mass., recalls that in the nineties George Putnam, driver of one of the ice carts operated by his father, Otis F. Putnam, ice dealer in Salem, often used to say to her: "Well, Lydia held us up today, and how she did abuse us for mistreating the horses!"

lovable, more domestic, more retiring than her sister. Though mentally as vigorous, she was less ambitious for public recognition, preferring patient, quiet study, secluded gardening, collecting of flowers, rocks, and birds' eggs, and enjoyment of her many pet cats. Among the latter were a yellow tabby named "Buttercup," an enormous grey woolly "Walt Whitman," and a meek, pitiful stray which was christened "Evangeline."

With these three unusual women Jones Very lived until the death of his mother on May 3, 1867; and after that date, with his sisters. In the winter his life was exceedingly regular. All the morning he studied and wrote and prayed, or else read in his Greek Bible, remaining in his little west room under the gambrel roof—the room called "The Prophet's Chamber," lined with books, and packed with manuscripts of his own poems and with the letters from a vast number of celebrated folk who corresponded with him. In the afternoon, if the weather was pleasant, he walked for long distances, frequently to Ship Rock or up the turnpike among the "Pastures." Sometimes he went with friends—Cyrus A. Bartol, Frank Sanborn, or Charles T. Brooks[54]—but oftenest alone or in company with a farmer, a hunter, or a fisherman whom he met on the way. On stormy winter days he sat downstairs in the living room with his sisters, who, more mindful of the health of their flowers than of themselves, sat wrapped in shawls and coats in a temperature adapted to the green plants which filled the pots in the south window. But summer brought the glorious days for Jones Very; it was then that he could live in the garden made lovely by its eighteen varieties of trees, its boxwood borders, and its beds of roses, peonies, larkspur, pinks, lilacs, marigolds, lilies, and lad's love. There were three bowers, one for each member of

---

[54] Describing these walks, in a letter to the Essex Institute for the Jones Very Memorial Meeting (*Bulletin of the Essex Institute*, XIII, Jan.-June, 1881, 29-30), the Reverend Charles T. Brooks wrote: ". . . When I met him, the first thing that impressed me was always that peculiar sweet smile which I remembered of old. Now and then I enjoyed a walk with him, which, by his leading, would always be to the pastures. . . . What I remember . . . is the way in which he would stop, after expressing some thought about nature, man or God, that he seemed to fear might appear commonplace from its simplicity, and then turning round and fixing upon you an earnest look, as if he would show by his piercing glance that there was a depth in his thought concealed from superficial minds by its very transparency."

the family. Lydia's, placed nearest the house, they called "Boffin's Bower"; Frances's, halfway down the walk toward the river, they appropriately named "Forget-me-not Bower" because it was bordered with the flowers the owner loved; and Jones's, at the foot of the garden and in the most secluded spot available, they tagged "Inspiration Point." Here the poet sometimes read, but oftenest wrote his sonnets, or just meditated.[55] In the spring and summer afternoons he walked to his favorite spots by the seashore or far inland, communing through natural objects with their Creator. He knew where the hepaticas, the violets, and the Mayflowers first bloomed, where the rarest birds built nests, and where even the most timid animals placed their young; and for all of these he felt a personal love and showed a deep understanding. Children in their strolls through the "Pastures" saw his spectral figure clothed in ministerial garb and surmounted by a high silk hat, and they noticed the large umbrella which seemed never to have been opened. But they were not afraid; on the contrary, they were attracted to him, for they saw, too, his wrapt expression as he lovingly examined wild flowers, and they frequently walked with him along the turnpike and through the woods, fascinated by the man's loving-kindness. Miss Carrie Martin, of Salem, recalls that once when, as a child, she was picking houstonia, Jones Very gently leaned over her and said, "Never leave one. Gather the whole bunch. One will be lonesome."

It was this intimate association through a long period of years that furnished material for much of Very's poetry. One has only to glance through the complete edition, edited by Clarke, to see how many titles belong to Salem—its history,[56] its folk,[57] its scenes, its flora, and fauna.[58] Truly, Very is the laureate of Salem; and,

[55] For a description of the garden before Jones Very's death, see Lydia Very's *An Old-Fashioned Garden*.

[56] See the thirty-seven sonnets under the division titled "The Puritans," pp. 207-225; also, "On the First Church," p. 226; and many of the hymns, pp. 304-358.

[57] See "Sonnet—to the Rev. James Flint, D.D.," p. 235; "On Seeing the Portrait of Helen Ruthven Waterson," p. 473; "To the Memory of the Rev. James Chisholm," p. 474; "To the Misses Williams," p. 474; "Salem," p. 499; "Old Houses of Salem," p. 522; "Captain Samuel Cook," p. 513; "To the Memory of Alpheus Crosby," p. 513; and many others.

[58] They are too numerous to list; see pp. 359-440, under the caption "Poems Descriptive of Nature."

unlike her more famous son, Hawthorne, he sang of her lovingly. Whenever public exercises of any nature were held, Jones Very was generally asked to contribute the words for a special hymn, and often he furnished the stanzas requested. His career as hymnologist extended from June 22, 1836, when his "Hymn" for the dedication of the New Stone Church of the North Society in Salem was sung, to January 2, 1879—four months before his death—when he wrote "We welcome, with the opening year" to celebrate the installation of the Reverend George Herbert Hosmer as pastor of the East Church in Salem.[59] Many of Very's hymns are today included in Protestant hymnbooks, among the more popular being "Father, Thy Wonders Do Not Singly Stand" (an adaptation of his sonnet, "The Spirit Land"), "We Go Not on a Pilgrimage,"[60] and "The Prayer" (Wilt Thou not visit me?).[61] Of the first and the second hymn, Miss Harriet Wilkins, of Salem, reports: "We sing them often in our church."[62] In a letter dated August 24, 1900, and addressed to Professor G. M. Hammell, of Tennessee, Lydia Very wrote concerning "The Prayer": "One of my friends lately visiting Europe attended Church in London, and the first hymn sung was 'Wilt Thou not visit me?' The occupant of the pew told her it was a great favorite there. Dean Stanley says that he (Very) was the best hymn writer in America, and when he came here said that the person whom he most wished to see was Jones Very."[63]

As the years passed by, Jones Very gradually withdrew more and more from society. But his reputation as one of America's important minor poets was steadily growing. The edition of *Essays and Poems* was ultimately out of print, but in spite of repeated requests for another edition, Very showed no eagerness to publish his works further. When Griswold brought out *The Poets and Poetry of America* in 1843, Very was one of the eighty-eight poets

[59] See in the library of the Essex Institute (Catalogue Number: BR–922–H82) a program of the exercises. The poem is not included in the Clarke edition or in any other. See Chapter VIII, p. 175.

[60] *Clarke*, p. 80 and p. 287, respectively.

[61] Omitted from *Clarke*, but found in *Andrews*, p. 111, and in the 1839 edition, p. 175.

[62] Letter to the author, dated Dec. 29, 1935.

[63] G. M. Hammell, "Jones Very—A Son of the Spirit," *The Methodist Review*, LXXXIII (Jan., 1901), 20-30.

whose work was included in the anthology; and in the eleventh edition, published in 1852, eighteen of his poems appeared with a brief biographical sketch and a sound criticism. *The North American Review* ignored Very, along with Poe, in its criticism of Griswold's first edition, the reviewer emphasizing the worth of Bryant, Dana, Whittier, Longfellow, and Holmes;[64] but by 1856 the periodical had modified its attitude to such an extent that the reviewer of Griswold's sixteenth edition stated: "Jones Very has written some of the best sonnets in our language."[65] By 1863 Very's poetry (the sonnet—"The Railroad") was considered important enough to be used for illustrative material in a review of Matthew Arnold's *Poems;* and as proof of the poet's higher imagination and his ability to interpret the deep significance of the commonplace, the reviewer continued:

Each trite object stands for something beside itself, and bears a burden of admonishing suggestion to pierce the soul. Thus Jones Very, contemplating the most mechanical and prosaic thing, a railroad, and seeing how it marches straight on its course, lowering down, lifting up, thrusting aside, whatever would divert or impede it, in a lofty mood of inspiration, addresses it in these lines. . . . In this marvelous instance we see the creative spirit of poetry converting even a railroad into a living and flaming prophet of God.[66]

When Leigh Hunt and S. Adams Lee edited *The Book of the Sonnet* in 1867, they included Very's "The Robin," "Morning," "Thy Beauty Fades," and "The Spirit Land,"[67] and they spoke of the author as being "responsible for a larger number of sonnets than any other writer of New England."[68] His masters were declared to be the "old metaphysical rhapsodists of the sixteenth and seventeenth centuries, such as Donne, Herbert, Vaughan, etc.," and, like them, he was said to suffer from a "vague mysticism" of reflection. "Nevertheless," the editors continued, "in his highest moods, he is sincere, tender, fanciful; and the flow of his verse, though at one time monotonous, at another involved, is for the most part musical and pleasing."

[64] LVIII (Jan., 1844), 1-39.
[65] LXXXII (Jan., 1856), 236-244.   [66] XCVI (Jan., 1863), 131-132.
[67] These are included in Volume II of this work.
[68] I, 117.

Emerson, who, according to Edward Emerson and Waldo Forbes, "used to praise 'The Strangers' and 'The Barberry Bush,' "[69] chose to read these poems as illustrative of Very's work when he gave his readings at Chickering Hall during the winter and spring of 1869, and accompanied the poems with interesting comments.[70] Bryant, too, included "The Latter Rain," "Nature," and "The Spirit Land" in his anthology, *A New Library of Poetry and Song,* published the following year. But Evert and George Duyckinck paid a more substantial tribute in 1877, when they included eight of Very's poems in *The Cyclopaedia of American Literature.*[71]

But Jones Very was only mildly concerned over any judgment of his work. His life by this time had become even more introspective than formerly, and often he seemed entranced and sat for hours with scarcely a movement of his body to indicate physical life. The death of his brother Washington had been a severe blow, but his mother's death in May, 1867, was a loss almost too great even for one of his superlative faith and will-lessness. In the agony of his grief he wrote the simple yet tender poem,[72] "Our Dear Mother."[73] Indeed, the years were taking their toll. His roommate at Harvard, James Chisholm, had long since succumbed to fever while occupying a pastorate in Norfolk, Virginia; Thoreau had died in 1862, and Hawthorne in 1864. Apparently he did not attend the funeral of either friend,[74] but he afterwards visited Sleepy Hollow Cemetery and paid his tribute in the sonnet, "On Visiting the Graves of Hawthorne and Thoreau."[75] Often loneliness swept over him, for in spite of his companionship with nature and his sense of the nearness of God, he sometimes craved vital human sympathy, as is indicated by his letter to his lifelong friend, Robert C. Waterson, in 1868:

[69] See Note in Emerson's *Journals,* V, 383.

[70] *Ibid.,* X, 283-285, under date of March 21, 1869.

[71] Very is discussed in II, 385-386; his poems used are: "To the Painted Columbine," "The Wind-Flower," "The New Birth," "Day," "Night," "The Latter Rain," "Nature," "The Prayer."

[72] Mrs. Very died May 3, 1867; the MS is dated "May, 1867."

[73] *Clarke,* pp. 479-480.

[74] *Journals,* X, 39. Emerson lists the pallbearers among whom Jones Very's name does not appear.

[75] *Clarke,* p. 519.

Those were indeed pleasant and precious days, when we enjoyed so much each other's companionship at Cambridge. Then thoughts and feelings were freely interchanged and our lives were blended in one. There is nothing which we miss more in our manhood than that delightful communion which we enjoyed with early friends. Such an intercourse and communion it is we are toiling all our lives to find,— not perhaps to be renewed here, but which we hope is reserved to continue forever in heaven.[76]

No doubt Lowell would have welcomed Very as a guest at meetings of the Saturday Club, but the Salem recluse would have been unhappy in such a group of Boston Brahmins and popular literati. Even for the celebration of the three hundredth anniversary of Shakespeare's birth, he had been content to remain in Salem and write a sonnet.[77] Indeed, he lived much in the past. Once he was visited by the Reverend William Hooper, whom he had known since childhood and whose career, like Very's, had started as a cabin boy and had ended as a minister. They took from the wall a picture of the bark *Aurelia,* and spent an afternoon in delightful conversation of their boyhood.[78] But such pleasant reminiscences were only brief interludes in a decade of loneliness. Sometimes he recalled the days when he had visited Emerson at Concord, and he longed to see the man again; but the dread of meeting him when aphasia had dulled the Concord sage's mental powers kept him away from Emerson. Death or old age had already claimed most of those dear to him, and he resignedly awaited his turn. When William Cullen Bryant died in 1878, Very paid his tribute to the man who had praised his sonnets by writing a short elegy;[79] and he sang his swan song in the hymn for the installation of the Reverend George Herbert Hosmer early in 1879. In January, 1880, James Freeman Clarke, in the ninth of his twelve lectures before the Lowell Institute in Boston, selected Emerson and Very as the best representatives of mysticism in America.[80] In quoting and discussing Very's sonnets, Clarke stressed the fact that

[76] *Andrews,* p. 27.
[77] "On the Three Hundredth Anniversary of Shakespeare's Birthday," *Clarke,* pp. 493-494. The MS is dated May, 1864.
[78] See Poem No. 59 in Brown University MSS.
[79] *Clarke,* pp. 523-524.
[80] See his *Events and Epochs in Religious History,* chap. ix, pp. 291-298.

this mystic "imitated no one, and seemed the growth of the soil," that his sonnets "had a purity like that of the air in a bright December day in New England" joined to a "sad, hopeful, adoring strain." He asserted further: "Some of these . . . will not perish."

But Very's knowledge of such praise affected him only slightly and was of short duration. About the middle of April, 1880, he became ill, but he was so patient in enduring suffering that his sisters failed to realize his extreme danger. At length when a physician had been summoned, he pronounced the case one of malignant erysipelas. Some idea of the confusion and mental anguish at the Very home is conveyed by the message and the confused grammar on the postal card addressed to Mr. George Whipple, of the Essex Institute:

Salem, May 1st/80

Will Mr. Whipple please tell the one who fancies my painting that my brother is *very sick* and I can make no different arrangement—the picture*s* if sold must be sold as they are and the buyer can put it into any other frame.

Yours,

L. L. A. Very.[81]

Death came on Saturday, May 8, 1880.[82] A hush fell on Federal Street, for the earth-life of a mystic had closed. Miss Wilkins, then a child living across the street from the Very home, recalls that her elders moved about their tasks with the gravest quiet, speaking only when necessary, and then in low and reverent tones. The funeral, held at nine o'clock on the following Tuesday morning, was private, and was marked by the severest dignity and extremest simplicity.[83] The "brave saint" was reverently interred beside his

---

[81] See the Very MSS in the Margaret W. Brooks Collection, preserved in the Essex Institute, Salem, Mass.

[82] See Salem *Observer*, Saturday, May 15, 1880; Salem *Gazette*, Tuesday, May 11, 1880, Friday, May 14, 1880, Friday, May 21, 1880; Salem *Register*, Monday, May 10, 1880, Thursday, May 13, 1880, Monday, May 17, 1880, Thursday, May 20, 1880; Salem *Post*, Wednesday, May 12, 1880; Boston *Evening Transcript*, Friday, May 11, 1880; and Boston *Sunday Herald*, May 16 and June 6, 1880.

[83] See, in the Essex Institute files, an invitation to Dr. Henry Wheatland and Mr. George Whipple, of the Essex Institute, reading as follows:

"May 8, 1880.

"The funeral of Rev. Jones Very will take place Tuesday Morning, May 11th at 9 o'clock. His sisters will be pleased to have you attend."

JONES VERY, AGE 60 YEARS
(From a portrait in the Essex Institute, Salem, Massachusetts)

brother Washington in the family plot in the Old South Burial
Ground (also known as the Danvers Burial Ground) on Boston
Street. There, on the north side of a massive granite pyramid, one
reads his simple inscription:

REV. JONES VERY

DIED MAY 8, 1880

AE 66 YRS. 8 MOS. 10 DS.

CHAPTER VII

VERY'S REPUTATION SINCE 1880

IMMEDIATELY after the death of Jones Very, his friends began their elegiac tributes. The first of these to be published was "Jones Very," and appeared, without the author's name, in the Boston *Transcript* for May 10, 1880:

> Manly and true, his flowing lyric verse
> Breathed of the freshness of an earlier day;
> His Saxon-English, simple, strong and terse,
> Gushed like a brooklet by our dusty way;
> The flowers and birds in him their kindred knew,
> And fairer bloomed and sang their sweetest song,
> And grander prospects opened to his view
> Than ever to our noisy world belong;
> He read the message in each floweret sent,
> And words of promise brightened all the sod;
> He felt a presence wheresoe'er he went,
> And like the prophets, daily walked with God.
> Go, gentle spirit, in his mansions sing;
> Thou leavest us a blessing with the spring.[1]

On May 14 the Reverend Charles T. Brooks, of Newport, Rhode Island, but a native of Salem, published in the Salem *Gazette* a forty-line memorial poem entitled "To the Poet Very"; and the editors of all the Salem newspapers printed accounts—strangely lacking in variety—of Very's life, and quoted Emerson, Dana, and Bryant. An unidentified author, but in all probability William P. Andrews, wrote an excellent and refreshingly informative article, published on May 16 in the *Sunday Herald* of Boston, only to be corrected by a long letter from Lydia Very three weeks later.[2] The *Harvard Register* for June, 1880, also included a brief account of Very's life and a short criticism of his verse.

On the evening of December 14, 1880, the Essex Institute held a

[1] This sonnet is undoubtedly the work of William P. Andrews, since the ideas expressed strikingly resemble those in *Andrews*, p. 30.

[2] "Jones Very Again," in the edition of June 6, 1880.

memorial meeting for Very.[3] At that time William P. Andrews read a paper entitled "The Life and Spiritual Experience of Jones Very, the Poet," in which he incorporated reminiscences and bits of criticism gleaned from many letters Very had received from Emerson, Dana, and Bryant. Edward A. Silsbee also spoke at length on Very's literary excellence and place in American poetry, and the Reverend George H. Hosmer concluded the meeting by reading a number of letters from men unable to attend the memorial exercises but eager to express their high regard for Very as a saintly man and an unusual poet. Among such letters were those of a group of prominent ministers—James Freeman Clarke, Robert C. Waterson, Charles T. Brooks, Henry W. Foote, William Orne White, William Silsbee, and George D. White—all of whom eulogized Very almost excessively. Thomas Wentworth Higginson, Edwin M. Stone, and Professor Andrew P. Peabody also communicated with the Institute,[4] but their letters, being only mildly eulogistic, were not read publicly. Emerson, of course, had been asked to contribute something, but he was ill at the time and his daughter, writing for him, replied briefly if not curtly:

Concord, Dec. 11th, 1880.
Dear Sir,
    Mr. Emerson has somewhere among his papers a few notes of his intercourse with Mr. Very. He will try to find them, and if they seem to him such as it would be well to send you shall have them. But I think, as there are two ifs in the way, it is more probable that they will not come than that they will.
Yours truly,
Ellen T. Emerson.[5]

In 1883, the year following Emerson's death, Charles Eliot Norton edited *The Correspondence of Thomas Carlyle and Ralph Waldo Emerson,* in the first volume of which he graciously referred

[3] For an almost minute account of the meeting, see: "The Life and Services of Literature of Jones Very. A Memorial Meeting. Tuesday, Dec. 14, 1880," *Bulletin of the Essex Institute,* XIII (Jan.-June, 1881), 1-35. (The pamphlet really contains 37 pages, those following p. 18 being erroneously numbered 17 and 18 instead of 19 and 20.)

[4] See in the Essex Institute files: "Letters to the Institute concerning Jones Very's Death and the Memorial Meeting in Dec. 1880."

[5] *Ibid.*

to Very's *Essays and Poems* as follows: ". . . a little volume, the work of an exquisite spirit. Some of the poems it contains are as if written by a George Herbert who had studied Shakespeare, read Wordsworth, and lived in America."[6]

Partly because of the love William P. Andrews bore for Very, and partly as a result of his serious study of the poet's life and poetry, this gentleman began, in collaboration with Lydia and Frances Very, to prepare for the press a new edition of Very's poems. In the meantime he contributed articles on Very to the *Harvard Register*[7] and *Century*,[8] the first of which opened with an elegiac sonnet to his friend.[9] *Poems by Jones Very* was published by Houghton, Mifflin and Company in 1883, and was sold in the bookstores for one dollar. Because of its attractive format and its careful editing, it is the best of the three published volumes of Very's works. The "Memoir" prepared by Andrews is almost invaluable for students of Very, for Andrews had access to all of Very's manuscripts and letters, the latter of which, with only a few exceptions, have since been destroyed.[10] The account is written with great sympathy and understanding, but always with excellent restraint; the regrettable defects are the inaccuracies in dates, the confusion in chronology, particularly with regard to the relationship of Very and Emerson, and the failure to specify dates and authors of several quoted letters. The reason for publication of the second edition is given as follows: "That edition [the one of 1839] was never reprinted, though it was long since exhausted; and among Mr. Very's letters many requests from Mr. Dana and other friends were found for more copies, for which they had searched the bookstores in vain."[11]

The poems are arranged "with a view of showing the history" connectedly of Very's remarkable spiritual experience; and the divisions are appropriately classified as "The Call," "The New Birth," "The Message," "Nature," "Song and Praise," and "The Beginning

---

[6] I, 334.   [7] March, 1881, pp. 131-136.
[8] "An Inspired Life," II (Oct. 1, 1882), 859-862.
[9] The same author published a long poem "To the Poet Very" in the Salem *Gazette* for Feb. 23, 1883.
[10] They were burned after the death of Lydia Very in 1901.
[11] *Andrews*, p. 26.

and the End." All of the poems which Emerson selected for the first edition are included, and to these have been added others, making a total of 138. Especially pleasing are the thirty-seven nature poems, among which is Emerson's favorite, "The Barberry Bush";[12] and the entire collection splendidly represents Very at his best. One gets from a careful reading of this volume a feeling of profound respect for Very's poetic genius, a reverence for the purity of the man's life, and a deep and abiding faith in the beauty and spiritual significance of nature. Interesting, particularly to a biographer, is the poem called "The Sight of the Ocean,"[13] in which he expresses the "sad, lonely feeling" he could not control whenever he viewed the sea. Truly, the ocean seldom attracted Very pleasantly; sometimes it fascinated him, but the end of all such experiences was like that expressed in the last stanza of the poem:

> As night o'er the ocean its shadow threw,
> And homeward the weary sea-bird flew,
> I turned from the dark and rocky height,
> With grateful heart to my hearth-stone bright.

Another poem reveals Very's reaction to Poe's works, particularly "The Raven," and reads:

> A sad refrain I heard, from poet sad,
> Which on my soul with deadening weight did fall;
> But quick another word, which made me glad,
> Did from the heavens above me seem to call.
> The first was Nevermore; which, like a knell,
> Struck on my ear with dull funereal sound;
> The last was Evermore; which, like a bell,
> In waves of music filled the air around.
> Forevermore with loved and lost to be,
> No more to suffer change, nor grief, nor pain;
> From partings sad to be forever free,—
> Such was that sweet bell's music:—its refrain
> Blended with voices from the heavenly shore,
> Each whispering to my heart, Forevermore.[14]

But since the selected poems express primarily Very's spiritual experience and his intense mysticism, the sonnet titled "The River" is more representative of the collection, and, because it appears in

[12] P. 103.   [13] Pp. 120-121.   [14] P. 146.

neither of the other editions of Very's work, it deserves to be quoted
here:

> Oh! swell my bosom deeper with thy love,
> That I some river's widening mouth may be;
> And ever on, for many a mile above,
> May flow the floods that enter from thy sea;
> And may they not retreat as tides of earth,
> Save but to show from Thee that they have flown,
> Soon may my spirit find that better birth,
> Where the retiring wave is never known;
> But Thou dost flow through every channel wide,
> With all a Father's love in every soul;
> A stream that knows no ebb, a swelling tide
> That rolls forever on and finds no goal,
> Till in the hearts of all shall opened be
> The ocean depths of thine eternity.[15]

The Andrews edition was well received by the critics. *The Literary World* (Boston) for June, 1883, declared Very to be a "mystic
of the Old World type, a brother in spirit to Tauler and Madame
Guyon, who, like them, lost the present in the unseen, and trans-
figured the homely scenes of a common life with a glow of Hebrew inspiration."[16] He was compared with Herbert and William
Blake; but the reviewer very correctly declared further that "in
the naturalness and facility with which he pierces through the
material, outward fact, to the spiritual lesson beneath, he rivals the
dictionary of correspondences, and deserves the name of a poetic
Swedenborg." In July, 1883, Samuel Longfellow earnestly com-
mended "this little volume of poems" to the readers of *The Index*[17]
by concluding his brief review with the statement that "These are
the hymns of a soul that has not heard about God, but heard him
and walked with him." George Batchelor, writing for *The Dial*
(Chicago), found Very's sonnets to excel because of their "spiritual
interpretation of nature,"[18] and in this particular to have no rivals
in American literature. *The Atlantic Monthly* found many of the
poems to be "commonplace," some to be "but feeble repetitions of
sentiments that had been better expressed before"; but the best

[15] P. 45.   [16] XIV, 205.
[17] N.S., IV (July 5, 1883-June 26, 1884), 10.
[18] IV (July, 1883).

were declared to give "evidence of original power, genuine feeling, and unconscious art."[19] Ten of the religious and seven of the pure nature poems were quoted, and "to read him" was declared to be "like reading Vaughan." A reviewer for the New York *Tribune* believed Very "a New England mystic in whom was blended the Buddhist ecstasy and a sweet, sedate Puritanism."[20] Thus Very's poems were received by the critics of 1883.

But there were some people who were reading Very for actual pleasure rather than for the purpose of contributing reviews to periodicals. Among these was Gamaliel Bradford. On April 26, 1884, when he was barely twenty years old, he made in his *Journal* a three-paragraph entry concerning Very. "I have found a new poet," he wrote enthusiastically; and then, apologizing for his failure to appreciate Very long ago, he continued: "But that was at a period when everything Hebraic angered me . . . and I read so carelessly as to mistake simplicity for commonplace, the purity of Very for the stupidity of Longfellow."[21] This admiration continued throughout Gamaliel Bradford's life; and, thirty years later, when exulting over his reading, he added: ". . . and with all this diversified entertainment necessarily blends the large, solemn pre-occupation with God which was the whole of Jones Very."[22] It was only natural, then, that Bradford should have included a critical study of Very in his *Biography of the Human Heart,* published in 1932.[23]

The thousand printed copies of the Andrews edition[24] were practically exhausted in less than three years, and the publishers suggested to Lydia and Frances Very that another edition be prepared for the press. They, under the sponsorship of James Freeman Clarke, who wrote a biographical sketch of Very, and Cyrus A. Bartol, who contributed a short preface, attempted to edit a com-

[19] LII (July, 1883), 123 ff.
[20] The article here referred to was reprinted in the Boston *Evening Transcript* for Tuesday, Aug. 28, 1883. The date of the *Tribune* printing has not been ascertained, because files of that newspaper have been unavailable.
[21] *The Journal of Gamaliel Bradford,* ed. Van Wyck Brooks, p. 39.
[22] *Ibid.*, p. 280.
[23] Chapter VII, "Jones Very," pp. 185-212. For Bradford's further interest in Very, see *The Letters of Gamaliel Bradford,* ed. Van Wyck Brooks (Boston: Houghton Mifflin Co., 1934), pp. 38, 77, 78, 99, and 162.
[24] Letter to the author from Houghton Mifflin Co.

plete edition of their brother's poems and his three essays under the title *The Works of Jones Very*. Five hundred copies were published in October, 1886.[25] This edition was exceedingly unfortunate for the furtherance of Very's reputation, for the book contains 526 pages and is too ponderous looking for a lover of either nature sonnets or religious verse. One who has the patience to hunt diligently can find a number of really good new poems scattered among the 676 listed,[26] but many of the pieces are trite or even mediocre, and perhaps should never have been published.[27] Very's range is, of course, narrow; many of his poems are very similar in language and subject matter; and a number of widely different poems have identical titles. For example, there are four poems called "Nature" and four others bearing such similar titles as "Nature Repeats Her Lessons," "Nature's Help for the Soul," "Nature Teaches Only Love," and "Nature Intelligible"; and to these should be added six poems identified merely by the title "Song." Had the editors made an index of first lines, as did Andrews for the edition of 1883, some of the confusion could have been avoided. At least the title of one included poem would not have been omitted from the table of contents,[28] and fifteen poems which had appeared in the Andrews edition would not have been omitted entirely.[29] The same precaution also might have prevented the inexcusable repetition of twenty-three poems (sometimes with identical titles, at other times with different ones),[30] one of which occurs three times.[31]

[25] *Ibid.*

[26] Among these are such nature poems as "The Yellow Violet" (p. 372), "The May-Flower" (p. 376), "The Wood-Wax" (p. 377), "The Houstonia" (p. 384), "The Return of the Columbine" (p. 427), and "The Barberry-Pickers" (p. 428); and the thirty-seven sonnets under the division called "The Puritans," pp. 207-225.

[27] Such are "On the Completion of the Pacific Telegraph" (p. 232), "The First Atlantic Telegraph" (p. 272), "Voting in an Old Church" (p. 462), "The Lesson of History" (p. 465), "The Youth and the Stream" (p. 486), "The Comphene Lamp" (p. 507), and "The Telephone" (p. 272).

[28] "Health of Body Dependent on the Soul" (p. 521).

[29] These are (in *Andrews*): "Day unto Day Uttereth Speech" (p. 46), "The Swift" (p. 124), "The River" (p. 45), "To—on the Death of His Friend" (p. 138), "The Prison" (p. 68), "The Prophet" (p. 76), "The Winter Rain" (p. 87), "The Beginning and the End" (p. 156), "The Star" (p. 41), "Labor and Rest" (p. 89), "The Fruit" (p. 104), "The Mountain," (p. 78), "The Tenant" (p. 115), "The Morn" (p. 121), and "To Him That Hath Shall Be Given" (p. 37).

[30] These occur as follows:

p. 98 and p. 248—"The Hours."

Man's Sympathy With Nature.

There is a sighing in the wood,
A murmur in the beating wave;
The heart has never understood,
To tell, in words, the thoughts they gave.

Yet oft we feel an answering tone,
When wandering on the lonely shore;
Or listening through the night alone,
As inland swells the ocean's roar.

And oft beneath the wind-swept pine,
Some chord is struck the strain to swell;
Nor sounds, nor language can define,
'Tis not for words, or sounds to tell.

Thou hear'st in these that Mighty Voice,
Whose goings forth, unknown to all,
Bid sounding wood, and wave rejoice,
And fill with music Nature's hall.

And, in the speechless human heart,
It speaks, where'er man's feet have trod,
Beyond the lips deceitful art,
To tell of Him, the Unseen God!

The confusion which the Clarke edition must have produced in even a patient reader is indicated by a sentence in the opening paragraph of a review written by G. Bradford, Jr., for *The Unitarian Review*: ". . . Though this last volume contains much which we do not find in Mr. Andrews's edition, we shall, nevertheless, refer to his as containing all that is best and most illustrative of Very's genius, and as being better arranged for the convenience of the general reader."[32] The entire review, then, is based on the Andrews edition. Indeed, had the publishers and the Misses Very been satisfied with a further printing of this edition, Jones Very's poetry might be better known today.

After the publication of Clarke's edition, one hears little of Very during the remainder of the nineteenth century. Charles F. Richardson in his *American Literature: 1607-1885*, published in 1895,[33] considered Very briefly in the second volume of his work, declaring his sonnets to be packed with "rich and weighty words" but

---

p. 101—"The Weary and Heavy Laden" and p. 244—"The Soul's Rest."

p. 104 and p. 278—"The First Shall Be Last."

p. 108 and p. 251—"The Temple."

p. 117—"Thy Neighbor" and p. 254—"Thy Better Self."

p. 118—"Compassion" and p. 246—"Christ's Compassion."

p. 171—"The Hour" and p. 284—"The Life of the Hour."

p. 130—"The Slave-Holder" and p. 257—"The Day Not for Gain."

p. 178 and p. 420—"Nature."

p. 197—"The Silent" and p. 364—"Man's Sympathy with Nature."

p. 199—"Give and It Shall Be Given unto You" and p. 284—"Spiritual Debtors."

p. 230 and p. 465—"Outward Conquests Not Enough."

p. 232 and p. 432—"The Comet."

p. 233 and pp. 421-422—"Nature Repeats Her Lessons."

p. 252—"The Revelation of the Spirit through the Material World" and pp. 437-438—"The Sunset."

p. 294 and p. 326—"The Soul's Freedom."

p. 308 and pp. 357-358—"The Help of the Spirit."

pp. 311-312 and pp. 514-515—"Congregational Singing."

p. 314 and pp. 346-347 and pp. 508-509—"The Light Still Shining in the Darkness."

p. 328 and p. 521—"Health of Body Dependent on the Soul."

p. 331 and p. 438—"The Child's Answer."

p. 356 and p. 489—"Hymn on the Early Spring."

p. 473 and p. 517—"The Indian's Petition."

[31] "The Light Still Shining in the Darkness," see pp. 314, 346-347, and 508-509.

[32] "Jones Very," XXVII (Feb., 1887), 111-118.

[33] New York: G. P. Putnam's Sons, pp. 233-234.

"harmed by a semi-Buddhistic Christian Quietism." Two years later Charles Dudley Warner used eleven of the poems in his *Library of the World's Best Literature;* and in his criticism of the man, declared that he was "one of the choicest of that noteworthy group of New England idealists."[34] After 1900, one discovers Very's poems in at least twelve anthologies,[35] and one finds critical articles in *The Methodist Review,*[36] the *Howard College Bulletin,*[37] *The New England Quarterly,*[38] and *The American Review.*[39] Scholars in Germany also became interested in Very, particularly in his mysticism and his love of nature. Anton E. Schonbach considered him favorably in his *Über Lesen und Bildung,*[40] published in 1900; and three years later Albert Ritter translated the "Memoir" and ninety-two of the poems which appeared in the Andrews edition.[41] In 1913 the Boston *Evening Transcript* reminded its readers of the centenary of Very's birth.[42] It would seem, then, that the man's reputation is being definitely though slowly established in the twentieth century.

The most ardent of the recent admirers of Very is Louis Untermeyer. In the Preface to his *American Poetry from the Beginning to Whitman,* he considers Very and T. H. Chivers as "two independents, who, scorned in their time, are now recognized as geniuses";[43] and he strongly censures Bliss Carman because he found "room for much inconsequential verse" in *The Oxford Book of American Verse,* published in 1927, but even failed to mention Very.[44] Untermeyer, as if to correct the error of Bliss Carman,

[34] New York: R. S. Peale and J. A. Hill, XXVI, 15, 323-315, 329.

[35] See the list, arranged chronologically, at the conclusion of "Primary Sources" in the Bibliography.

[36] Professor G. M. Hammell, "Jones Very—A Son of the Spirit," LXXXIII (Jan., 1901), 20-30.

[37] Percy Pratt Burns, "Jones Very," LXXX (June, 1922), 42-66.

[38] Carlos Baker, "Emerson and Jones Very," VII (March, 1934), 90-99.

[39] Yvor Winters, "A New England Mystic," VII (May, 1936), 159-178. Mr. Winters reprints this article in *Maule's Curse—Seven Studies in the History of American Obscurantism,* published by New Directions in 1938. In an appendix he includes twenty-two of Very's poems.

[40] Very is discussed in Chapter IV, "Ralph Waldo Emerson und sein Kreis," pp. 81-133.

[41] *Jones Very der Dichter des Christentums* (Linz, Wien, Leipzig: Oesterreichische Verlagsanstalt).

[42] "Jones Very, a Poet of Mysticism," Saturday, Oct. 25, 1913.

[43] P. 51.   [44] Pp. 51 and 475.

× The Prisoner
My soul's very

All men around me running to and fro
~~Find~~
Are finding life in what to me is death;
I have no limbs that where I please will go,
Nor voice that when I wish will find a breath;
Here, where I stand, my feet ~~take~~ fixed root;
This way or that I cannot even ~~the~~ move;
A prisoner, ever bound both hand and foot,
While I a slave to mine own choice would
'Tis hard to wait, but grant me ~~but~~ ~~this~~ set free;
                                        prove;
And they; how narrow their ~~confined~~ short bounded lot!
~~Within my orbit worlds untold will be~~
My sun the centre of their worlds will be,
In systems moving where they shine forgot;
                twinkling glancing
Their rays too feebly ~~~~ through the
                                        night,
Where I shall shine with all day's lustre
                                        bright

includes eleven of Very's sonnets, preceded by a brief biographical and critical sketch. The concluding paragraph of the latter represents, in brief, the conclusion which any unprejudiced student of Very must form after a careful and thorough consideration of the mystic's life and works: "In the textbooks of the history of literature, Very is almost always a cursory appendage to the Transcendental group. Actually, he had no counterpart in America. If he reminds one of any preceding poet, it is the English Herbert. The metaphysical note, though more limited than Herbert's, is as pure; the imagery, while not so subtle, is as apposite. It is a queer circumstance that such poetry should be neglected and its author practically unknown."[45] To Mr. Untermeyer's statement, one should add that it is doubtful that such verse as Very wrote can ever be popular. As Bradford rightly states, "Very's breadth is too slight in proportion to his depth."[46] His work is uneven; his religious phraseology is, to many readers, repellent; and his passionate idealism is out of keeping with a materialistic civilization. Could he have written a popular narrative poem—something like *Snow-Bound* or *The Courtship of Miles Standish*—to keep his name alive among the masses, his nature poems and his religious verse might be more generally known today. But since his genius was lyrical and mystical rather than narrative, the really exquisite sonnets which treat of nature and God—most of which are in the edition of Andrews—are the works upon which his reputation must rest. The outmoded prose essays and the mediocre, unimpassioned poems can well be forgotten. It is the hope of Very's admirers that an edition somewhat similar to the one of Andrews may yet come from the press and thus preserve for American literature the unique genius of Emerson's "brave saint."

[45] *Ibid.*, p. 475.   [46] *Op. cit.*

CHAPTER VIII

POEMS IN MANUSCRIPT

THERE ARE two large collections of manuscripts left by Jones Very, one in the library of the Andover Theological Seminary, at Cambridge, Massachusetts, and the other in the Harris Collection of American Poetry at Brown University, Providence, Rhode Island. The first collection was presented to the owners by "the Misses F. E. and L. L. A. Very, of Salem, Mass.," on March 22, 1895; the second collection was purchased—the larger bulk in 1903 from Goodspeed's, in Boston; the "Lines on Mt. Auburn"[1] and other verse in 1929 from Lull, another bookdealer.[2] Just how these manuscripts came into the hands of Goodspeed's and Lull is not known.[3]

Among the manuscripts at the Andover Theological Seminary are only nine poems which have not been published, to which may be added two poems which have been preserved only on programs. These eleven poems, which are hymns and religious sonnets, are recorded in this chapter exactly as they occur in manuscript, and, for convenience, are numbered. The manuscript material at Brown University contains fifty-nine unpublished poems.[4] These are varied in length, subject matter, and literary value. Many of the poems are dated; some have titles and others have none; a few are partly punctuated, but others ignore punctuation almost entirely. They, like the manuscripts at Cambridge, are recorded in this chapter exactly as they are found in the manuscripts. The first eight

---

[1] See Bibliography for a list of the MSS.

[2] From records in the library at Brown University.

[3] Miss Harriet I. Wilkins, of Salem, Mass., recalls that shortly after the death of Lydia Very, in 1901, a stranger, representing himself as being from Brown University, persuaded Mrs. Cooper, housekeeper and caretaker at the Very homestead, to allow him to enter the house and to examine manuscript material. The result, so Miss Wilkins recalls, was that the stranger walked away with some material which Mrs. Cooper in her simple ignorance had given him.

[4] It is barely possible, should complete files of the newspapers published in Salem, Mass., ever be available, that some of these poems may prove to have been published; but lacking such evidence, and knowing that the poems do not appear in any printed edition of Very's works, it seems only logical and just to treat them as poems existing only in manuscript form.

Eternal Life

My life as yet is but an infant's walk,
With tottering steps and words half-uttered slow;
But I shall soon in nobler accents talk,
And grown to manlier stature, firmer go;
I shall go out and in and pasture find
In him who leads me safe forever on;
The spirit's fetters then shall I unbind,
And sin from me forever shall be gone;
Eternal life will be the gift bestowed,
By him who loved us while yet dead in sin;
Such love forever from the Father flowed,
But we were not prepared the crown to win;
Oh bless his Name, who calls us on to heaven;
And him in whom the promises are given.

The Redeemed

I hear the prints of my ascended Lord,
Ye cannot hurt me now, for I am pure;
And hear, forever hear his holy word,
And shall forever in the Truth endure;
Behold the love the Father hath for me,
That He should call his son a child of earth;
And from the guilt of sin forever free,
And bid me know in Him a purer birth;
Come, worship with me on the holy hill,
Come, be a brother with a brother's love,
He will our hearts with deeper rapture fill,
And we though here shall taste his joy above;
And in our midst, though here, our Lord shall be,
And we, while here on earth, his face shall see.

poems are obviously early productions, as the dates and occasional ungrammatical or awkward structure indicate. The seventh poem was intended for the Salem *Observer*, but it never appeared in that newspaper. Poems numbered 9 through 15, those numbered 21 through 49, and those numbered 52 through 57 are religious sonnets, most of which, if one have patience to supply the missing punctuation as he reads them, will prove to be representative of Very's better verse. The fifty-first poem, "Endicott," undoubtedly was written for the group of sonnets headed "The Puritans," found in the Clarke edition,[5] but for some reason was omitted from that publication. Number 16 is a hymn; numbers 17, 18, and 50 are religious poems in four-line stanzas; number 19 is a bird lyric tinged with the religious; and numbers 20, 58, and 59 have autobiographic significance. A number of these pieces have been referred to in previous chapters of this study.

In the Essex Institute, at Salem, Massachusetts, is a program of the installation exercises for the Reverend George Herbert Hosmer,[6] in which is printed a hymn written for the occasion by Jones Very. This poem (numbered 60) concludes the list of manuscript poems incorporated in this chapter.

MANUSCRIPTS IN THE ANDOVER THEOLOGICAL SEMINARY, CAMBRIDGE, MASSACHUSETTS

1.   This Mortal Shall Put on Immortality

This mortal body quickly dies,
Struck by disease and pain;
In vain we gaze, our longing eyes
Behold it not again.

'Tis but a tent, a house of clay,
Where for a time we dwell;
For years, or for a single day
No one of us can tell.

Mysterious union of the soul,
Of spirit with the clod;
One being, Man, a perfect whole,
The image of his God!

[5] Pp. 207-225.

[6] "Order of Exercises at the Installation of Rev. George Herbert Hosmer, over the East Church, Thursday, January 2, 1879."

O Keep that image pure and bright
Of body and of mind,
And keep the glory still in sight,
For which it was designed.

Since not for suffering, or disease,
God formed us of the dust;
But that we might our Maker please,
And place in Him our trust.

Who through his Son the promise gave,
That man shall never die;
But triumph o'er the opening grave
In immortality!

                              JV

2.   Hymn

The Forms of Nature and the Unity of Their Origin

Seek not in outward things,
The origin and birth
Of animal, and plant, and seed,
In air, or sea, or earth;
In vain their history we trace
Through ages vast, through time and space.

From One Eternal Mind
Have come the forms we see;
Those countless forms, whose difference make
Nature's variety;
Each stamped with impress of its kind
And each to its own sphere confined.

No atom but obeys
The One Creative Will;
Whose Word, beneficent and good,
The universe doth fill;
Without which naught was made, or born,
Which was before Creation's morn.

Globule and secret cell
A history contain;
Which Science, with its marvelous powers,
Still seeks to read in vain;
To the All Perfect Mind alone
Their origin, and types are known.

In Nature's primal plan
Prophetic types are seen;
Which lead us onward up to Man,
Their end, and destiny;
A unity of mind and thought
Through every form and being wrought.

But, in her labyrinth lost,
Too oft we miss the clue;
Which, midst her ever varying forms,
Runs through the old and new;
And in phenomena we rest,
As of the truth itself possest.

Rest not, O Soul, till thou
That clue, that thread shall find;
Without whose constant, guiding help,
We wander dark and blind;
In endless mazes led astray,
Missing the strait and narrow way.

For this still upward leads;
Steep is the Mount of Thought;
Which we, aspiring still, must climb,
Till to the summit brought;
Where, with clear vision, we discern
Nature's vast realm, her mysteries learn.

3.   Yet Once More

The heavens are shaken! not the solid earth,
But the high heavens, the spirit's own abode;
Through the dark souls whence sin springs armed to birth,
The miracle of miracles is showed!
There mountains shake, there breaks a startling voice
Unknown amid its sinful depths before;
The guilty dare not, when it speaks, rejoice;
But fain within its presence would adore;
Fly! fly! it is the spirit's voice you hear,
It is an angel sent to thee from heaven,
To tell thee that the marriage feast is near,
And but a moment's warning can be given;
Oh haste! the robe, the robe of white put on,
E'er that for thee that moment shall be gone.

4.   The Eagles

The eagles gather on the place of death
So thick the ground is spotted with their wings,
The air is tainted with the noisome breath
The wind from off the field of slaughter brings;
Alas! no mourners weep them for the slain,
But all unburied lies the naked soul;
The whitening bones of thousands strew the plain,
Yet none can now the pestilence control;
The eagles gathering on the carcass feed,
In every heart behold their half-formed prey;
The battened wills beneath their talons bleed,
Their iron beaks without remorse must slay;
Till by the sun no more the place is seen,
Where they who worshiped idol gods have been.

5.   Winter

There is a winter in the godless heart
More cold than that which creeps upon the year;
That will not with the opening spring depart,
But presses on though summer's heats are near.
Its blasts are words that chill the living soul,
Though heard in pleasing phrase and learned sound;
Their chilling breath nor triple folds control,
They pierce within though flesh and blood surround.
How dead the heart whence drives the arrowy shower!
The full-blown rose hangs drooping at its breath,
The bursting buds of promise feel its power,
And fixed stand incased in icy death;
And e'en the soul which Christ's warm tears fill,
Its sleety accents falling thick can chill.

6.   Repent, for the Kingdom of Heaven Is at Hand

Repent, repent, the day of wrath is near!
Who shall abide the terror of the hour?
Repent, the son of righteousness is here,
Thou hast no stay save in his rock-built tower;
The rains descend, the tempest speeds its way;
They pour upon the houses built with hands,
That melt before the torrents; walls of clay
Dissolved roll onward with the rolling sands;
Where is the house that stood before secure

With gates and mighty bulwarks lifted high?
It stood not on the strong foundation sure
That rain and tempest's shock can still defy,
And, when the storm around has ceased to roar,
Stand still unmoved where once it stood before.

7.   The New Jerusalem

There are towers; where they are,
In the topmost sky;
Thou from here hast never seen,
With thy clouded eye.

There are houses, temples there,
In that world of bliss;
Yet thou canst not see them here,
From a place like this.

There I see the Son of Man,
Of that world the light;
Seen by all; their sun by day,
And their moon by night.

There are beings, they who went
From thy presence here;
From their mansions looking down
On thine earthly sphere.

Cherubs there, and white-robed men,
Angels born to love;
High! how high their golden home!
Dwelling there above.

8.   Still a Day to Live

Still a day to live, still a day to live,
The thought to my mind doth wisdom give;
For what in a day, may not be done?
What may not be lost? What may not be won?

In a day we may turn from the evil away,
Resist the temptations that lead us astray;
In a day we may goodness forever secure,
And thus our high calling of God may make sure.

As bright from the east upriseth the sun,
Let the morning with prayer and with praise be begun;
Commune with thy Maker, and ask for his care,
He hears, and will bless thy heart-spoken prayer.

In the hours of thy business, thy pleasure, thy rest,
Let the thought of his Presence on all be impressed;
'Twill strengthen for toil and thy pleasure make pure,
And give thee the riches that ever endure.

Each hour heed the voice that to duty may call,
Though that duty to thee seem but trivial or small;
Each deed, timely done, to remembrance how sweet;
Be quick, for the moment of action is fleet.

For the night quickly cometh, when labor is o'er,
And the sun at his rising shall see us no more;
When fruitful, or faithless, no more we can say,
"I have still, I have still yet to live for a day!"

9.   Hymn

The Good Fight

The battle is within,
And not on outward plain,
'Tis there the victory we win,
The crown of life we gain.

Our word, our thought, our deed,
That battle still makes known;
We are not from the conflict freed,
Till sin be overthrown.

Not with an outward foe
Must thou the battle wage,
A mightier contest thou must know
Than warrior's martial rage.

The world doth claim the soul,
As well as outward things;
It seeks the spirit to control,
Its hidden, vital springs.

The motive thou must scan,
Which doth thy spirit move;
For 'tis the motive makes the man,
And doth his virtue prove.

Thou needst a heavenly power,
A mightier strength than thine;
To guard thee in temptation's hour,
O, ask for strength divine.*

* MS has parentheses around the word *ask,* and underneath it in pencil is written
the word *seek.*

Watch, pray, that thou mayst be
A victor in the strife;
And God from sin shall set thee free,
And give eternal life.

10.   Welcome

Written for the Essex Institute Fair, Held at Salem,
Sept. 4th, 1860.

We welcome to our Hall and Fair
All who would aid in Learning's cause!
The noble work we fain would share,
Which man to clearer knowledge draws.

With still increasing light it beams,
As we the world around explore;
From earth and sky its radiance streams,
That all may see, believe, adore.

The beast, the bird, the fish, the shell,
The flower, the crystal from the mine,
Have each some word of truth to tell
Of the Creator's vast design.

But oft with uninstructed eye,
And soul unmoved, on these we gaze;
And e'en the glories of the sky
No knowledge show, call forth no praise.

From Learning's hall to Nature's page
With more enlightened minds we turn;
Delighted still, from youth to age,
New charms to see, new truths to learn.

As Nature, to her children all,
Opens her realms of wonder wide;
Aid us that Learning's sun-lit hall,
To none who seek, may be denied.

11.   Song*

Written for the Valedictory Exercises of the Senior Class of
Harvard University, Tuesday, July 19, 1836.

(Tune—"Auld Lang Syne")

No more around the social board
Shall rise the laugh of glee;
The song that stirred our bosoms once
Has hushed its melody.

* This poem is copied from a program of the exercises held at Harvard University.

Chorus

Youth's cherished spot! what wreaths of joy
Around thy memory twice!
While throbs the heart's warm beating pulse,
'Twill tell of "auld lang syne."

The glance of love, the friendly word,
Shall be returned no more;
Nor answer when our footsteps tread
The scenes they loved before.

Chorus.

They who upon our pathway shed
Life's gladdest beams are here,
Upon the shrine where we have knelt
To shed the parting tear.

Chorus

We linger—struggling accents rise
Each friendly ear to greet;
In one farewell our hearts would breathe
Whole years of memory sweet.

Adieu! we cannot speak the thoughts
Our swelling breasts would speak,
For feeling's deepest, fullest tide,
The tongue's vain words are weak.

Chorus

We linger, etc.

MANUSCRIPTS IN THE HARRIS COLLECTION OF AMERICAN POETRY,
AT BROWN UNIVERSITY, PROVIDENCE, RHODE ISLAND

1.   Lines on Mount Auburn, December, 1833

Sing heavenly Muse, of that fair mountain sing,
Where rest in peace the honored dead; and where
As the seasons roll around their heads, their
Children oft shall come, and o'er them drop the
Tear of grateful memory; and from their
Example learn the better how to live,
The better how to die. Learn from them
As if the glorious sun his rays still shed
Upon them, as lifes swift current still through
Their veins ran warm: as if before them were

Those forms so well remember'd, and they stood
Attentive to receive a parents wish
Respected. Hallowed Spot! where still the dead
Seem yet to live, yet to give instruction
The more regarded since from them it comes.
Here as with devious steps we wander through
Thy thickets dard, or near some tomb o'er which
The flowers of spring in beauty wave deep musing
We shall from worldly thoughts and worldly cares
Withdraw ourselves and deep communion hold
With those long since departed, and raise our
Souls to him whose never ceasing goodness
Crowns our life. Here oft let youth retire from
Life's gay scene from pleasures chantry round to
Learn that though they live by worldly pleasures
Compassed round, and though the flowers of spring are
Breathing there in richest fragrance, and the
Woods are in their greenest verdure crowned that
As those flowers by winter's crewel blast their
Fragrance and their beauty soon will lose so
They on earth shall flourish but awhile; that
Soon their flowering spring by the chill blast
Of age shall wither; and thus may they be
Led to place their happiness on things not
Fleeting but eternal in the heavens.
Here, too, may manhood come from restless cares
Of life withdrawn and learning here from those
Whose life was most employed in duties to
Their country and to man most useful, death
Spares not even manhood, life's most active
Scene, he shall from this lesson learn to live
A better and a happier man.
And here may age whose silver locks proclaim
Life's winter learn that their example still
Shall live and unborn generations
Revere their memory. And let them learn
"The storms of Wintry Time will quickly pass
And one unbounded Spring encircle all"
"Where they shall flourish in immortal youth
Unhurt amid the war of elements
The wreck of matter and the crush of Worlds."

2.   Lines Suggested by Hearing the Beach, December 21, 1883,
         at F. Peabody's Mills, South Salem.

The silent moon is rising
O'er the hills of purest snow,
The silent river's flowing
In its deep bed below.

The bustle too is dying,
Around the noisy mill;
The workmen home are hying,
And all is hushed and still.

3.

Haunts of my youth farewell! a while I leave
You in your loveliness! A while I go
To visit other scenes, more fair, perhaps, but none
I love so well. Resistless as thy stream,
Fair river, when thou pour'st along swollen with
Autumnal rains, is love of home within
The breast of man. So Afric's wretched son
With eye bent on his fast-receding home,
Far drop'd his scanty fare, heeds not his chains,
But with the tear-drops starting in his eye,
Exclaims—"There I was born. There is my home."
The wanderer of the long years, whom oft
Encountered dangers never learned to shed
A tear, weeps like a child when he beholds
The smoke of much-loved Ithaca. Beauty's
Fabled Goddess, since on earth no more she
Deigns to dwell, has left with thee, O home, her
All-enchanting love. Dearer to Lapland's
Sons, her snow-clad plains, her ice-bound rivers,
Her mountain tops, the residence of storms,
Than the green sunny plains, the vine-clad hills,
The winding streams of favor'd Italy.
And ye, my youthful haunts, though some there are
On which my eyes could well a summer's day,
Nor heed the sun, blushing to leave so
Fair a scene, nor evening's soft approach warning
My lingering footsteps home, though some there are
Which those who look on fairer scenes would pass
Contemptuous by—yet all to me are
Beautiful. Round all alike, O home, thy

Charm is thrown. I love you all. The yellow
Leaves at my return perhaps will rustle
In the autumnal blast, or winter's snows
May hide my wandering path; still will I trace
It out: for there's no winter in my love
For thee, no age but death. Amid the snows
Of age 'twill like the evergreen appear
As fresh as in my vernal prime.

4.

Home of my youth! Where first my lot was cast
To Thee I dedicate my feeble song
Upon whose hills how swift the moments passed
As linked with flowers the days moved easily on
Though hills more fair and streams more bright than thine
May lure my eye as from thy paths I stray
While memorys ray shall on their summits shine
What spot shall seem more fair to me than they.

For if may be—would that a worthy lay
Might bear my love for thee to distant time
Far as thy sons oer all trackless way
Have borne thy name to India's sunny clime.
A blessing rest alike on thee and thine
On those whose bark shall rove from strand to strand
Whereer they are whatere their lot may be
Sweet be the name of their own fatherland.

5.

The moon was shining on the deck
The stars looked out upon the sea
The sail had dwindled to a speck
That was upon our lea.

I crept beside the grey-locked man
Whose words I loved to hear so well
He knew my wish and thus began
His ocean tale to tell.

"The ship from Hamburgh held her way
And playing round her stately form
The waves curled bright their wreaths of spray
All heedless of the storm.

The ship seemed glad to feel once more
Around her roll the deep blue main
As onward bounding from the shore
She heard its voice again.

And I was young my boy as thou
And all around seemed strange and new
I watched the ocean's deep green brow
I watched the heavens so blue.

I looked behind—my home had fled
And seemed afar like distant cloud
My mother all I loved seemed dead
I wept and sobbed aloud.

6.

As long as Ceres gives the grain,
And Bacchus yields the wine;
So long shall in my breast remain,
The thoughts o'auld lang syne.

Then fill your cups my hearty friends,
We'll have a cheerful time;
We'll use the gifts that Bacchus sends,
And drink to auld lang syne.

7.   For the Salem *Observer*

"Ambitione inani pectus caret"

Knowest thou what ambition gains
As reward of all its pain?
Knows't thou what the precious spoils
It receives for all its toils?

See, with what an eager eye,
Yon child pursues the butterfly;
Mark his looks of joy and pleasure,
As he strives to seize the treasure.

Now on yonder rose it stands,
Running with extended hands
He would grasp the brilliant toy;
Flying from the eager boy.

Now within a tulip's cup,
'Tis from sight almost shut up;
Fill'd with joy yet mixed with fear,
Cautiously he's drawing near.

See the prize is now obtained,
The long-eluding object's gain'd;
He opes his little hand with joy,
Why that tear? say why? my boy.

Ah, its golden splendor's fled,
What thou soughtst, alas! is dead;
Thy rude grasp has crush'd the fair,
See ambition's prize is there.

       Salem, June 2, 1834. I.

8.

What more delightful than to wander forth
In spring, before the sun has chas'd away
The freshness of the morn; or shook the dew
From off the tender grass? Nature seems
As young as when the morning light first broke
On Eden; as calm the river's surface;
And the birds as sweetly tuned their morning
Hymn. Beneath the shade of oak reflected
In the sleeping stream, I set me down,
And muse and gaze on the unrival'd scene.
Would that my thoughts could speak, my tongue describe
The pleasures that a scene like this affords!
No—language is too feeble to give them
Utterance. Would to him whose feelings have
Been swallowed up by love of gold; to him
Whom mad ambition drives; to him whose sense
Is clay'd by luxury's empoison'd cup,
Would that to them the happiness I feel
I could describe! 'twould strike the fetters from
The slave of gold; 'twould stop ambition's mad
Career, and dash the bowl from palsied hands
Of luxury. The birds their joy express
In notes of sweetest harmony; without
A wave the peaceful river glides along;
Words fail to give my feelings utterance.
The pleasure within my breast surpasses
Far, that which prompts the sweetest lay

Of bird; more calm my breast than the smooth stream,
With looks more joyful than the azure vault;
In silent gratitude I raise mine eyes
To heaven.

June 8, 1834

9.   I Am the Way

The way is simple for I am the light
By which thou travelest on to meet thy God.
Brighter and brighter still shall be thy sight
Till thou hast ended here the path I trod;
Before thee stretches far the thorny way,
Yet smoothed for thee by him who went before.
Go on it leads you to the perfect day
The rest I to the patriarch Abraham swore
Go on and I will guide you safely through
For I have walked with suffering feet thy path
Confide in me the Faithful and the True
And thou shalt flee the approaching day of wrath
Whose dawn e'en now the horizon's border shows
And with its kindling fires prophetic glows.

10.   The Kingdom of God Is Within You

My Kingdom is within you seek it there
Ye shall not seek in vain who work within
You shall within it find the good and fair
The living spirits freed from death and sin
Thou canst not buy with gold and silver ore
The treasures that my kingdom can afford
They are for those who love me kept in store
And they who love me keep my holy word
Repent be quick to do what first thou did
There is but one the strait and narrow way
Fear not when thou art faint and must be chid
But only bear lest thou from me should stray
For I am life and they who seek me find
The keys of heaven I hold to loose and bind.

11.   My Church

This is the rock where I my church will build
Harder than flint its sure foundations are.
Though few now pass the door it shall be filled

The gates of Hell shall not my triumph bar
Seek and thou too the door shall find
Knock and thou too shall enter in
I hold the keys and who but me can bind?
And who but me can loose the bonds of sin?
Eternal life shall those who worship here
Forevermore receive at my right hand
I call thee too my wedding day is near
Haste lest without the bridal hall you stand
And you be found not with the garment on
Which all who live with me on earth have won.

12.   The Charge

I speak in you the word that gave you birth
Fear not I call you to attend my voice
Walk humbly on thy path lies through the earth
But thou shalt in the latter day rejoice
If thou to all hast spoken ever true
What thou hast heard from me who send you forth
For every secret thing is brought to view
When I before all men proclaim your worth
Speak boldly then for 'tis not you they hear
But Him who in you speaks the living word
Nor those who kill the body need you fear
They cannot hear who have not of me heard
My sheep shall hear thee for I bid thee call
And hasten at thy summons one and all.

13.   The Sabbath

Thy rest has come thy long expected rest
The spirit sees at last her Maker God
Within His presence ever to be blest
Nor longer feel for sin His chasening rod
The Sabbath has begun its sacred hours
No more can aught of earthly passion stir
The service of thy shrine demands my powers
And earth no longer can its claim defer
Oh when shall all its service be complete
And I have done thy perfect will on earth
That Christ my name before thee may repeat
And wake me as a witness of his birth?

When shall I wake and know that day of love
That endless Sabbath kept for me above?

14.   The Invitation

There is no sound but thou dost hear my voice
And in the silence of thine heart obey
Thou shalt with me before the throne rejoice
When I have led thee in the living way
Follow my steps they lead to God and life
Where thou no more shalt fear no more shalt fall
For I will give the weary rest from strife
And they with me shall dwell who hear my call.
Come then partake the feast for you prepared
I have come down to bid you welcome there
For those who have with me the dangers shared
I will with them my Father's blessings share
Come hasten on thy Brothers wait within
Strive for in me thou shalt be free from sin.

15.   The Preacher

The world has never known me bid them hear
My word it speaks will they but hear its voice
I will uphold them banish every fear
And in my name alone fore'er rejoice
Thou has been by my Holy Spirit led
And it shall lead you still as gently on
Till thou hast on the word I give you fed
And in my name the Crown of Life have won
Come hasten on thou shalt not want for I
Will be your guide your rest and your defence
Be strong I wipe the tears from every eye
And to my Father's house will lead you hence
Put on thine armor daily fight with me
And you my glory soon in joy shall see.

16.   Hymn

Thou who keep'st us each together
Who as one in heart may meet;
We are called we know not whither;
Thou wilt guide our wandering feet.

Homes we leave, the world's warm greeting
Spoken round the household fire;
We have known in friendship meeting
All the heart can here desire.

Yet Thou givest all we borrow
From these brightened scenes around,
And Thou biddst us rise and follow
Him who hath acceptance found.

Though through thorny ways his leading,
And untried the path before;
We as children all things needing
Here a Father's love adore.

He has spoken; Him Thou hearest;
He descends from heaven to save;
Thou that on the billow fearest,
"Faith! Walk firm the rocking wave"!

"Little flock be not ye troubled,
Thine the kingdom of the son;
Though earth's weight of woe be doubled,
He the crown of Light hath won."

17.   The Still Small Voice

The Lord passed by! A mighty wind
The lofty mountains rent
The ancient trees by the strong blast
Like pliant reeds were bent.

But in the wind the Lord was not
Nor in the earthquake dire
Which shook the solid mountain's base
Nor in the flaming fire.

But after these, a still small voice
The listening prophet heard
And in his mantle wrapt his face
He knew it was the Lord.

The War is past, with earthquake shock
That shook our native land,
And quenched the fierce consuming flame
By his divine command.

And now the still small voice we hear
Unheard amidst its strife
That bids the sons of men return
Unto the paths of life.

O may we heed that still small voice
That speaketh from above!
And to its words of Peace and Love
Forever faithful prove.

18.

Thou know'st not what thy Lord will say
Thou knowst not him but He knows thee
And though from here he's far away
Can still thy every action see.

While thou wert busy here and there
So He was here and He is gone
Thou oft has time enough to spare
But He thy Lord and Master now.

Then quickly do the thing thou wouldst
And quickly say the thing thou't speak
Nor to thyself a moment trust
For he who trusts himself is weak.

19.

Sing on! how exquisitely sweet
Those notes are to the ear!
And yet thou deem'st they are not sweet
For this earth's flowers to hear.

Sing tender, sweeter then, thou bird,
Pour forth thy very soul
In tones enchanting to be heard
Let nought thy song control.

And is not this enough? Ah no!
'Tis not enough for thee
More! beautify thy warbling flow
In melting melody!

And yet again, then try it again!
And what canst thou add more?
A holier, more entrancing strain
Indeed thou try'st to pour!

Ceasing! why not that strain prolong?
Why droopest thou thy head?
Oh bird! in warbling out thy song,
Thy very spirit fled.

And thou art dying now—thy note
Has ta'en thy life away
Thy soul did on those carols float
From thee it could not stray.

Note: There is a bird of Africa of whom it is said, that
        sometimes it sings itself to death.

20.   Lines

                To the Spout near My Window

Old water spout that standeth there
So straight and motionless and slim
Thou art my minstrel and I bear
Life's burdens better for thy hymn.

For thou hast music sweet to me
As the swept harp's soft floating strain—
A soothing plaintive melody,
Waked by the showering, tinkling rain.

It mingles with night's passing dreams,
Or gently lifts sleep's heavy wing;
Nor thunder's roar, nor light'nings gleams
Forbid thee that mild song to sing.

When folded dripping clouds have long
Wearied and dimmed my upward view,
Those constant notes bid faith be strong,
And wait till opens Heaven's bright blue.

In sultry noonday's fiery glare,
That liquid voice thou'lt never try,
But waitest till the mountain air
Sweeps the cloud's unsealed fountains by.

And often, when the summer's sun
Has scorched and hardened the dry earth,
Swift tiny torrents down thee run
To tattle of the new shower's birth.

Murmur away! and from thy voice
This treasured lesson will I learn—
In the clouds' shadows to rejoice,
Since fortune's rays blast while they burn.

21.   Come Unto Me

Come all ye weary. I will give you rest
The rest for all my Fathers love prepares
Come and in me and him be wholly blest
And I will free you from the world of cares
For I am meek and lowly learn of me
And you shall find in me the promised peace
Come learn of me though blind your eyes shall see
And every joy I give shall never cease
The marriage feast is ready hasten in
For those who tarry shall their lateness mourn
Come and your robes I'll wash from every sin
And in my arms shall every son be borne
Till freed from every danger he shall be
A child of light and all my glory see.

22.   Flee to the Mountains

The morn is breaking see the rising sun
Has on your windows cast his burning light
Arise the day is with you onward run
Lest soon you wander lost in murky night
I will be with you 'tis your day of flight
Hasten the hour is near you cannot fly
Leave all for me who stops can never fight
The foe that shall assail him from on high
They come the plagues that none can flee
Behold the wrath of God is on you poured
Oh hasten find the rest He gives in me
And you shall fear no fear in me restored
They cannot pause oh hasten while you may
For soon shall close around thy little day.

23.   Blessed Are They That Mourn

Blessed are they that mourn my life is theirs
The life I led on earth they too shall lead
Its joy and sorrows and its weight of cares

Shall all be theirs for in my name they bleed
Happy their lot for so I bid them grow
And finish here the work my Father gave
And when the weary day its end shall know
They shall through me rejoice them o'er the grave
Happy their death for they shall live again
When I in triumph come to claim the few
Who in my name the cross within have worn
And by their toils have found me just and true
Happy thrice happy those who seek my face
They shall not want for they shall find my grace.

24. Faith

Hast thou but faith thou shalt the mountain bid
Remove and it shall walk nor longer stand
Thy weakness to oppose and nobly chid
Its giant heights shall not at thy command
Be strong the worldly trys thine infant might
And soon thy stature shall resist my rod
Be sober and in wisdom much delight
And thou shalt then be called a child of God
Hasten the way before thee yet extends
Far on where yet thou little dreamst to go
Be wise and seek in me who knows its ends
And you no more shall wander to and fro
But onward run till you the race have won
And from my precepts here my Father's will have done.

25. Redeeming the Time

Be up betimes there is no need of rest
Save what is given and thou wilt take no more
My love will grow and make thee wholly blest
When thou hast drank the streams that freely pour
When nought of sloth nor folly marks the way
Thy spirit daily holds for I am there
Thy path lead onward to the perfect day
Come and thou shalt with me my Kingdom share
Come for the needy cry aloud for bread
Do not withhold thy hand but inward pray
Give and for you the richest feast they'll spread
When they in me have learnt the better way
Pray always cease not prayer by day or night
Tis so thy course shines brighter and more bright.

26. Relief

Oh give me of thy waters pure and clear
For my soul pants beneath this sultry hour
There is no spring nor running river near
That can assuage the burning fever's power
Oh grant me of thy spirit now to taste
Such as it was to me when I obeyed
Then may I walk amid this scorching waste
Nor sink its waters has my thirst allayed
I rise and now can run I now can bear
The heaviest burthen thou might on me place
Oh give but of thy rich grace to share
And I no more will wet with tears my face
Nor mourn that hope hast left me but press on
Though mountains rise thy will shall still be done

27. Joy

Thou hast a moon for every cloudy night
And soon the mourner shall rejoice again
Fight well the sun shall come with cheery light
And thou no more thy tearful look retain
The spirit is now slow it comes when thou
Hast learnt by chastening of His healing love
Who bade them for a time 'neath sorrow bow
That gentle peace might visit from above
Oh give the chastener welcome he will bring
Strength and his rod shall guide thy feet aright
And though thy tears may fall they are the spring
When gushing joy shall pour thee new delight
And thou shalt bless the hand that gave the pain
For it but fell that thou might joy again.

28. The Creation

I said of old when darkness brooded long
Upon the waste of waters Be thou light
And forthwith sprang the sun rejoicing strong
To chase away the mystery of the night
Behold an earth the heavens are hung above
Ascend the sons of men ascend be free
Rise and fulfill my perfect law of love
Believe the Father speaks he calls to thee
Drop every burthen that might clog thy way

Rejoice for thou art called my race to run
The oft besetting sin cast far and pray
That you with joy may end what is begun
Rejoice and look on high for thence shall fly
He whom thou hearst to bear thee to the sky.

29.   The Snare

My kingdom is within you haste to find
Its glorious dawn bright streaming in the west
Open thine inward eye for thou art blind
Behold the morning waits go cleanse thy breast
For see its herald he who goes before
And with his warning voice prepares the way
Quick oer your hearts his cleansing water pour
And you shall see the rising of my day
Go not from place to place it comes not so
But as the lightning shineth from the east
And to the west its forked branches go
E'en so unnoticed has its light increased
Till in its circling brightness all shall stand
And none escape who slight Johns true command.

30.   The Yoke

My yoke is easy and my burthen light
For he who finds me loves and can obey
From him has fled the darkness of the night
He is prepared to cast this life away
And follow me who onward lead the few
That have prefered the life I gave to gold
They shall not want for glories ever new
Shall on their eyes with every hour unfold
See a new heaven is theirs a rising earth
That shall not from their vision disappear
There shall the meek rejoice them in their birth
The troubled be at rest, there shall no fear
Come to disturb the blessed abode I give
But all in joy and peace with me shall live.

31.   The Promise

I come the rushing wind that shook the place
Where those once sat who spake with tongues of fire
Oer thee to shed the freely given grace

And bid them speak while I thy verse inspire
The world shall hear and know that thou art sent
To preach glad tidings to the needy poor
And witness that by me the power is lent
That wakes the dead, the halt and lame can cure
Thy words shall breathe refreshment to the mind
That long has borne the heavy yoke of pain
For thou art to the will of Him who lives resigned
And from thy sorrows reap the promised gain
And gather fruits with Him who with thee sows
Nor can men steal thy goods, for none thy treasure knows.

32.   The Path of Peace

Turn ye, turn ye who tread the wandring path
That leads not to my rest thorn-sprinkled oer
Why treasure wrath against the day of wrath
And garments buy for burning kept in store
Oh come and I will comfort you indeed
With peace no earthly hand can give your soul
Come buy of me against the time of need
Drink drink the wine from out my flowing bowl
Ye shall not want, your feet shall find again
The flowery path they lost in younger days
When every hour but added to your gain
Of pleasant fields and birds inviting lays
And you were lead from hill to streamlet on
Nor knew the day was ended till twas gone.

33.   Obedience

My word will teach obedience thou wilt learn
From me the perfect path the living way
Go forward for thy service now shall earn
For them a sure a never ceasing pay
Thou hast let them out to one untrue
Who will not give thee for thy labor given
Serve me within be inwardly a Jew
And thou shalt reign with me a priest in heaven
Thy way lies onward bright and brighter still
Till thou on earth hast fought the fight for me
And done within my Father's perfect will
Then from thy bondage here I'll set you free
And you shall mourn no more no more remove
But ever in me live and in me love.

34.

Grief

I bid thee weep but mourn not at thy lot
As though no comfort flowed for those who mourn
Thou shalt not sorrow always tears are not
But that by them thou mayst from sin be torn
Thou canst not weep for when my feet have traced
On to the goal whence I first came thy God
There every tear from memory effaced
Thoult smile and own as his the chastening rod
What son is he the Father does not strive
By sorrows porch to bring to me within
The plants his hand have raised have learnd to thrive
Through much affliction borne to them within
Be wise and He will lead you by the hand
Till you through tears shall see the promised land.

35.

The Reward

To him who hath to him I love to give
And he each day shall more and more abound
He shall the hidden manna eat and live
That only is in true obedience found
Come and its stores I'll open to your sight
They lie concealed save I the treasure show
None find my gold save those restored to light
Where nought of sin the spotless soul can know
There thou shalt live and feast with me in joy
A guest mid many that have owned my name
Arise henceforth thine ever blest employ
The praises of the Lamb thy lips shall claim
No more to feed on that which is not bread
No more to mourn and perish with the dead.

36.

'Tis Finished

'Tis done the world has vanished Christ remains
The only sure the only lasting trust
Look see its smouldering fire the iron chains
Are brook that bound my spirit to the dust
A life of love henceforth my sole employ
The Father's love in him so freely shown
Come hasten on and share with me the joy
That only from the cross by blood has flown
The joy I share to all is freely given

Who live the life he led on earth before
Come and e'en here thou hast the bliss of heaven
The robe put on the wedding robe he wore
And thou shalt be accepted at his feast
Nor fail of much he loveth e'en the least.

37.   Effort

I have not loved thee much my heart is poor
And cannot give like that thou givest me
Oh would with stronger zeal it might endure
And all thy gift in all thy suffering see
Lift up the feeble hands the bending head
Come rouse press on the goal is yet before
I will with stronger feet thy pathway tread
And reach while still I may the open door
That thou hast set for me and all who fight
The war with sin thou givest them to wage
Oh help me lest upon me fall the night
And I without shall feel the tempest rage
That now is rising in the lowering east
Oh quicken thou my steps to taste thy feast.

38.   The Task

The cross is hard to bear it weighs me down
E'en to the earth where on my feet must tread
Yet I by this must gain the wished for crown
And find the spirit in the body dead
Hard is the lesson patience gives to learn
Yet when tis just sweet comfort 'twill bestow
And thou wilt cheer me for I cannot turn
But must in thee to manly stature grow
Oh lift me up with every passing hour
Some higher and still higher sight to gain
Till I am raised above temptations power
And find in thee relief from every pain
For thou wilt give to those who ask aright
To taste thy cup and portion of delight.

39.   Spring

I have not lived the flesh has hedged me in
I have not known the joy to be with thee
But I must strive to loose the bonds of sin

That press me round and be forever free
Give me the victory oer the tyrant death
Whose sceptre rests now cold upon my heart
Breathe on me and reviving at thy breath
The chill that oer me steals will quick depart
And I revive like the ice frosted flower
That winter seizes in his rude embrace
When spring with kindly sun and loving shower
Creeps on from southern climes with welcome face
And chides the spoilers of her children fair
And once again restores them to her care.

40.   The Day

Break forth in joy my soul the sea retires
Its waters cease to roll across my head
I feel within new kindling of the fires
That seemed but (now) forever lost and dead
Awake give forth thy joy with voice of song
There is no death for him who walks with God
Obey and in the land He gives live long
And none shall lay thy head beneath the sod
Awake to sin is sleep death is the night
That (steals a)round the spirit when it sins
The morning comes rise witness the delight
With which the ransomed soul the day begins
Come for this freedom waits thy spirit too
Oh see she brings all (that) we lost to view.

41.   The Strong Man

There is no night I cannot sleep again
For I have learned of patience to obey
And light and darkness cannot now retain
The Spirit that has made the life of Christ its day
There is no slumbering when he reigns within
Each hand puts forth each foot its vigor shows
Life rules and motion is in every limb
Thou sawst me dead now all within me grows
And strengthens with each pulse all things are small
I can do all things in the spirit strong
I will not boast in vain see see them fall
The iron ramparts that withstood so long
Increase my strength oh Thou who gave me life
That I in Thee may still renew the strife.

42.   The Warrior

Where are ye, ye who mocked my arm of late
I triumph now your hour of mirth is past
Bow down I come in strength of Christ elate
Boast not; I breathe; ye fall before the blast.
Ye hills retire; open thou raging sea
My steps are onward now; ye cannot stay
The God of battles—lo He fights for me
Submit before His feet prepare the way
Ye iron breasted armies too I scorn
Away how feeble is the spear or sword
I am of Him who gives the quicking spirit born
And mild forever wield the conquering word
Its power shall beat in atoms mountains high
And through the parting sea shall lead me dry.

43.   The Shelter

There is no joy like that in finding Thee
Thou art my shelter from each storm that blows
He walks abroad his way is safe and free
Who loves and in new commandment goes
For him there waits not who can do him harm
He knows no fear he sees no covert foe
He carries with him that which rage can charm
And bid the kindled fire of hate burn low
Love turns aside the malar pointed dart
The icy hand it warms and then restores
Who feels and knows not of its gentle art
That cures each wound that saddened grief deplores
Come and its healing touch shall give thee sight
And borrow from it joy to lend its light.

44.   The Harvest

The plant it springs it rears its drooping head
Strengthened with every shower that falls from heaven
See quickly at their touch its branches spread
And soon twill bless with flowers look they are given
The promised blessing cannot be delayed
But fast will follow every good intent
Tis not in vain thy mourning spirit prayed
Behold the rich reward in answer sent
Peace from the Father joy a full increase

For all thou sowed in sorrow in the earth
Thy joy shall bud and bloom thy new found peace
Grow with each day. Thine is the promised birth
Of all that dies it shall be raised again
See that thou sowest thick the springing grain.

45.

The Husbandman

I waited long but now my joy is great
For that which once I sowed begins to appear
Though slow yet sure my harvest tis not late
For Him who guides the oft revolving year
I watch not for the crops that dying earth
Yields from her bosom to the tribes of men
I watch for those who come of heavenly birth
A Father's care a Father's love have been
But lightly spent do they repay the toil
My hand upon my vineyard oft bestows
Come learn to reap for me the wine and oil
From every field in plenty overflows
I bid thee enter as a laborer now
Go forth and thou shalt pluck from every bough.

46.

The Last

Why hast thou tarried till the eleventh hour
Yet enter in thou shalt not want for hire
I will repay thou knowest I have power
To give thee all thy spirit can desire
Go in who reap for Me shall find their gain
In ever new and ever fresh employ
Thou reapest let no hour thy hand restrain
Be strong fill up the measure of thy joy
It shall overflow for He who gives the meat
Has stores no time nor hunger can exhaust
He shall provide thee hasten gain thy seat
At his son's board lest thou from him be lost
And reap not of the full reward he gives
For he that sups with him he ever lives.

47.

The Call

Come thou and labor with me I will give
To (him) who works abundant work to do
Arise gird on thine armor tis to live

That thou must struggle now and strongly too
There is no pause the conflicts soon begin
Arm thee with all thy patience all thy zeal
The gates of vice are open enter in
Nor fear thy foe though armed in thriple steel
I charge thee welcome none who bear the sword
Be true spare not though thou must slay thy nearest friends
Remember Him who arms thee with his word
And forth in his own name his servant sends
Be true for He thy crown can take away
And He thy spirit by his word can slay.

48.   The Promise

The words I give thee they are not thine own
Give them as freely as to thee they're given
And thou shalt reap the grain thy hands have sown
When thou hast reached in peace the opening heaven
Come I will give thee kindred friends and wife
Such as no earthly lot can have in store
Thou shalt receive them for eternal life
And earth shall yield her many myriads more
My mansion is prepared come enter in
Put on the wedding dress and you shall be
A welcome tenant freed from every sin
Henceforth to walk from bondage ever free
In the last day I come it cometh soon
Be wise thy morning hour shall reach its noon.

49.   Joy

The joy thou giv'st no man can take away
For it is born of him who lives within
He comes the power of death o'er all to slay
And cleanse the heart of every secret sin
Thou shalt not see his face and mourn again
Save that thy mourning works thee double joy
For he can rich reward thy slightest pain
And give thee hope when sorrows here annoy
Come know with me the riches of his grace
Freely he offers them to all beside
And he will show us soon his Father's face
And bid the stream of grief, however wide
Its waters here may roll, be dry and we
No more within its waves tossed to and fro shall be.

50.
The Good

The useful and the sweet the fair and true
Do grow together the same plant always
From the deep truth the flower comes forth to view
With scent and beauty the design to praise.

And good the earth or wave that deep or thin
Gives all to all yet nothing takes away
Itself itself forever holds within
The unfolded whole of all that can decay.

For Truth and Beauty are but tree or plant
And that we eat but fruit and smell but flowers
The spirit cannot things of earth of long want
It dwells not in Time's autumn fading bowers.

But there where all in all the hand, the face
And breath like fragrance mingling with the air
Reveals a form that Perfect Love will trace
The Holy One within the House of Prayer.

51.
Endicott

Amidst a band of worthies bold and true
The noble Endecott was in the van
The gallant leader of the suffering few,
Who gloried in the name of Puritan.
Austere and strict was he, yet kind and pure,
Above the common level he had risen;
And, taught by Persecution to endure,
His hopes, like theirs, were fixed on God and heaven.
His wife and children with him, too, embark,
His firm attachment to the cause to prove;
What precious freight was trusted to that ark!
Of Faith and Hope, of Purity and Love;
When were such treasures on the ocean cast
The sport of the wild waves, and stormy blast?

52.

Here let the Church her holy mission prove
Of Truth and Liberty, of Love and Joy,
The image of that heavenly House above
Which naught again shall threaten or destroy
Within her walls wide as the social state
Through countless years may all the people throng

With joyful hearts and countenances sedate
To bow in worship and to join in song.
No more without her fold may Childhood stray
To wander in the desert parched and wild
Forgetful of the strait and narrow way
By Pleasure's voice from virtue's path beguiled
But happy in her sacred courts remain
Its heart still young its robe without a stain.

53.   So Is Every One Who Is Born of the Spirit

It bloweth where it listeth hark the sound
Ye know not whence it comes nor where it goes
Its fruit shall in your borders to be found
Yet know ye not the stalk from which it grows
Go learn whence comes these words of heavenly truth
Cleanse ye the fountain whence their murmurs flow
And you though old shall still renew your youth
And of the life the Spirit leads shall know
Go count the steps that measure out the path
That leads through John for he must come before
Then shall you flee the approaching day of wrath
And enter safely through the accepted door
For I am sure who promise seek my rest
The star the east beheld shines sinking in the west.

54.   The Seed

Wouldst thou behold my features cleanse thy heart
Wash out the stains thy will impresses there
And as the clay-stamped images depart
Thou shalt behold my face how wondrous fair
How changed from that thine outward eye must see
It wears no form its searching glance can know
From flesh and blood it now has wrought it free
And in the Spirit learns from Christ to grow
That which thou sowest is not that which springs
From the dead grain thou givest to the earth
Each moments toil an added luster brings
To deck the spirit when it springs to birth
From out the seed in Christ that long has lain
Buried beneath the snowy-crusted plain.

55.   The Apostle

I am the First and Last declare my Word
For I have sent thee an apostle forth
Thou hast from Me the Living gospel heard
Thou shalt proclaim its truth from south to north
The farthest west the early east shall hear
My name that by the earth shall hallowed be
And they shall bow before my shrine in fear
And own my truth and it shall make them free
And thou if thou shalt keep my holy name
A priest shall be before the living God
And through the world the Father's truth proclaim
Ruling the nations with his chastening rod
And walk from glory on to glory still
Till thou in me has done his perfect will.

56.   The Message

There is no voice but it is born of Me
I Am there is no other God beside
Before Me all that live shall bow the knee
And be as in a fiery furnace tried
Warn them for I have told thee of my love
Bid them prepare my supper to attend
Thou has heard him who cometh from above
Let them receive thee for I am your friend
Though they have scorned the servants that I sent
Year after year within each stubborn breast
Let them give back the vineyard I have lent
Them yet another year to find my rest
And sent my son let them thy word receive
And in the Christ that in thee speaks believe.

57.   I Am the Bread of Life

I am thy life thou shalt upon me feed
And daily eat my flesh and drink my blood
For nothing else than me canst thou have need
Thou art a spirit I the spirits food
Come eat and thou shalt ask for bread no more
Come drink and thou shalt never thirsting cry again
I shall live in thee an increasing store
A spring forever swollen by the rain
Drink freely thou hast found the stream of life

In deeps where few have sought its healing wave
Thou hast fought well with sin the mortal strife
And hath found him who hath the power to save
Abide in me and I will lead you on
Till you the Father's home in me have won.

58.   To Charles W. Fell, Esq.

On His New Type Setting Machine

While men in war's dread service tax their powers
New weapons to invent to harm and slay;
A new invention, Charles, thou hast made ours,
And one prophetic of a brighter day;
When man with man no longer shall contend,
Save with the nobler weapons of the mind;
When War on earth forevermore shall end
And Peace all nations shall forever bind;
The Press with mightier powers the truth diffuse
And like the sun each darkened land illume;
And none the light of knowledge shall refuse
To those who sit in ignorance and gloom;
But all shall Liberty and Knowledge share,
Who see the sun, or breathe the vital air!

Salem, December 12th, 1864.

59.   The Barque Aurelia of Boston

The old Barque's picture we took from the wall,
In which I sailed over the sea;
Which our sailor-boy days did so brightly recall
To my boyhood's* companion, and me.

With our fathers once more we sailed over the main,
From country to country to roam;
New knowledge of earth, and its nations to gain,
Yet never forgetful of home.

The ocean so lonely, so vast, and so grand,
Seemed again on our vision to rise;
By night and by day, in calm and in storm,
As its wonders first greeted our eyes.

The sailors' quaint speech, and their strange dress and ways,
Again to my fancy appeared;
Yet their honest, kind hearts I remember to praise,
For to them was the ship's boy endeared.

And the* port where we lay, and the winter time spent
Where first our acquaintance began;
What pleasure has time to those early days lent
Since each has become a grown man!

The river, the shipping, the flat boats we view,
Slaves, and Indians we ne'er saw before;
At every turn we see something new,
As the city again we explore.

And with us was one, whom our hearts loved so well,
Long since from the earth passed away;
How oft of his looks does memory tell
Board the barque, or at school, or at play!

With him, too, have gone, to the fair world above,
Our fathers, the seamen we knew;
Where cherished for aye are friendships and love
Which on earth have proved faithful and true.

> Capt. Samuel Cook,
> With the respects of
> Jones Very.

* Rev. William Hooper
* New Orleans.
1871

60.   Original Hymn

                     By Rev. Jones Very

We welcome, with the opening year,
Our Pastor, to this ancient fold;
With words of love, and hope to cheer,
The gracious Gospel, never old.

In cultured ground the seed is sown,
As in a good and fruitful soil;
Long has this field the blessing known
Of faithful laborers' care and toil.

As come the swift returning years,
May nobler aims our spirits raise;
Faith triumph over doubts and fears,
More grateful hearts, inspire our praise.

Our Father, may thy gracious word
Quicken in all the life divine;
Till we from error, sin, restored,
Through Christ, thy Son, are wholly thine.

EPILOGUE

Frances and Lydia Very, having inherited both their mother's[1] and their brother Jones's[2] estates, continued to reside in their old home at 154 Federal Street until their deaths. Frances died on November 9, 1895, having been stricken in front of her home while talking to a friend. Her estate was willed to her sister. Lydia lived alone for several months; but at length, because of her enfeebled condition, she took into her home as companions and protectors Mr. and Mrs. Charles A. Cooper. They were kind but illiterate folk, who had no sense of appreciation for the letters and other manuscript material stored in the Very home; and when Lydia Very died on September 10, 1901, they proceeded to burn all such. Little was saved from the flames, and students interested in Jones Very have thus suffered an irreparable loss. Miss Harriet I. Wilkins discovered and saved for the Essex Institute the letter from Emerson previously quoted, but other messages from Emerson, Howells, Lowell, Whittier, Thoreau, Elizabeth Peabody, Hawthorne, and Celia Thaxter were destroyed.

Lydia Very willed the homestead and two thousand dollars to the Essex Institute, on provision that the Very burial plot be cared for and that the home be known as a memorial to her brothers Washington and Jones.[3] Today, it stands as a neat reminder of the simplicity and saintliness of an American mystic. On the right front of the structure is a bronze tablet, bearing the names of the Very brothers, the dates of their births and deaths, and—as an

[1] See, in the Essex County Court Records, *Probate Book* 425 (Wills), p. 31, the will of Mrs. Lydia Very. After providing that debts be paid, the will reads, in part: "The residue of my real and personal estate, I give and devise to my children, Jones Very, Frances E. Very, and Lydia L. A. Very, to share and share alike. I make no provision for the children of my deceased son." The will is dated June 24, 1853.

[2] See, as in n. 1 above, *Book* 409, p. 201.

[3] See, as in n. 1 above, *Book* 516, pp. 72-74. The furnishings in the home were left to Mrs. Cooper; the rest of the personal estate—about $20,000—was willed to friends long since dead. Nothing was left to her nephew, Frank Washington Very. The Essex Institute also acquired portraits, sketches, and other items of interest.

especial tribute to Jones—Hawthorne's statement from "A Virtuoso's Collection":

A Poet Whose Voice is Scarcely Heard Among Us
By Reason of its Depth

The only living relatives of Jones Very are the children of his
nephew, Frank Washington Very,[4] no one of whom ever saw or
corresponded with his father's immediate kin. The nearest approach made to a meeting with Frances and Lydia—those eccentric,
strong-willed nature-lovers—was during the celebration of Salem's
three-hundredth anniversary, when two residents of the city im-
personated Frances and Lydia Very as a part of Salem's tribute to
the memory of its former prominent citizens.

[4] See list under n. 50 of Chapter VI, p. 120.

APPENDICES

I

THE TRIAL OF LYDIA VERY*

1826 July 11 To the hon. Daniel A. White, judge of probate of the county of Essex.

The complaint of John Pickering of Salem, in the county of Essex, esquire, as he is administrator with the will annexed, of the goods and estate of Jones Very, late of Salem, aforesaid, mariner, deceased, humbly shews: That the said J. V. died possessed of certain personal estate consisting (among other things) of a sum of money on hand amounting to $1250, as appears by a certain memorandum in the hand writing of the said deceased, annexed to his last will and testament. That the said sum of money as your complainant is informed and does verily believe, was deposited in the dwelling house occupied by the said testator and there remained at the time of his decease in the hands and custody of Lydia Very his widow, who has rendered no account thereof, and your complainant has probable cause to suspect and does suspect that the said Lydia Very has concealed, embesseled or conveyed away the said sum of money. Wherefore, your complainant prays that the said Lydia Very may be called before your honor and examined upon oath in the premises according to the form of the statute in such case made and provided; and as in duty bound will ever pray.

Jno. Pickering, adm.

Essex Co. Probate Court, July term A.D. 1826. John Pickering, adm. of Jones Very, petitioner & c. v. Lydia Very.

Examination of said Lydia Very, on oath, under the petition of said administrator, viz.

Interrogatory 1. At the time of the decease of the above named Jones V. your husband, or about that time, had he any money?

Answer. I do not know what amount.

Int. 2. In what part of the house, or in what place did he use to keep his money?

Ans. If he had any, he used to put it in his writing desk.

* Essex County *Probate Book* 405, pp. 482-485. Spelling, punctuation, grammar, etc. are reproduced here as they are found in the source.

Int. 3. How short a time, previous to his death, had he any money on hand, and of what kind was it? and where was it?

Ans. The day before he died, I saw the gold, but don't know the amount,—that was in the writing desk.

Int. 4. What was done with the writing desk or where is it?

Ans. It stood at the side of his bed, under a table, it is in the house now.

Int. 5. Was there any silver money or bank bills in the desk?

Ans. Not to my knowledge.

Int. 6. What was your occasion of taking notice of the gold?

Ans. I went to the desk to look for the paper that he had written about one o'clock the day before he died, which was afterwards proved to be his will.

Int. 7. At what time did you go to look for that paper?

Ans. The next morning after his death.

Int. 8. Was the gold you mention lying alone in the desk or in a bag, and when did you last see it?

Ans. It was in a bag. I saw it last at one o'clock the day before he died.

Int. 9. What became of it then, and where is it now?

Ans. I do not know.

Int. 10. Did you take it up or take hold of it at that time?

Ans. No.

Int. 11. Who was in the room with you when you saw it as last mentioned?

Ans. My sister (Frances Very) and my son, a boy about 12 years old.

Int. 12. Did you occupy the house after his decease, and do you now occupy it?

Ans. Yes.

Int. 13. Have you seen any of the money since your husband's decease, if yea, how much?

Ans. None of it, I mean the gold and silver above mentioned.

Int. 14. Do you know of any of it having been laid out since for the use of the family or for any other purposes?

Ans. No.

Int. 15. Have you ever mentioned to anybody that there was gold or other money left on hand by your husband, and have you mentioned how much there was?

Ans. I do not recollect; I have not mentioned how much there was.

Int. 16. Have you not mentioned to Mr. Benj. Cheever that there was money on hand, and did you not tell him what had been done with it, or what would be done with it?

Ans. No.

Int. 17. Have you not had any conver'n with Mr. Cheever about it? if yea, state what you told him?

Ans.   The morning after my husband died, Mr. Cheever came in. I mentioned that there was a $20 bill in his pocketbook; I told him my family was necessitated for wearing apparel and asked him if it was proper for me to get it; he told me it was and took the money and charged it for me; I bought hats and other things for my boys that they stood in need of, to wear to their father's funeral; this is all the conversation I ever had with Mr. Ch'r about money.

Int. 18. Have you not had conversations with any other person or persons about the money left by your husband?

Ans.   Not to my knowledge except about the gold only.

Int. 19. Have you not spoken of the gold or any other money to Mrs. Sarah Farrell?

Ans.   No; she called at the home one day and asked how I did, and then went out; I have not seen her since.

Int. 20. Did you not speak of the money to Mr. Isaac Very, your husband's father; if yea, what did you state to him?

Ans.   He told me that on the paper he had there was $1250 mentioned, and he wished me to bring it forward, the day after my husband was buried; and he spoke of a quadrant and sextant and spy glass that belonged to my husband; I told him I was his wife and these were his children, and I thought we had the best right to them; he told me there was no proof that I was his wife; I told him I had a certificate up chamber that had been there twelve years, he said I need not trouble myself to go for it, as I should not find it there, and I did not find it to my sorrow; he told me again to bring forward the money to put at interest; I told him I did not know anything about the money only the gold; and about that I told him that I expected his wife had got it; that was all I ever told him about the money; as to the quadrant, sextant, and spy glass, Mr. Foster, my attorney, advised me not to give them up until they were appraised.

Int. 21. Was there a watch belonging to the estate; if yea, what is become of it?

Ans.   It was lying upon the bed in the room, and I asked the gentleman to appraise it: they looked around and went out of the room, but they did not appraise that, nor a number of small things that were there.

Int. 22. What other things were there which you understood not to be appraised?

Ans.   There were some old chairs and other things which the appraisers abserved were not worth taking notice of, as some articles of crockery, not worth, perhaps, more than a few shillings.

Int. 23.   What kind of bag was the gold in? and have you seen the bag since either with anything in it or empty?

Ans.   It was a canvas bag; I have not seen it since.

Int. 24.   Do you know in whose hands the bag was after you saw it, or in whose presence it has been at any time since?

Ans.   No.

Int. 25.   How did you know what was in the bag when you saw it in the desk?

Ans.   Because it lay open; that is, not tied, as it lay.

Int. 26.   Did you send to Capt. I. Very at the time of your husband's death, and make any enquiries of him respecting any paper?

Ans.   I asked his daughter to ask her father about the paper that my husband had made the day before at one o'clock; she told me afterward that her father had got it; and that it had been given to him by his wife, to whom my husband had given it. I did not say to Capt. Very that I had any paper corresponding to one that he had, containing an account of my husband's property.

Int. 27.   Did you not tell Mr. Cheever that there was a sum of money, about $250, which you were willing to pay over or to give up belonging to the estate?

Ans.   I never did.

Int. 28.   Did you not mention anything about the money to Mrs. Clough or Mrs. Lydia Very at any time?

Ans.   I never did, nor anything about the estate. In respect to the 6th. int'g, I wish to be understood that the "occasion" there mentioned, was when I noticed that the gold was missing, and not when I saw it in the desk; the last time I saw the gold was the day before he died at one o'clock.

Lydia Very

II

POEMS PUBLISHED IN THE SALEM *Observer* BUT NOT INCLUDED IN ANY EDITION OF JONES VERY'S WORKS*

1.   [August 10, 1833]

  The earth is parched with heat, flowers droop and die,
  The clouds of dust fly whirling through the sky;

* Spelling, punctuation, grammar, etc., are reproduced here as they are found in the source. The publication date of each poem is enclosed in square brackets.

The cattle lowing seek the friendly shade,
By lofty rock or some dark forest made.
The traveller spent with toil, by heat oppressed,
Near some tall oak, exhausted, sinks to rest;
And dreams of home, of all his soul holds dear,
Dreams not, alas! of fatal danger near.
Dark low'ring clouds o'er heaven's bright azure run,
A bloody redness vails the scorching sun.
The river's surface, late so green and bright,
Holds back its waves, dark as the shades of night.
Hushed is the wind, nor e'en a zephyr blows,
All nature sunk in deep profound repose.
The farmer leaves his fields, with terror flies,
And often turning views the angry skies.
See now the waves rise higher than before,
In wild commotion lash the sounding shore.
See through the air the leaves and stubble borne,
The slender tree from the thick grove uptorn.
Hark through the leaves, with peal and awful sound,
Rolls the deep thunder startling all around.
The lofty hill ee'n from the centre shakes,
The bravest heart o'ercome with terror quakes;
See on the ground, by that resistless stroke,
The wretched traveller, the blasted oak,
In equal lot, by equal force o'erthrown:
He sunk in death, he uttered not a groan;
He saw no flash, he heard no awful peal,
From life to death insensibly to steal
Him God decreed; why then aught men to mourn,
From earthly joyes to heavenly he was borne.
The thunder ceased, the gloomy clouds had fled,
Wide o'er the earth, refreshing zephyrs shed
The sweet perfume of many a laughing flower,
Or sighed with soothing notes through many a silver bower.

2.   Lines   [August 24, 1833]

Written on Reading Stuart's Account of
the Treatment of Slaves in Charleston

Oh slavery! thou bane of human kind;
Thou tyrant o'er the body and the mind;
To all that's just, to all that's right a foe,
Thou fill'st the world with misery and woe.
Ah! many a wretch by thee is caused to mourn;

From friend, from relative, from country torn,
From all the joys that e'er his soul held dear,
Beneath thy cruel scourge is doomed to fear.
By curst desire of gain, by thirst for gold,
The unhappy victim of thy crime is sold.
Is sold! to whom? would I could bide the shame!
To man; O traffic base, disgraceful to the name;
To man, with reason and with freedom blest,
O'er all creation placed the first, and best;
Alas! how fallen from that station be,
Who, blest with reason, proud in being free,
Can from his proper sphere a being draw,
Deprive of rights, of liberty, and law;
Deprive, (What's far more cruel than the rest,)
Of all the gifts with which himself is blest.
Would that my lips the tale could never tell,
The tale of horror, known, alas! too well.
Would that the world had never seen the day,
When man his fellow man should thus betray,
Would rather every ship that sailed the main,
For such base traffic, such degrading gain,
Had sunk with all beneath the raging sea,
Where they from slavery ever would be free:
Free from a tyrant's power, who often rends
Parent from children, friend from dearest friend;
Free from a life of wretchedness and woe,
Free from all toil and suffering here below.
Ah! who could read the story of that woe?
And who if reading half their sorrow know?
Would that by me their wrongs could half be told,
Would that their sufferings I could half unfold.
Before our God and their's those sufferings rise,
He sees their wrongs, he hears their helpless cries:
Soon may those wrongs and sufferings have an end,
Man be not foe to man, but friend.

August 13, 1833   I.

[April 26, 1834]

3.

Hast thou ever heard the voice of nature,
In the whirlwind's roar, the zephyr's gentle
Breath, in the fierce eagle's cry, when darting
Forth he seeks the spoiler of his nest,
In the soft whispering voice of love with

Which the dove salutes his mate? or hast thou
Seen nature put forth her force in various
Forms, the lightning rend the solid oak,
The lofty cedars bend like reeds before
The blast, the madden'd ocean lash the shore
With foam, or hast thou seen the rising sun,
When first he looks forth on a summer's day,
Or, when his beams fall fiercer down, the cattle
Seek the cool refreshing shade, slaking their
Thirst in some hoarse-murmuring brook?
Hast thou ever seen such sights or heard such sounds,
And never thought of Him, who rides upon
The whirlwind, who in the gentle zephyr breathes,
Who to the dove, the eagle gave their notes
Of rage or love, who from his awful hand
The lightning hurls, the lofty cedars bend,
And with his nostrils heapeth up the waves,
Who made the brook to run to quench the thirst
The cattle feel in summer's sultry reign?
If on thine ear or sight all these have fell
Unheeded, and thou hast lived unmindful
Of a God, who gave thee sight to see and
Ear to hear, and for these thy senses formed,
Harmonious sounds, and ever varying
Beauties; learn oft as upon thy sight or
Ear they fall to think of him who made them.

April 7, 1834.   I.

4.   Death of Lafayette   [June 28, 1834]

He is gone, loaded with years and honors!
He who before the rich rewards of Kings
Preferred to succor the distressed, and raise
His arm in freedom's holy cause, is gone!
Mourn France a son, who shed around thy name
A never fading splendor! He caus'd no
Widow's tears to flow, he caus'd no orphans
"To demand their sire with tears of artless
Innocence." Heaven hasten'd not to snatch from
Our admiring gaze; but granted riches
And honors, length of days to show,—that e'en
Upon earth, virtue is oft rewarded.
Columbia's daughters weep! But for him

Your children, now perhaps in bondage,
Might cause to curse the day that gave them birth.
And yet her sons lament! lament for him,
Who in his youthful days your fathers arm
Upheld, revived their drooping hopes, and gave
Them vigor to resist their haughty foe.
Ye mountains veil your heads in clouds and mourn
For him, who around your summits cast glory
More bright than noon-day sun! Ye waving pines
Sigh louder in the blast; for he, who gave
You liberty's fair soil, is now no more.
And thou, O boundless ocean, mourn! for ne'er
Again thy waves shall bear to freedom's coast,
One more worthy of thy lamentation.
Fairer, Lafayette, than summer's day thy
Latter years, and thou on whom a nation's
Blessings fell, shall now receive a nation's tears.

Salem, June 21, 1834

5.   Old Age   [July 5, 1834]

Say not, that in old age
No joys, no pleasures dwell;
That it is but a page,
Which only sorrows tell.

Say not, in age we find
Nought but a wintry shore;
Round which the northern wind,
And raging ocean roar.

Say not, that like the tree
Search'd by the light'ning's wing;
That thus old age will be,
A sear'd and barren thing.

Say not, 'tis like the sun
Sinking in western skies
When storm-clouds have begun
To shut him from our eyes.

O no, 'tis like the shore
Beneath Italian skies;
T'wards which with moon-lit oar
The joyful boatman plies.

O no, 'tis like the tree
When golden autumn's near;
But with maturity,
It hails its latest year.

It sinks, as sinks the sun
From our admiring eyes;
Whose daily course is run,
Fair as we saw him rise.

Salem, June 30.   I.

6.   Lines   [July 12, 1834]

Suggested by Seeing a Butterfly Sculptured upon a Tomb

Fit emblem of th'immortal soul! though thou
Art soaring high, thou didst inhabit once
A dark and loathsome mansion. Such is man,
Like to the worm, which once thou wast, he creeps
Encumber'd now by earthly bonds, which check
His eager flight, and to a narrower
Sphere confine his untried powers; lest perhaps
The soul ascending premature might fall
Supported by too feeble wing. Attend
O man! and learn thy destiny, which hand
Divine has traced on natures works. Seasons
In their ceaseless round proclaim it; darkness
And light, and ocean's ebb and flow in turn
Succeeding; sun and moon oft veil'd in dim
Eclipse; calm succeeding tempest; nature
Through all her works proclaims it, from the orbs,
That wheel their courses through the void immense,
To insect fluttering in the summer's breeze,
All, all proclaim the destiny of man.
Learn then O man! from such unnumber'd signs,
Where lies thy happiness, whence thy being
Sprang and whither tends: if with an upward
Hight thou hop'st to soar, when from this earthly
Coil thou'st freed; plume thy wings while here below;
Cast off what then may clog thy flight, and bear
Thee down. Passions fierce attack, attack most
Direful; lust, poisoning the relish
Of the soul for all that's pure; indolence,
With slow yet ceaseless course eating its way,
Like rust, into the mind, and deadening all

Its energies: these and thousand nameless foes,
That strive to fix thy thoughts on things below
Thy noble destiny, repel; then, like
The Phoenix, thou shalt rise triumphant from
Thine ashes and, on untiring pinions,
Heaven-ward borne shalt seek thy resting place.

Salem, July 6th.   I.

7.   Kind Words   [July 19, 1834]

Turn not from him, who asks of thee
    A portion of thy store;
Though thou canst give no charity,
    Thou canst do what is more.

The balm of comfort thou canst pour
    Into his grieving mind.
Who oft is turn'd from wealth's proud door
    With many a word unkind.

Does any from the false world find,
    Nought but reproach and scorn;
Does any, stung by words unkind,
    Wish that he ne'er was born;

Do thou raise up his drooping heart;
    Restore his wounded mind;
Though nought of wealth thou canst impart,
    Yet still thou canst be kind.

Thy kindness, like the summer's shower,
    Shall cheer him on his way
Through the false, hollow world; its power
    Shall reach his latest day:

It stays not here, but, as the rain,
    Which ocean's bosom drinks,
Drawn by the sun ascends again,
    To heaven from which it sinks;

So, drawn by thee, thy words shall wing
    Backward their course to thee;
And, in thy breast, shall prove a spring
    Of pure felicity.

Salem, July 16, 1834.   I.

8.   Pleasure   [August 2, 1834]

Goddess of pleasure, where thy golden car?
Rides it on zephyrs through the unclouded sky?
Or mov'st thou with silken soils and silver
Oars down the smooth river, sported around
By daughters of the sea, fann'd by the wings
Of smiling lovers; or on its shady bank
Do'st thou repose, lull'd by distant music
Stealing soft o'er its calm bosom? or sit'st
Thou in more cool retreat, some grotto dark
Of living marble hewn by natures hand,
Catching the sound of nightly water-fall
Borne on the wind? Though 'neath unclouded skies
The votaries seek thee, where the zephyrs sport
Around, and scatter odors from their wings;
And though down the stream of life, with silken
Soils wafted by prosperous winds, they glide;
Thee seeking in ever-varied worldly
Joys; and though from busy scenes of life
Retir'd, some on the shady bank have woo'd thee;
Or in grottos dark recess; deluded.
How oft hast thou, like the false flickering
Light, which leads the weary trav'ller astray,
Danc'd round them in thy golden car, &, when
They sought to enter, fled their eager grasp.
Ask him, who, lead astray o'er treach'rous bogs.
Is wand'ring; ask of him where shines the light,
Which that he follows seems:—"At home," he says.
There, pleasure, rest thy golden car. The mind
Is its own home. In fair and stormy sky
Alike thou dwell'st, thy back alike is steer'd
Down the calm stream, and through the raging sea.
It is the mind, communing with itself,
That cast a sunshine on the paths of life;
That midst adversity's dark hour can see
Above a clear unclouded sky; that rides
As undisturb'd upon the troubl'd waves
Of active life, as in the calm heaven
Of retirement who seeks thee not within
In vain he wooes thee on the skady bank;
In vain he courts thee in the grotto's dark
Recess. Though burst his stores with India's rich
Produce, yet still he will be poor; nations

May bow beneath his sway, yet weaker he
Shall be than those who call him master. Let
His table groan, and let his cup o'erflow;
If he neglects the banquet of the mind.
Drinks not from out that inward fount, which he
Who drinks of never thirsts, still he shall live
In want, in want shall die.

Salem, July 22, 1834.   I.

9.   Sleigh Ride   [January 10, 1835]

Hurra, hurra, away they go
Far over the hills and fields of snow;
Away they go with mirth and glee,
Like the prison'd bird that's just let free.

Away, away, away they fly
Swiftly beneath the bright spangled sky;
The mirthful laugh chimes in full well
With the merry jingle of many a bell.

And many an eye is laughing there,
That would with those isles of light compare;
That glance from under the brow of night,
And kindle the heart with soft delight.

And there full many a cheek now glows,
That rivals the hues of the fairest rose;
Which spring in its warmest vale could show,
But these are blushing on hills of snow.

Oh! say not that winter is mirthless, then,
Though the snow lays deep on mountain & glen;
Yet with laughing eyes and hearts of glee
Away we'll fly like a bird let free.

January 5th.   I.

10.   The Ice Ship*   [April 16, 1836]

In 1775 Capt. Warrens, the master of a Greenland whale
ship, fell in with an English ship surrounded with icebergs.
The last page of her log-book ran thus: Nov. 14, 1762. We
have now been imprisoned in the ice seventeen days. The fire
went out yesterday, and our master has been trying ever since

* The title of the manuscript in the Andover Theological Seminary reads "The
Frozen Ship."

to kindle it; but without success. His wife died this morning.
There is no relief. Capt. Warrens learned on his return to
England, that the ship had been missing thirteen years.

Why rings not back the welcome shout
From yonder ice-bound ship?
Why floats not her glad standard out,
With bright'ning sunbeams lit?

Why hear we not the hum of life,
Amid that silent throng;
The laugh, the joke, with joyance rife,
The merry seaman's song.

Ah, mailed in ice their bodies stand!
Each fixed and glaring eye
Seems gazing on the wondering band,
That now are gathering nigh.

Each icy hand still grasps the rope,
It held when life was there;
When round their hearts yet lingered hope,
And wrestled with despair.

Speak, ye cold lips! say what ye lock
Within that marble breast;
Though deep *our* souls the tale should shock,
It cannot break *your* rest.

Say! what sharp pangs your bosom rent,
When the low, flickering fire,
Its last warm rays of life had lent;
And left you vain desire.

Where were your thoughts, when round your frame
Claspt the cold, icy night;
Gathered they round the hearth's warm flame,
Lighting fond faces bright?

When to your last loud cries of woe,
No human accents spoke;
And, roaring deep, the waves below
In fetters o'er you broke;

Did you unraise the trembling prayer
To Him, who rules the sea;
And triumph o'er your soul's despair
And mortal agony?

Ye answer not: no voice can wake
That tale within your breast;
Nor human thoughts of suffering break
Your calm eternal rest.

Beyond this chaning, troubled sphere,
Your spirit rests above;
Where neither death, nor mortal fear,
Again its peace can move.

II.   Washington   [August 20, 1836]

The Father of his country stood
And saw awake the glittering plain;
As morn on mountain height and wood
Returned to look again.

As in his boyhood's earliest hour,
In nature's forest home untrod,
The noblest form of human power
Kneels childlike to his God.

His sword, that through the battle cloud
Flashed terror on his country's foe,
Its lightening hides beneath the shroud
Of verdure waving low.

He, who amid the battle's shock
Spoke calmness to the struggling brave,
And stood like sea-encompassed rock
Unshaken by its wave;

Trusts not the warrior's proudest boasts—
The thunders of the tented field;—
He kneels before the God of hosts,
Of all that live the shield.

From hence was kindled in thy breast
That holiest flame of liberty;
That made thy country's cause the blest,
And gave her sons like thee.

From hence it caught the sacred flame,
That lit with hope her deepest night;
And blazes still around thy name,
A halo of undying light!

I.

12.   The Autumn Leaf   [October 1, 1836]

Thou fair yet lifeless leaf! on whom decay
Seems beautiful, red glowing as thou hangest
Beneath the earliest touch of autumn's hand;
I pluck thee fluttering from thy parent vine,
Before the rude wind tears thee from its fond
Embrace to toss thy form in idle play,
Shrivelled and brown upon the winter air:
For thou art as a tablet to the thoughts
That now are gushing fresh, as if my soul
Had drunk a new life amid these lofty shades,
And felt its being moved by sympathy
With unseen power.
Brief monitor of frail humanity!
Why has decay, that steals from off the cheek
The bloom of health, traces the aged brow
With lines of care, dimming the burning eye,
And snatching from the form its lofty grace,
Why has it wrought on thee so fair a change?
And why in tints of beauty robed thy form
Brighter than decked before thy vernal prime?
Heaven's teaching[s] are not lost on humble hearts.
Though written on the leaves, and strown upon
The faithless winds, still will its messages
Forever reach the heart that loves its God.
'Twas well to touch thy death with gayest hues,
Even as the day sinks wrapt in gorgeous clouds,
For thou wert born to live but on the eye,
A thing of outward sense; of whose green youth,
And vigorous noon, and glittering age the child,
In lisping words, recounts. Thou wast not born,
Like him who gazes on thy splendor now,
To light a hidden sould with brighter hues
Thou wait upon the colored dawn, and hang
Upon the dying leaf; and, while decay
Deals rudely with his outward life, and clouds
Impatient gather to obscure its glory,
To shape like him, from out a world of change
A spirit into those eternal forms
Of Love, and Majesty, and Beauty, which,
Thou here by feeble glance of sense unseen,
The all-holy eyes of God approve.

                                       I.

13. The Word [December 15, 1838]

The Word, it cannot fail, it ever speaks;
Unheard by all save by the sons of heaven;
It waits while time counts on the appointed weeks,
The purpose to fulfill for which 'twas given.
Unchangeable its ever fixed command,
When human feet would from its precepts stray;
It points their pathway with its flaming hand,
And bids them keep the strait and narrow way.
And when by its unceasing counsels led,
The child would seek again his Father's face,
Upon its stores of heavenly manna fed,
He gains at last through grief his resting place,
And hears its praise from angels' countless throng,
And joins forever in their new raised song.

I.

14. The City [March 2, 1839]

And thou hast placed me on a lofty hill,
Where all who pass may mock and pierce me through;
Oh how can I in Christ be humble still,
Save that I learn with him thy will to do;
I cannot now from sight of men be hid,
Oh may my life thy heavenly rest proclaim;
That they may see in me the works that bid
The disbelievers glorify thy name;
Oh make them see thy light, the light from heaven,
That they may be its children too with me;
And when, through suffering here, thy peace is given,
Thy nearer presence with me let them see;
And hear from him who but one talent gave,
That they with him shall many cities save.

15. Spring [March 9, 1839]

The stem that long has borne the wintry blast,
Encased with ice or powdered o'er with snow;
Shall, when its chilling breath has breathed its last,
Its springing leaves and bursting blossoms show;
So ye, on whom the earth's cold wind has blown,
While there you suffered for your master's name;
The kindness of the Father soon shall own,

And in the spirit you bear his love proclaim;
Endure, that you the glorious light may see,
That soon will rise upon the perfect soul;
Press on, and you accepted soon shall be,
And see the son and he shall make you whole;
And on the Father's name forever call,
And from his perfect wisdom never fall.

16.   The Bride   [July 27, 1839]

I sought of Thee my promised wife,
    She of the golden hair;
But though I toiled with manly strife,
    Thou gave me one less fair.

Again I toiled, and many a day
    My hands to labor flew;
But Thou withheld again my pay,
    And gave me one less true.

And still once more my limbs they plied
    Their strength to serve Thee Lord;
But Thou wouldst not, though long I tried
    With her my pains reward.

But still for her I loved in youth,
    My nerves again are strung;
And I will serve Thee still in truth,
    As when my limbs were young.

And though the snows fall on my head,
    And lightless grows my eye;
She of my youth I still may wed,
    And dwell with her on high.

I.

III

A Defense of Jones Very's Sanity by the Reverend James Freeman
Clarke, and Poems Published in *The Western Messenger* but
Not Included in Any Edition of Jones Very's Works

[VI (March, 1839), 308-314]
Religious Sonnets
By Jones Very,– Salem, Mass.

We received, last month, twenty-seven sonnets of a spiritual nature
chiefly, from the gentleman whose name stands at the head of this
article. They were accompanied by the following note:

Rev. J. F. Clarke, Editor Western Messenger:

Hearing of your want of matter for your Messenger, I was moved to send you the above sonnets; that they may help those in affliction for Christ's name is ever the prayer of me his disciple, called to be a witness of his sufferings and an expectant of his glory. If you should ask for more as I have them so will they be communicated freely. Amen.

The hope of Jesus be with you when you are called to be a partaker of his temptations.

Jones Very.

We propose to communicate a part of them in this number, reserving the remainder for the next. They have been read by ourselves with no uncommon emotions of interest, and we trust will be equally interesting to our readers.

We hope it will not be considered indelicate if we introduce them with a few words about their author, as some acquaintance of his mental history and experience seems indispensable to a just comprehension of their meaning. If possible, we should place ourselves upon his standing point of thought, in order to be aware of their significance.

We had the pleasure of meeting Mr. Very, a few months since, in the city of Boston. We had heard of him before, from various quarters, as a young man of much intelligence and of a remarkably pure character, whose mind had become extremely interested within a few months, upon the subject of religion. He was said to have adopted some peculiar views on this important theme, and to consider himself inspired by God to communicate them. Such pretensions had excited the fears of his friends, and by many he was supposed to be partially deranged. The more intelligent and larger sort of minds, however, who had conversed with him, dissented from this view, and although they might admit a partial derangement of the lower intellectual organs, or perhaps an extravagant pushing of some views to their last results, were disposed to consider his main thoughts deeply important and vital.

And here we may remark that the charge of Insanity is almost always brought against any man who endeavors to introduce to the common mind any very original ideas. And especially is this the case with moral and religious truths. He who insists on taking us out of the sphere of thought which is habitual to us, into a higher and purer one, is regarded by us with alarm and dissatisfaction. We must either yield ourselves to him, and suffer our minds to be taken out of their customary routine, which is always painful—or we must find some way to set aside his appeals to our reason and conscience and disarm them of their force. The easiest way is to call him insane. It is a short and ready explanation of his whole conduct. It relieves us at once of all further trouble about him. Nobody is obliged to attend to the "insane

ravings" of a maniac. The moment therefore this word is applied to
a man, were he sage, prophet, or apostle—were he Socrates or Solon,
were he Jesus or Paul—all men are authorized to look down upon him
with pity. And it is so much more soothing to our vanity to look
down than to look up, that it is no wonder that the worldly-minded,
the men of sluggish and shallow intellects, and those who have arranged
and systematized their opinions, are pleased with this excuse for pitying
the man whom they ought to reverence. With them too go all those
teachers, priests and prophets, who have attained an influence over the
public mind, and love the exercise of that better than the attainment of
new truth. The fear of innovation, error, change allies itself to these
other motives, and so by common consent the prophet is declared a
maniac. "He has a devil, and is mad, why hear ye him?" was said of
the saviour of men. "Paul, thou art beside thyself, much learning has
made thee mad." And so have many other earnest souls, who spurn
the worldly and mean thoughts and practices of those about them, who
longed for an introduction to a brighter day into the darkness of time;
reformers and enthusiastic philanthropists, Wesleys, Penns, Foxes, been
called delirious by their own age, and been deified by the following one.
"Your fathers stoned the prophets, and ye build their sepulchres."

It is also, however, to be remarked that the intense contemplation
of any vast theme is apt to disturb the balance of the lower intellectual
faculties. While the Reason, which contemplates absolute truth, is active
and strong; the understanding which arranges and gives coherence to
our thoughts, may be weakened and reduced to a state of torpor. When
this reaches an extreme point, it becomes delirium or mono-mania.

But even in these cases it may be a question which is the worst
delirium, that by which a man, possessing some great truth, has lost
the use of his practical intellect– or that other wide-spread delirium, in
which the mind is enslaved to the lowest cares and meanest aims, and
all that is loftiest and greatest in the soul is stupefied and deadened in
worldliness. When, for instance, we have seen a man in whose intellect
all other thoughts have become merged in the great thought of his connection with God, we have had the feeling very strongly, which we
once heard thus expressed, "Is this Mono-Mania, or is it Mono-Sania?"

With respect to Mr. Very, we have only to say that the intercourse
we have ourselves had with him has given no evidence ever of such
partial derangement. We have heard him converse about his peculiar
views of religious truth, and saw only the workings of a mind absorbed
in the loftiest contemplations, and which utterly disregarded all which
did not come into that high sphere of thought. We leave it to our
readers to decide whether there is any unsoundness in these sonnets.
To us, they seem like wells of thought, clear and pellucid, and coming
up from profound depths.

Mr. Very's views in regard to religion, as we gathered them from himself, were not different from those heretofore advocated by many pure and earnest religionists. He maintains, as did Fenelou, Mme. Guion and others, that all sin consists in self-will, all holiness in an unconditional surrender of our own will to the will of God. He believes that one whose object is not to do his will in anything, but constantly to obey God, is led by Him, and taught by Him in all things. He is a Son of God, as Christ was the Son, because he *always* did the things which pleased his Father. He professes to be himself guided continually by this inward light, and he does not conjecture, speculate or believe, but he *knows* the truth which he delivers. In this confidence however, there is nothing of arrogance, but much modesty of manner.

[VI (March, 1839), 311]

The Wolf and the Lamb Shall Feed Together*

The wolf, why heeds he not the sportive lamb,
But lies at rest beside him on the plain?
The lion feeds beside the browsing ram,
The tyger's rage is curbed without a chain;
The year of peace has on the earth begun!
And see ye not bestowed the promised sign,
The prophets by the spirit moved have sung,
To close the world's long strife with day benign?
Look not abroad, it comes not with the eye;
Nor can the ear its welcome tidings hear;
Nor seek ye Christ below, nor yet on high,
Behold the Word to thee is also near;
E'en at thy heart it speaks, Repent! Obey!
And thine eye too shall hail the rising day.

[VI (March, 1839), 312]

Behold He Is at Hand That Doth Betray Me

Why come you out to me with clubs and staves,
That you on every side have fenced me so?
In every act you dig for me deep graves;
In which my feet must walk where'er I go;
You speak and in your words my death I find,
Pierced through with many sorrows to the core;
And none that will the bleeding spirit bind,

* Spelling, punctuation, grammar, etc., are reproduced here as they are found in the source.

But at each touch still freer flows the gore:
But with my stripes your deep-dyed sins are healed,
For I must show my Master's love for you;
The Cov'nant that he made, forever sealed,
By blood is witnessed to be just and true;
And you in turn must bear the stripes I bear,
And in his suffering learn alike to share.

[VI (March, 1839), 313]

Forbearance

The senseless drops can feel no pain, as they
In ceaseless measure strike the barren ground;
But o'er its trodden surface constant play,
Without a pang that there no life is found;
Yet oft the word must fall on stony fields,
And where the weeds have shot their rankness high;
And nought the seed to him who sows it yields.
But bitter tears and the half-uttered sigh;
But these are rife with precious stores of love,
For him who bears them daily in his breast;
For so the Father bids him hence remove.
And so attain His everlasting rest;
For thus He bares with thee when thou wast blind
And so he bids thee bear wouldst thou his presence find.

The Fragments

I weigh out my love with nicest care,
Each moment shall make large the sum I give,
That all who want may find yet some to share;
And bless the crumb of bread that helps them live;
Of thy rich stores howmuch has wasted been,
Of all thou giv'st me daily to divide;
I will in future count it for my sin,
If e'en a morsel from the poor I hide;
Help me to give them all Thou giv'st to me,
That I a faithful steward may be found;
That I may give a good account to Thee,
Of all the seed thou sowest in my ground;
That nought of all Thou givest may remain
That can a hungry soul in life sustain.

[VI (April, 1839), 366]

The New Jerusalem

I saw the city, 'twas not built by hands,
And nought impure can ever enter in,
'Twas built by those who keep the Lord's commands,
And in his blood have washed away their sin;
Thrice happy those who see the pearly gate
Before their earthly vision distant rise;
And keep the path though narrow still and straight
Through many a stormy hedge their journey lies;
Behold within the mansion of thy rest!
Prepared by Him who in it went before,
Behold the peace that makes the spirit blest!
By him who loved thee kept for thee in store;
Press on, the crown he won shall soon be thine,
And thou amid the just a star in heaven shall shine.

[VI (April, 1839), 367]

The Cross

I must go on, till in my tearful line
Walks the full spirit's love as I on earth;
Till I can all Thou giv'st again resign,
And he be formed in me who gave me birth;
Wilt thou within me bruise the serpent's heel,
That I through Christ the victory may win;
Then shall the peace the blessed in him must feel,
Within thy bosom here on earth begin;
Help me to grasp through him eternal life,
That must by conflict here by me be wrought;
With all his faith still aid me in the strife,
Till I through blood like him the prize have bought;
And I shall hang upon the accursed tree,
Pierced through with many spears that all may see.

Nature

Nature would speak through her first master man,
He will not heed her kindly calling voice;
He does not call her name as he began,
For in his Maker he cannot rejoice;
Yet still she woes (woos) him back with many a call,
That e'en his nature finds it hard to spurn;
And would surrender to his asking all

That now with anxious toil he scarce can earn;
She pleads, but pleads in vain; He will not hear,
But o'er her holds the rod his passions gave;
And thinks she will obey through coward fear,
And be like him of her own self the slave;
But ever fresh she rises 'neath his rod,
For she obeys in love her sovereign God.

[VI (April, 1839), 370]

The Mustard Seed

Plant the small seed, the mustard grain within,
And it shall spread its limbs from shore to shore;
But first it must in smallest root begin,
And seem to yield too little for thy store;
But thou hast sparing sown, it cannot grow
When thou dost not thy field in order keep.
Wilt thou no rain or sun on it bestow,
And think a plenteous harvest thou shalt reap?
Not so the earth rewards the farmers toil;
Not so the heart will yield its rich increase;
Wouldst thou in time partake the wine and oil,
Wouldst thou within thee find the promised peace,
Sow daily, sow within the precious seed,
And thou shalt find rich crops in time of need.

Eden

Thy service Father! wants not aught beside
The peace and joy it to thy servant brings;
By day in Christ a constant prayer t'abide,
By night to sleep beneath thy outspread wings;
To keep thy ground from thorns and poisonous weeds,
That Thou might'st sow in me the fruitful word;
Is all Thou ask'st, is all thy goodness needs,
This the command that Adam from Thee heard;
Oh may I better serve Thee, Lord! than he,
And may my garden be forever clean;
From noisome weeds, unsightly branches free,
Within it may thy Presence still be seen;
And wilt thou speak with me forevermore,
And I forget to sin as I have sinned before.

The Thorns

I cannot find thy flowers, they have not blown,
The cruel winter will not let them live;
The seed in every heart thy hand has sown,
Yet none will back to Thee the blossom give;
Their roots without the bosom daily grow,
And every branch blooms inward and unseen;
The hidden roots unslightly length they show,
And hide the limbs that thou hast clothed in green;
They will not like the plants that own thy care,
The heavy laden boughs extend to all;
They will not of the flowers Thou giv'st them share,
But drink the rain that on their bosoms fall,
And nought return but prickly briar and thorn,
That from the enclosed heart thy children warm.

[VI (April, 1839), 371]

My Meat and Drink

I do not need thy food, but thou dost mine;
For this will but the body's want repair,
And soon again for meat like this 'twill pine,
And so be fed by thee with daily care;
But that which I can give thou needs but eat,
And thou shalt find it in thyself to be;
Forever formed within a living meat,
On which to feed will make thy spirit free;
Thou shalt not hunger more, for freely given
The bread on which the spirit daily feeds;
This is the bread that cometh down from heaven,
Of which who eats no other food he needs;
But this doth grow within him day by day,
Increasing more the more he takes away.

Forgive My Trespasses

Thy* trespasses my heart has not forgiven,
To the full answer that my Lord would ask:
The love in him to me so freely given,
Is for my feeble strength too great a task:
Increase oh Father! swell the narrowing tide,
Till the full stream shall reach from shore to shore;
I have not yet each sinful thought denied,

* MS reads *My,* which makes sense.

Heal up for me the freshly bleeding sore.
Let me not waste the life my Savior gave,
On the vile lusts that war against the soul;
May sin in him forever find its grave,
And all my being own his just control;
And fixed forever is his perfect law,
May I more freely from thy fountain draw.

[VI (April, 1839), 372]

The Watchman

I place thee as a watchman on a tower,
That thou mayst warn the city of the dead;
The day has come, and come the appointed hour,
When through their streets my herald's feet shall tread;
Prepare ye all my supper to attend!
I have prepared it long that you might eat;
Come in, and I will treat you as a friend,
And of the living bread shall be your meat;
Oh come, and tarry not; for your's shall be
The honored seats around your Father's board;
And you my son's your master's face shall see,
And to my love forever be restored;
And you my promises to Abr'am given
Shall find fulfilled to all his seed in heaven.

[VIII (January, 1841), 424]

"The Settler"

When thou art done thy toil, anew art born;
With hands that never touched the spade or plough,
Nor in the furrows strewed the yellow corn,
Or plucked the ripened fruit from off the bough:
Then shall thou work begin;– thy plough and spade
Shall break at early morn the virgin soil;
The swelling hill and thickly wooded glade
With changing aspect own the daily toil;
Thy house shall strike the eye, where none are near,
For thou hast travelled far, where few have trod;
And those who journey hence will taste thy cheer,
And bless thee as a favored one of God;
For He it was who in this pathless wild,
Upon thy good intent so richly smiled.

Jones Very

[VIII (February, 1841), 449]

Time's House

The stones of time's old house with pelting storms,
That on it long have beat from day to day,
Are loose; the door is gone, and smoke deforms
The boards within and walls of plastered clay;
Long have his children strove to keep it whole;
By many a wile he's taught them to make good.
The waste that creeping years have from it stole,
And long its walls the ruin have withstood.
But now within and out the storms assail.
Its beams rock to and fro with every gust;
And fears o'er cherished hopes at last prevail,
Nor longer to its threatening roof thy'll trust;
But cease to patch each rent with jealous care,
And learn at last to live beneath the open air.

                                        Jones Very

[VIII (February, 1841), 462]

Death

Men live and die in secret; none can see
When going out or lighting up the flame,
Save the all-seeing eye;– frail mortals, we
Call death and life what are but so in name;
Death is that shunning Him who bids thee die,
Which thou but disobedience learnst to call;
Words cannot hide thee from the searching eye,
That sees thy corse beneath their sable pall;
And life the lifting up that thou dost feel,
When thy feet follow where he bids thee go;
A life beyond disease, or severing steel,
That nought but him who gives it, fear below;
This be thy life, and death shall flee away,
For thou hast learned forever to obey.

                                        Jones Very

[VIII (February, 1841), 467]

The Dwellings of the Just

I saw the dwellings of the Just,
    No sun was in their sky;
Nor candle lit their rooms by night,
    [They saw without an eye.]

They walked upright as fearing none,
　　Each step so true they trod;
They moved as those who have been taught
　　The perfect law of God.

All day they labored, yet at rest,
　　As in His sight, who lives.
Who to each one his rightful place,
　　And rightful portion gives.

And shadowy night was blessed to them,
　　As His who gives the day;
And sweet the sleep it brought to these,
　　Whose joy was to obey.

Jones Very

[VIII (February, 1841), 472]

The Beehive

The hive the honey-bee has found,
With loaded wings and heavy sides,
Stands in the garden fenced around,
Where she, called Industry, resides.

In and out her menials fly,
On their journeys one by one,
As she sends them far and nigh,
Telling each what must be done.

Are there flowers on crag, in dell,
Overloaded with their sweets;
Quick the humming insects tell
Heard within their wild retreats.

Do they bloom on open field,
Or the sheltered plots of men;
Not the smallest is concealed,
There her messengers have been.

All the day in quiet haste,
Thus they do their mistress' will;
Suffering not a drop to waste,
That may go her hive to fill.

Jones Very

[VIII (April, 1841), 551]

The Fox and the Bird

The bird that has no nest,
The Fox that has no hole;
He's wiser than the rest,
Her eggs are never stole.

She builds where none can see,
He hides where none can find;
The bird can rest where'er she be,
He freely moves as wind.

Thou hast not found her little young,
E'en though thou'st sought them long;
Though from thine earliest day they've sung,
Thou hast not heard their song.

Thou hast not found that Fox's brood,
That nestle under ground;
Though through all time his burrow's stood,
His whelps thou'st never found.

The Word

The Word where is it? hath it voice,
That I may hear it and be free;
Hath it a form, that I may know;
A touch, that I may feel; and see?

Where does it dwell? above, below?
Or is it where e'en now I tread?
I would be near it when it calls,
And bids awake the slumbering dead.

'Tis near me; yet I hear it not—
—That voice that cometh down from heaven—
And hide myself in shrinking fear,
When wide above the earth is riven.

Oh strengthen in me faith to rise,
And go where'er it leads the way;
That I may live with it as one,
And all that it commands obey.

IV

A Poem Published in *The Dial* but Not Included in Any Edition
of Jones Very's Works*

The Evening Choir

The organ smites the ear with solemn notes
In the dark pines withdrawn, whose shadows fall
Motionless on the moonlit path which leads
To the house of God, within whose porch I stand.
Behold the stars and larger constellations
Of the north hemisphere; glitter more bright
Their ranks, and more harmonious they seem,
As from within swells out the holy song.
The pillars tremble with the waves of sound!
There is in these deep tones a power to abide
Within us; when the hand is mouldered
Of him who sweeps its keys, and silent too
Her voice, who with the organ chants so sweet,
We shall hear echoes of a former strain,
Soft soul-like airs coming we know not whence.
I would that to the noisy throng below,
Which paces restless through the glimmering street,
Might reach this anthem with its cadence soft,
And its loud rising blasts. Men's ears are closed,
And shut their eyes, when from on high the angels
Listen well pleased, and nearer draw to the earth.
Yet here the blind man comes, the only constant
Listener. In the dim-lighted church within
Some pew's recess, retired he sits, with face
Upturned as if he saw, as well as heard,
And music was to him another sense:
Some thoughtless at the gate a moment stand,
Whom a chance-wandering melody detains,
And then, forgetful, mingle with the tide
That bears them on; perchance to wonder whence
It came, or dream from a diviner sphere
'Twas heard.
                    Tomorrow is the Sabbath-time;
Refreshed by sleep this tired multitude,
Each hurrying to and fro with thoughts of gain,
And harried with the business of the world,

---

* *The Dial*, III (July, 1842), 98-99. Spelling, punctuation, grammar, etc., are
reproduced here as they are found in the source.

Men with children mixed clamorous and rude,
Shall, all at once, quit their accustomed streets,
And to the temples turn with sober pace,
And decent dress composed for prayer and praise.
Yon gate, that now is shut upon the crowd,
Shall open to the worshippers; by paths
Where not a foot's now heard, up these high steps
Come arm in arm the mother, father, child,
Brother, and sister,—servants and the stranger
Tarrying with them, and the stated priest
Who ministers in holy things. Peace be
On this House, on its courts! May the high hymn
Of praise, that now is sung preparative,
Quiet the rough waves that now are breaking
At its base, and threatening its high walls.
I would not, when my heart is bitter grown,
And my thoughts turned against the multitude,
War with their earthly temple; mar its stones;
Or, with both pillars in my grasp, shake down
The mighty ruin on their heads. With this
I war not, nor wrestle with the earthly man.
I war with the spiritual temple raised
By pride, whose top is in the heavens, though built
On the earth; whose site and hydra-headed power
Is everywhere;—with Principalities,
And them who rule the darkness of the world,
And spirits of wickedness that highest stand.
'Gainst this and these I fight; nor I alone,
But those bright stars I see that gather round
Nightly this sacred spot. Nor will they lay
Their glittering armor by, till from heaven's height
Is cast Satan with all his host headlong!
Falling from sphere to sphere, from earth to earth
Forever;—and God's will is done.

v

A POEM PUBLISHED IN *The National Anti-Slavery Standard* BUT NOT
INCLUDED IN ANY EDITION OF JONES VERY'S WORKS*

The Vagrant at the Church Door

For years he had not seen his native place—
For years he had not spoken to a friend—

* *The National Anti-Slavery Standard* (New York), XXIV, No. 20, Saturday,
Sept. 26, 1863.

For years he had not stood within a church;
And now he lingered in the dusky porch,
And watched the congregation one by one,
Cheerfully enter, and devoutly bend
In silent adoration. Many a face,
Familiar long ago, glanced toward his own—
Perhaps with wonder, for they knew him not.
And he was sadly changed, since in this spot
His happy boyhood swiftly passed away.
Strange fascination! Now he needs must stay;
For in the echoes of the choir, he hears
A melody familiar to long past years
And sweet associations. Soon his tears
Tell how the vagrant's spirit has been moved.
All that he dreamt, all that he ever loved,
All that youth's prophecy said "might have been,"
All the grim shadows of the wasted past,
In dim procession moved before him now.

The vagrant passed his fingers o'er his brow,
And seemed bewilder'd—crazed—until at last
The dawning of a hopeful smile was seen
Upon his face. The music of the psalm
Died out in whispering echoes; and the voice,
In earnest accents, of the village priest,
Was heard in prayer. Once more the vagrant glanced
Within the church, and then he entered in.
Beneath a column's shadow sat entranced
The poor world-weary man. A holy calm
Encompassed him, and made his heart rejoice—
The past dissolved as though it had not been.

The service ends. The rolling organ ceased.
The verger came to where the vagrant sat
Mute as a statue. "Come, my man," said he,
"The church is closing; take your stick and hat,
And let me shut the doors." Then wonderingly
The verger looked again, and muttered low,
"Poor soul, I knew him thirty years ago—
I little thought he would come here to die."

                                        Jones Very

BIBLIOGRAPHY

PRIMARY SOURCES

Very, Jones. *Bowdoin Prize Dissertations,* in Archives of Widener Library at Cambridge, Mass. Vol. VI (1835-1839). Nos. II and IV are Jones Very's.

—— "Captain Jones Very" (bears date of "Salem, Jan., 1872"), Salem *Register,* Monday, May 17, 1880.

—— *Exhibition and Commencement Performances—1834-1835,* in Archives of Widener Library at Cambridge, Mass.

> No. 12. Tuesday, April 28, 1835.
> No. 12. Tuesday, May 3, 1836.
> No. 12. ("Order of Exercises for Commencement")
> > An English Oration. "Individuality."

—— *Essays and Poems.* Boston: Charles C. Little and James Brown, 1839.

—— "How Long?" *The Harbinger,* II (June 6, 1846), 404.

—— Manuscripts in the library of the Andover Theological Seminary, Cambridge, Mass.

> *Poems.* Several hundred, unbound, and wrapped in paper.
> *Sermons.* Nos. 1-105, bound in one volume—gift of the Misses F. E. and L. L. A. Very, of Salem, Mass. Rec'd. March 22, 1895.

—— Manuscripts in the Harris Collection of American Poetry in the library of Brown University, Providence, R. I.

> POEMS:
> > a. MSS Book 1, Portfolio, Very MSS.
> > b. MSS Book 3, Portfolio, Very MSS.
> > c. MSS Book 4, Portfolio, Very MSS.
> > d. Lines on Mount Auburn and other MSS Verse; bought from Lull in 1929.
> > e. Scrapbook—MSS Poems of Jones Very.
> > f. MSS Book signed Jones Very AE 12.
> LETTERS:
> > Wm. Allen to Jones Very—2 letters.
> > Jones Very to Wm. Allen—2 letters.
> SERMONS:
> > Nos. 1-28.
> > All, except Poem 4, acquired from Goodspeed's, Boston, in 1903.

—— Manuscript (early draft) of "Epic Poetry." (At top of outside page is written in Very's handwriting: "Written in April—delivered July, 1836.") In Lydia Very MSS (E—Vs73.1, 1897, 2: The Essex Institute).

—— *Poems and Essays,* complete and revised edition, with a biographical sketch by James Freeman Clarke and a preface by C. A. Bartol. Boston and New York: Houghton, Mifflin & Co., 1886.

—— *Poems by Jones Very,* with an introductory memoir by William P. Andrews. Boston: Houghton, Mifflin & Co., 1883.

—— Poems in *Harvardiana:*

II (Jan., 1836), 137-139: "King Philip."

II (Feb., 1836), 199: "The Stars"; 200: "The Snow Bird."

II (March, 1836), 231-232: "The Painted Columbine."

II (April-May, 1836), 248: "My Mother's Voice"; 262-264: "The Arab Steed."

II (June, 1836), 326: "The Humming Bird."

II (July-Aug., 1836), 377: "Lines to —— on the Death of a Friend."

—— Poems from the Salem *Observer:*

1. Aug. 10, 1833: no title ("The earth is parched with heat, flowers droop and die"); dated July 24, 1833; signed "I".

2. Aug. 24, 1833: "Lines—Written on Reading Stuart's Account of the Treatment of Slaves in Charleston"; a slavery poem; dated Aug. 13, 1833.

3. April 26, 1834: no title ("Hast thou ever heard the voice of nature"); dated April 7, 1834; signed "I".

4. June 28, 1834: "Death of Lafayette"; dated Salem, June 21, 1834; signed "I".

5. July 5, 1834: "Old Age"; dated Salem, June 30; signed "I".

6. July 12, 1834: "Lines—Suggested by Seeing a Butterfly Sculptured upon a Tomb"; dated Salem, July 6; signed "I".

7. July 19, 1834: "Kind Words"; dated Salem, July 16, 1834; signed "I".

8. Aug. 2, 1834: "Pleasure"; dated Salem, July 22, 1834; signed "I".

9. Aug. 16, 1834: no title ("Give me an eye, that manly deeds"); dated Salem, Aug. 9; signed "I".

10. Aug. 30, 1834: no title ("I saw a child whose eyes had never drank"); dated Salem, Aug. 25, 1834.

11. Jan. 3, 1835: "The New Year" ("All hail new year! though clad in storms thou com'st"); no date, Salem; signed "I".

12. Jan. 10, 1835: "Sleigh Ride" ("Hurra, hurra, away they go"); dated Jan. 5.

13. April 11, 1835: "The Snow Drop" ("Hail early Harbinger of Spring"); Salem, April 8; "I".

14. Aug. 1, 1835: "Eheu! Fugaces, Posthume, Posthume, Labuntur Anni" ("Fleeting years are ever bearing"); no date; signed "I".

15. Aug. 8, 1835: "The Humming Bird" ("I cannot heal thy green gold breast"); Aug. 1; "I".

16. Aug. 22, 1835: "Nature" ("I love to sit on the green hillside"); Aug. 15; "I".

17. Aug. 29, 1835: "Religion" ("Gather around thee treasures brought"); Aug. 24; "I".

18. Dec. 5, 1835: "A Withered Leaf—Seen on a Poet's Table" ("Poet's hand has placed thee there"); Nov. 24; "I".

19. Dec. 26, 1835: "The Stars" ("Night's wanderers! why hang ye there?"); Dec. 22; "I".

20. Jan. 2, 1836: "The Snow Bird" ("And hast thou come to gaze on me"); Dec. 25; "I".

21. Jan. 9, 1836: "Memory" ("Soon the waves so lightly bounding"); Jan. 4; "I".

22. April 16, 1836: "The Ice Ship" ("Why rings not back the welcome shout"); no place or date given; "I".

23. April 23, 1836: "The Painted Columbine" ("Bright image of my early years"); "I".

24. June 4, 1836: "My Mothers Voice"; preceded by the following: "The following beautiful Stanzas were written in a Lady's Album, a few weeks since, by Jones Very, of Salem, a young poet who has occasionally furnished articles of the same description for one of the papers published in this city. It is sufficient to say that Mr. Very, in this, as well as in all his other productions gives evidence that he possesses a fine poetical talent—a spirit alive to whatever is beautiful in nature, or lovely and attractive in the human heart. There is a music in the numbers, and an eloquence in the tone of 'My Mother's Voice' which will make every bosom thrill. (Landmark)."

25. June 11, 1836: "The Arab Steed"; "I".

26. Aug. 20, 1836: "Washington"; preceded by two prose paragraphs ("The Father of his country stood"); "I".

27. Oct. 1, 1836: "The Autumn Leaf" ("Thou fair yet lifeless leaf! on whom decay"); "I".

28. June 25, 1836: article headed "New Stone Church" mentions Very's hymn as follows: "The following Dedication Hymn, composed by Mr. Jones Very, a member of the North Society, was sung on the occasion: 'The weight of years is on the pile. . . .' "

29. Dec. 31, 1836: "The Winter Bird" ("Thou singest alone on the bare wintry bough"); "I".

30. April 15, 1837: "The Canary Bird" ("I cannot hear thy voice with others ears"); "I".

31. April 22, 1837: "The Tree" ("I love thee when thy swelling buds appear"); "I".

32. Dec. 2, 1832: "The Voice of God" ("They told me, when my heart was glad"); "I".

33. Dec. 23, 1837: "The Windflower"; "I".

34. Dec. 30, 1837: "Beauty" ("I gazed upon thy face—and beating life—").

35. Jan. 6, 1838: "Beauty" and "The Windflower" preceded by the following: "Owing to some typographical errors in the two following original Sonnets, (from an esteemed poetical correspondent), which have appeared in the Observer, we republish them corrected."

36. April 21, 1838: "A Sonnet" ("Thy beauty fades and with it too my love"); "I".

37. June 9, 1838: "The Robin" ("Thou needst not flutter from thy half-built nest") and "The Columbine" (Still, still my eye will gaze long-fixed on thee"); "I".

38. Aug. 18, 1838: "The Stranger's Gift" ("I found far culled from fragrant field and grove"); "I".

39. Oct. 27, 1838: "The New Birth" ("Tis a new life—thoughts move not as they did"); "I".

40. Nov. 10, 1838: "In Him we live, and move, and have our being" ("Father! I bless thy name that I do live"); "Enoch" ("I looked to find a man who walked with God"); "I".

41. Nov. 17, 1838: "Love" ("I asked of Time to tell me where was Love"); "The Son" ("Father I wait thy word. The sun doth stand"); "I".

42. Nov. 24, 1838: "Day" ("Day I lament that none can hymn thy praise"); "Night" ("I thank thee, Father, that the night is near"); "I".

43. Dec. 1, 1838: "The Morning Watch" ("'Tis near the morning watch"); "The Coming" ("The day begins—it comes—the appointed day"); "I".

44. Dec. 15, 1838: six sonnets: "The Latter Rain"; "The Slave"; "The Bread from Heaven" ("Long do we live upon the husks of corn"); "The Spirit Land" ("Father! thy wonders do not singly stand"); "Worship"; "The Word" ("The word! it cannot fail; it ever speaks"); each signed "I".

45. Dec. 22, 1838: four sonnets: "The Living God" ("There is no death with Thee! each tree and plant"); "Time" ("There is no moment but whose flight doth bring"); "The Heart" ("There is a

cup of sweet or bitter drink"); "The Violet" ("Thou tellest truths unspoken yet by man"); "I".

46. Dec. 29, 1838: four sonnets: "The Serpent" ("They knew that they were naked and ashamed"); "The Soldier of the Cross" ("He was not armed like those of eastern clime"); "The Trees of Life" ("For those who worship thee there is no death"); "The Spirit" ("I would not breathe when blows thy mighty wind"); "I".

47. Jan. 5, 1839: four sonnets: "John" ("What went ye out to see"); "The Presence" ("I sit within my room and joy to find"); "The Lost" ("They wander, straggling sheep without a fold"); "The Dead" ("I see them crowd on crowd they walk the earth"); "I".

48. Jan. 12, 1839: four sonnets: "The Robe" ("Each naked branch, the yellow leaf or brown"); "Life" ("It is not life upon Thy gifts to live"); "The Will" ("Help me in Christ to learn to do Thy will"); "The War" ("I saw a war yet none the trumpet blew"); "I".

49. Jan. 19, 1839: four sonnets: "The Priest" ("Grant me forever of thy word to hear"); "The Weary and Heavy Laden" ("Rejoice ye weary! ye whose spirits mourn!"); "The Flight" ("Come forth, come forth my people from the place"); "The Resurrection" ("The dead! the dead! they throw their grave clothes by"); "I".

50. Jan. 26, 1839: "The Word" ("There is no voice but that which speaks in Thee"); "My Father's House" ("My father's house, I find no entrance there"); "The Servant" ("The servant Thou hast called stands ready shod"); "I Was Sick and in Prison" ("Thou hast not left the rough-barked tree to grow"); "I".

51. Feb. 2, 1839: four sonnets: "The Laborer" ("Father, I thank Thee that the day begins"); "Sacrifice" ("Thou dost prefer the song that rises pure"); "The Grave Yard" ("My heart grows sick before the widespread death"); "Thy Brother's Blood" ("I have no Brother —they who meet me now"); "I".

52. Feb. 9, 1839: four sonnets: "The Son of Man" ("The Son of Man, where shall he find repose?"); "The Father" ("Thou who first called me from the sleep of death"); "Rachel" ("Where are my children, whom from youth I raised"); "The Ark" ("There is no change of time and place with Thee"); "I".

53. Feb. 16, 1839: four sonnets: "The Hours" ("The minutes have their trusts as they go by"); "The Earth" ("I would lie low, the ground on which men tread"); "Christmas" ("Awake ye dead! the summons has gone forth"); "The Christ" ("'Tis not by water only, but by blood"); "I".

54. Feb. 23, 1839: four sonnets: "The Things Before" ("I would not tarry, Look! the things before"); "Old Things Are Passed Away"

("The old creation Thou hast formed is dead"); "The Cup" ("The bitterness of death is on me now"); "The Harvest" ("They love me not, who at my table eat"); "I".

55. March 2, 1839: four sonnets: "The City" ("And Thou hast placed me on a lofty hill"); "The Rose" ("The rose thou show'st me has lost all its hue"); "The Jew" ("Thou art more deadly than the Jew of ole"); "Faith" ("There is no faith, the mountain stands within"); "I".

56. March 9, 1839: four sonnets: "The Tent" ("Thou springest from the ground, and may not I"); "Spring" ("The stem that long has borne the wintry blanket"); "The White Horse" ("The word goes forth! I see its conquering way"); "The Temple" ("The temple shall be built, the Holy One"); "I".

57. March 16, 1839: four sonnets: "The Corner Stone" ("The builders still reject my corner stone"); "The Good Ground" ("The word must fall; but where the well-tilled ground"); "My Sheep" ("I will not look upon the lands you own"); "The Beginning and the End" ("Thou art the First and Last, the End of All"); "I".

58. March 23, 1839: four sonnets: "Morning" ("The light will never open sightless eyes"); "Nature" ("The bubbling brook doth leap when I come by"); "The Temptation" ("Thou shalt not live e'en by the bread alone"); "Help" ("Thou wilt be near me Father, when I fail"); "I".

59. March 30, 1839: four sonnets: "The Reaper" ("There are no reapers in the whitening fields"); "Change" ("Father! there is no change to live with Thee"); "The Poor" ("I walk the streets and though not meanly dressed"); "They Who Hunger" ("Thou hearest the hungry ravens when they cry"); unsigned.

60. April 6, 1839: two sonnets: "The Sign" ("They clamor for a sign with eyeless zeal"); "Who Hath Ears to Hear Let Him Hear" ("The sun doth not the hidden place reveal"); "I".

61. April 13, 1839: "The Meek" ("I would be meek as He who bore her cross"); "The Tree" ("I too will wait with thee returning spring"); "I".

62. April 20, 1839: "The Clay" ("Thou shalt do what wilt with thine own hand"); "The Desert" ("Oh, but the desert blossom as the rose"); "I".

63. April 27, 1839: "The Altar" ("Oh Kindle up thine altar! see the brands"); "The First Shall Be Last" ("Bring forth, bring forth your silver! it shall be"); "I".

64. May 4, 1839: "Praise" ("Oh praise the Lord! let every heart be glad"); "Terror" ("There is no safety! fear has seized the proud"); "I".

65. May 11, 1839: "Humility" ("Oh humble me! I cannot hide the joy"); "The Prayer" ("Father, Keep them who walk in their own light"); not signed "I", but they are Very's poems.

66. May 18, 1839: "Forgiveness" ("Forgive me, Father, for to Thee I stand"); "Heaven" ("They do not toil in heaven; they live and love"); "I".

67. May 28, 1839: "The Rock" ("Thou art; there is no stay but in Thy love"); "Compassion" ("He saw them taxed with heavy burdens all"); no "I", but they are Very's.

68. July 13, 1839: "The Call" ("Why art thou not awake my son?"); "I".

69. July 20, 1839: "The Prayer" ("Wilt thou not visit me?"); "I".

70. July 27, 1839: "The Bride" ("I sought of Thee my promised wife"); "I".

71. Aug. 3, 1839: "My Garden" ("The Eyes that would my garden see"); "I".

72. Aug. 10, 1839: "The Unripe Fruit" ("I cannot wait, I cannot wait"); "I".

73. Aug. 17, 1839: "The Still-Born" ("I saw one born, yet he was of the dead"); "I".

74. Aug. 24, 1839: "Today" ("I live but in the present"); "I".

75. Aug. 31, 1839: "The Withered Tree" ("It stands 'mid other trees dry-barked"); "I".

76. Sept. 7, 1839: "The Hour" ("I ask not what the bud may be"); "I".

77. Sept. 14, 1839: "The Old Road" ("The road is left that once was trod"); "I".

78. Sept. 21, 1839: "The Clouded Morning" ("The morning comes, and thickening fogs prevail"); "The Fair Morning" ("The clear bright morning, with its scented air"); "I".

79. Sept. 28, 1839: "The Plagues of Egypt" ("I see them spreading o'er the land"); "I".

80. Oct. 5, 1839: "The Immortal" ("'Tis not that Thou has given to me"); by Jones Very.

81. Oct. 12, 1839: "The Dark Day" ("A darkness like the middle of the night"); "The Removal" ("When he who owns a house has come to thee"); by Jones Very.

82. Oct. 19, 1839: "The Rain" ("The rain descends; each drop some drooping flowers"); "The Frost" ("The frost is out amid our open fields"); by Jones Very.

83. Oct. 26, 1839: "The Serving Man" ("Lord thou hast many a serving-man"); by Jones Very.

84. Nov. 2, 1839: "Autumn Days" ("The winds are out with loud increasing shout"); "Autumn Leaves" ("The leaves though thick are falling; one by one"); by Jones Very.

85. Nov. 9, 1839: "The Good Samaritan" ("There journeyed from the south a man"); "The Birds of Passage" ("Whence come those many colored birds"); by Jones Very.

86. Nov. 16, 1839: "The Ramble" ("The plants that careless grow shall flower and bud"); "The Barberry Bush" ("The bush that has most briars and bitter fruit"); by Jones Very.

87. Nov. 23, 1839: "Yourself" ("'Tis to yourself I speak; you cannot know"); "Thy Neighbor" ("I am thy other self; what thou wilt be"); by Jones Very.

88. Nov. 30, 1839; "The Holy City" ("There is a house not built with hands"); by Jones Very.

89. Dec. 7, 1839: "The Bunch of Flowers" ("I saw a bunch of flowers, and Time"); by Jones Very.

90. Dec. 21, 1839: "The Worm" ("I saw a worm, with many a fold"); by Jones Very.

91. Dec. 28, 1839: "The Seasons" ("I will not call it Spring for me"); by Jones Very.

92. Jan. 18, 1840: "The Laborers" ("The workman shall not always work; who builds"); "The Unfaithful Servants" ("Thou hast no other hands than those that toil"); by Jones Very.

93. Feb. 1, 1840: "The Thieves" ("The night was dark and I alone"); by Jones Very.

94. Feb. 15, 1840: "The Strangers" ("Each careworn face is but a book"); by Jones Very.

95. Feb. 22, 1840: "The Light from Within" ("I saw on earth another light"); by Jones Very.

——— Poems in *The Western Messenger:*

VI (March, 1839), 311-314: "The Rail Road," "The Wolf and the Lamb Shall Feed Together," "Behold He Is at Hand That Doth Betray Me," "He Was Acquainted with Grief," "The Winter Rain," "Forbearance," "The Fragments," "The Fruit," "To Him That Hath Shall Be Given."

VI (April, 1839), 366-373: "The River," "The New Jerusalem," "The Cross," "Nature" ("Nature would speak through her first master man"), "Ye Gave Me No Meat," "Day unto Day Uttereth Speech," "Labor and Rest," "The Disciple," "The Mountain," "The Mustard Seed," "Eden," "The Thorns," "My Meat and Drink," "Forgive My Trespasses," "The Star," "The Watchman," "The Prison," "The Prophet."

VIII (May, 1840), 43: "The Prayer" ("Wilt Thou not visit me?"); (Jan., 1841), 424: "The Settler"; (Feb., 1841), 449: "Time's

House"; 462: "Death," "The Birth-Day"; 467: "The Dwellings of the Just"; 472: "The Beehive." (April, 1841), 549-552: "The Absent," "The Pilgrim," "A Word," "The Fox and the Bird," "The Word," "Faith and Light."

——— Very MSS from Essex Institute (Margaret W. Brooks Collection).

1. Power of Attorney to Lydia Very, made by Jones Very and Washington Very.

2. Letter to Dr. Henry Wheatland, concerning Wigwam Rock.

3. A postal card addressed to Geo. W. Whipple, Esq., the Essex Institute, Salem, Mass.

——— "The Evening Choir," *The Dial,* III (July, 1842), 97; "The World," *ibid.,* pp. 99-100.

——— "The First White Hamburg, and the First Muscat of Alexandria Grape-vine Imported into the United States," *Bulletin of the Essex Institute,* Vol. IV (1873).

——— "The Strangers," *The Index,* N.S., I, 101: "The Tree," *ibid.,* N.S., II, 450.

——— "The Vagrant at the Church Door," *The National Anti-Slavery Standard,* Vol. XXIV, No. 20, New York, Saturday, Sept. 26, 1863.

——— "The Very Family," *Essex Institute Historical Collections,* I (1859), 33-38, 116 ff.

ANTHOLOGIES CONTAINING VERY'S POEMS

Griswold, Rufus Wilmot. *The Poets and Poetry of America, to the Middle of the Nineteenth Century.* Eleventh Edition. Philadelphia: A. Hart, late Cary & Hart, 1852. Pp. 404-406: eighteen poems quoted, as follows: "To the Painted Columbine," "Lines to a Withered Leaf Seen on a Poet's Table," "The Heart," "To the Canary Bird," "Thy Beauty Fades," "The Wind-Flower," "Enoch," "Morning," "Night," "The Spirit-Land," "The Trees of Life," "The Ark," "Nature," "The Tree," "The Son," "The Robin," "The Rail-Road," "The Latter Rain."

Hunt, Leigh, and S. Adams Lee. *The Book of the Sonnet.* 2 vols. Boston: Roberts Bros., 1867. Vol. II contains "The Robin," "Morning," "Thy Beauty Fades," and "The Spirit Land."

Bryant, William Cullen, ed. *A New Library of Poetry and Song.* New York: Doubleday, Page & Co., 1870 and 1877. Contains "The Latter Rain," "Nature," and "The Spirit Land."

Emerson, Ralph Waldo, ed. *Parnassus.* Boston: James E. Osgood & Co., 1876. Contains "The Barberry Bush," p. 32; "The Strangers," p. 159.

Duyckinck, Evert A. and George L. *The Cyclopaedia of American Literature.* Philadelphia: William Rutter & Co., 1877. II, 385-387, contains: biographical sketch and criticism; also "To the Painted Columbine," "The Wind-Flower," "The New Birth," "Day," "Night," "The Latter Rain," "Nature" ("The bubbling brook doth leap when I come by"), "The Prayer" ("Wilt thou not visit me?").

Underwood, Francis H. *A Handbook of English Literature. American Authors.* Boston: Lee and Shepard, 1878. Pp. 604-605: "To the Painted Columbine" and "The Wind-Flower."

Stedman, Edmund Clarence, and Ellen Mackay Hutchinson, eds. *A Library of American Literature.* New York: Charles Webster and Co., 1889. VII, 217-219: "Yourself," "The Dead," and "The Silent."

Sunshine in the Soul. Boston: Roberts Bros., 1890. P. 95, "Sonnet" ("To tell my journeys where I daily walk"); p. 123, "The Idler."

Warner, Charles Dudley, *et al.,* eds. *Library of the World's Best Literature.* New York: R. S. Peals and J. A. Hill, 1897. XXVI, 15, 323-325, 329: "The Tree," "Day," "Night," "The Dead," "Man in Harmony with Nature," "The Giants," "The Humming-Bird," "The Builders," "The Wood-Wax," "Beauty," and "The Prayer."

Horder, W. Garnett, ed. *The Treasury of American Sacred Song.* London: Henry Frowde, Oxford University Press Warehouse, 1900. Pp. 81-85: "Nature," "Sabbatia," "Life," "The Presence," "The Spirit," "Labor and Rest," "The Prayer," "The Light from Within."

Stedman, Edmund Clarence, ed. *An American Anthology—1787-1900.* Boston and New York: Houghton, Mifflin and Co., 1901. Pp. 173 ff.: "The Idler," "The New World," "The Old Road," "Yourself," "The Dead," "The Gifts of God."

Rittenhouse, Jessie B., ed. *The Little Book of American Poets—1787-1900.* Boston and New York: Houghton, Mifflin and Co., 1915. Pp. 59-60: "Yourself" and "The Idler."

Hill, Caroline Miles, ed. *The World's Great Religious Poetry.* New York: The Macmillan Company, 1923. Pp. 308-309: "Health of Body Dependent on Soul" and "The Light from Within."

Snyder, Franklin B., and Edward S., eds. *A Book of American Literature.* New York: The Macmillan Co., 1927. Pp. 308-309: "The Soldier," "The Dead," "The War," "The Ark."

Quinn, Arthur, *et al.,* eds. *The Literature of America.* New York: Charles Scribner's Sons, 1929. I, 422: "The Dead."

Newcomer, Alphonso Gerald, *et al.,* eds. *Three Centuries of American Poetry and Prose.* New York: Scott, Foresman & Co., 1929. Pp. 611-612: "The Soldier," "The Dead," "The War," and "The Wild Rose of Plymouth."

The Home Book of Verse. Selected and arranged by Burton Egbert Stevenson. New York: Henry Holt & Co., 1930. P. 1293, "Nature" ("The bubbling brook doth leap when I come by"); p. 2070, "The Idler"; p. 1403, "The Tree."

Untermeyer, Louis, ed. *American Poetry from the Beginning to Whitman*. First Edition. New York: Harcourt, Brace & Co., 1931. Pp. 51 and 474-480: "The New World," "The Dead," "Enoch," "The Wind-Flower," "Morning," "The Tree," "The Strangers," "Night," "The Robin," "Day," and "The Prayer."

Foerster, Norman, ed. *American Poetry and Prose*. Boston and New York: Houghton, Mifflin and Co., 1934. I, 630: "The World."

Kreymborg, Alfred, ed. *An Anthology of American Poetry—Lyric America—1630-1930*. New York: Tudor Publishing Co., 1935. Pp. 92-93: "The Tree," "The Spirit Land," and "Nature."

Le Galliene, Richard, ed. *The Le Galliene Book of English and American Poetry*. Two vols. in one. Garden City, N. Y.: Garden City Publishing Co., 1935. P. 101: "The Dead."

Hymn and Tune Book (Unitarian). Boston: The Unitarian Society, n.d. "We Go Not on a Pilgrimage" and "Father, Thy Wonders Do Not Singly Stand."

Hubbell, Jay B., ed. *American Life in Literature*. 2 vols. New York and London: Harper & Brothers, 1936. I, 344-546: "Love," "Beauty," "The Soldier," "The War," "The Dead," "The Light from Within," and "Health of Body Dependent on the Soul."

Winters, Yvor. *Maule's Curse—Seven Studies in the History of American Obscurantism (Hawthorne, Cooper, Melville, Poe, Emerson, Jones Very, Emily Dickinson, Henry James)*. Norfolk, Conn.: New Directions, 1938. In an Appendix, pp. 216-232, "A Brief Selection of the Poems of Jones Very," one finds twenty-two selected poems.

SECONDARY SOURCES

A Catalogue of the Officers and Students of the University in Cambridge—1835-6, p. 15; 1836-7, p. 6.

Adams, Charles Francis. *Richard Henry Dana*. Boston: Houghton, Mifflin and Co., 1891.

"Allston, Washington." *D. A. B.*, Vol. I.

"Bartol, Cyrus Augustus." *D. A. B.*, Vol. II.

Bell, Margaret. *Margaret Fuller*. New York: Albert and Charles Boni, 1930.

Bennett, Charles A. *A Philosophical Study of Mysticism*. Reprinted with a preface by Rufus M. Jones. New Haven: Yale University Press, 1931.

Blankenship, Russell. *American Literature*. New York: Henry Holt & Co., 1931.

Boynton, Percy H. *Literature and American Life*. Boston and New York: Ginn and Company, 1936.

Bradford, Gamaliel. *Biography of the Human Heart*. Boston and New
York: Houghton, Mifflin and Co., 1932. Chapter VII, pp. 185-212,
"Jones Very."

—— *The Journal of Gamaliel Bradford*. Edited by Van Wyck
Brooks. Boston and New York: Houghton, Mifflin and Co., 1933.

—— *The Letters of Gamaliel Bradford 1918-1931*. Edited by Van
Wyck Brooks. Boston and New York: Houghton, Mifflin and Co.,
1934.

"Brooks, Charles Timothy." *D. A. B.*, Vol. III.

—— *William Ellery Channing—A Centennial Memory*. Boston:
Roberts Brothers, 1880.

Brooks, Van Wyck. *The Life of Emerson*. New York: E. P. Dutton
& Co., Inc., 1932.

—— *The Flowering of New England, 1815-1865*. New York: E. P.
Dutton & Co., Inc., 1934.

Cabot, James Elliott. *A Memoir of Ralph Waldo Emerson*, Vol. I. Bos
ton and New York: Houghton, Mifflin and Co., 1890.

The Cambridge History of American Literature. Edited by Wm. P.
Trent *et al*. New York: The Macmillan Company, 1933. 3 vols.

Channing, William Henry. *The Life of William Ellery Channing, D.D.*
Boston: American Unitarian Association, 1880.

—— *Thoreau: The Poet-Naturalist*. Boston: Roberts Brothers, 1873.

"Channing, Edward Tyrell." *D. A. B.*, Vol. IV.

Christy, Arthur. *The Orient in American Transcendentalism: A Study
of Emerson, Thoreau, and Alcott*. New York: Columbia University
Press, 1932.

Clarke, James Freeman. *Autobiography, Diary and Correspondence*.
Edited by Edward Everett Hale. Boston and New York: Houghton,
Mifflin & Co., The Riverside Press, 1891.

"Clarke, James Freeman." *D. A. B.*, Vol. IV.

Clarke, James Freeman. *Events and Epochs in Religious History*. Boston: James R. Osgood and Co., 1881. Chapter IX, "The Mystics in
All Religions: Section 4—American Mystics. Ralph Waldo Emerson. Jones Very," pp. 291-299.

Clarke, Sarah Freeman. "Reminiscences Concerning Elizabeth Peabody." Written for the memorial meeting, 1894. In MS collection
of Boston Public Library: MS 622.

Conrad, David Holmes. *Memoir of Rev. James Chisholm A. M.* New
York: Protestant Episcopal Society for the Promotion of Evangelical
Knowledge.

Cooke, George Willis. *An Historical and Biographical Introduction to
Accompany The Dial*. Cleveland: The Rowfant Club, 1902. Vol. II,
Chapter XXII, pp. 137-142.

—— *Poets of Transcendentalism.* Boston: Houghton, Mifflin & Co., 1903.

—— *Ralph Waldo Emerson: His Life, Writings, and Philosophy.* Fifth Edition. Boston: James R. Osgood & Co., 1882.

Cowper, William. *The Complete Poetical Works of William Cowper.* With a Memoir of the Author, by the Rev. H. Stebbing, A. M. New York: D. Appleton & Co., 1854.

Cross, Tom Peete, and Clement Tyson Goode. *Heath Readings in the Literature of England.* Vol. I. New York: D. C. Heath & Co., 1927.

"Dana, Richard Henry." *D. A. B.,* V, 59-60.

Donne, John. *Complete Poetry and Selected Prose.* Edited by John Hayward. New York: Random House, Inc., 1932.

Emerson, Edward Waldo, ed. *A Correspondence between John Sterling and Ralph Waldo Emerson.* Boston and New York: Houghton, Mifflin & Co., 1897.

Emerson, Ralph Waldo. *Journals of Ralph Waldo Emerson.* Edited by Edward Waldo Emerson and Waldo Emerson Forbes. Boston and New York: Houghton, Mifflin & Co., 1908-1914.

IV (1836-38), 423, 432.

V (1838-41), 98, 104-106, 110-111, 114, 133, 141, 143, 214, 220-221, 221, 223, 243, 289, 377, 381-383, 482.

VI (1841-44), 51, 131-132, 172, 198, 257-258, 290, 384-386.

VII (1845-48), 120 (this in midst of much discussion of Oriental mysticism, Swedenborg, etc.), 136-137, 555.

VIII (1849-55), 62, 211, 293.

IX (1856-63), 504, 524.

X (1864-76), 77, 108, 285.

—— In MS: letter dated Concord, Nov. 18, 1838, to Jones Very, urging him to continue writing verse, with a view toward publication of a book. In possession of the Essex Institute, Salem, Mass.

—— *The Complete Works of Ralph Waldo Emerson,* with a biographical introduction and a general index. Centenary Edition. 12 vols. Boston and New York: Houghton, Mifflin & Co., 1903.

I. *Nature, Addresses, and Lectures.*

II. *Essays, First Series.*

III. *Essays, Second Series.*

IV. *Representative Men.*

IX. *Poems.*

—— *The Letters of Ralph Waldo Emerson.* Edited by Ralph L. Rusk. New York: Columbia University Press, 1939.

Essex County Court Records:

I. *Grantees*—1820-1824.

II. *Will Book* 516, pp. 72-74 (Frances E. Very's will).

III. *Will Book* 517, pp. 32-34 (Lydia L. A. Very's will).

IV. *Will Book* 202, p. 136 (Washington Very's will).

V. *Will Book* 16, year 1825, p. 250 (Capt. Jones Very's will).

VI. *Probate Book* 405, pp. 482-485.

VII. *Deed Book* 268, p. 281 (Jones Very to Lydia Very).

Essex Institute Autograph Collection. Letter of Elizabeth Peabody to Robert C. Waterson, Feb. 26, 1838.

Foerster, Norman. *American Criticism.* Boston and New York: Houghton, Mifflin & Co., 1928.

Foerster, Norman, ed. *American Poetry and Prose.* Vol. I. Boston and New York: Houghton, Mifflin & Co., 1934.

—— *Nature in American Literature.* New York: The Macmillan Co., 1923.

Frothingham, O. B. *Transcendentalism in New England.* New York: G. P. Putnam's Sons, 1876.

Furness, Horace Howard. *Records of a Lifelong Friendship, 1807-1882: Ralph Waldo Emerson and Wm. Henry Furness.* Boston and New York: Houghton, Mifflin & Co., 1900.

Gay, Robert M. *Emerson: A Study of the Poet as Seer.* New Year: Doubleday, Doran & Co., Inc., 1928.

Goddard, H. C. *New England Transcendentalism.* New York: Columbia University Press, 1908.

Godwin, Parke, ed. *William Cullen Bryant: His Life and Works.* 6 vols. New York and Boston: D. Appleton & Co., 1884.

Gohdes, Clarence L. F. *The Periodicals of American Transcendentalism.* Durham, N. C.: Duke University Press, 1931.

"Gray, William." *D. A. B.,* Vol. VII.

Hale, Edward Everett. *James Russell Lowell and His Friends.* Boston and New York: Houghton, Mifflin & Co., 1899.

Hawthorne, Julian. *Nathaniel Hawthorne and His Wife.* Vol. I. Boston and New York: Houghton, Mifflin & Co., 1884.

Hawthorne, Nathaniel. *Mosses from an Old Manse.* Vol. II, "The Virtuoso's Collection," p. 272. Boston: Houghton, Mifflin & Co., n.d.

—— *The American Notebooks.* Edited by Randall Stewart. New Haven: Yale University Press, 1932.

—— *Twice-Told Tales.* Fourteenth Edition. Boston and New York: Houghton, Mifflin & Co., 1879. Pp. 89-91. Vol. I, "The Gentle Boy," pp. 76-115.

Herbert, George. *The Life and Writings of the Rev. George Herbert.* Lowell, Mass.: George Woodward, 1834.

Herbert, George and Henry Vaughan. *The Poetical Works of Herbert and Vaughan,* with a memoir of each. Two vols. in one. Boston: Houghton, Mifflin & Co., 1864.

Higginson, Thomas Wentworth. *Cheerful Yesterdays.* Boston: Houghton, Mifflin Co., 1898.

—— *Margaret Fuller Ossoli*. "American Men of Letters Series." Boston: Houghton, Mifflin & Co., 1885.

Historical Sketch of the Salem Lyceum, with a List of the Officers and Lecturers since Its Formation in 1830. Salem: Press of the Salem Gazette, 1879.

James, William. *The Varieties of Religious Experience*. New York: Longmans, Green and Co., 1917. Lectures XI, XII, XIII: "Saintliness"; Lectures XVI and XVIII: "Mysticism."

Lathrop, Rose Hawthorne. *Memories of Hawthorne*. Boston and New York: Houghton, Mifflin & Co., 1897.

Longfellow, Samuel. *The Life of Henry Wadsworth Longfellow*. 3 vols. Boston: Ticknor & Co., 1886.

Lowell, James Russell. *Among My Books*. First Series and Second Series. Boston and New York: Houghton Mifflin & Co., 1870 and 1876.

—— Annotations in his copy of *Essays and Poems* by Jones Very, 1839 edition, preserved in the Treasure Room, at the Widener Library, Cambridge, Mass.

—— *Letters of James Russell Lowell*. 2 vols. Edited by Charles Eliot Norton. New York: Harper & Brothers, 1899.

Macy, John. *The Spirit of American Literature*. New York: The Modern Library, n.d.

Metcalf, John Calvin. *American Literature*. Richmond: Johnson Publishing Co., 1921.

Michaud, Régis. *Emerson the Enraptured Yankee*. Translated from the French by George Boas. New York and London: Harper & Bros., 1930.

Milton, John. *Areopagitica and Other Prose Writings*. Edited with an introduction by William Haller. New York: The Macmillan Co., 1927.

Norton, Charles Eliot. *Henry Wadsworth Longfellow: A Sketch of His Life*. Boston and New York: Houghton, Mifflin & Co., 1907.

Norton, Charles Eliot, ed. *The Correspondence of Thomas Carlyle and Ralph Waldo Emerson, 1834-1872*. Vol. I. Boston: James R. Osgood & Co., 1883.

Parrington, Vernon Louis. *Main Currents in American Thought*. 3 vols. New York: Harcourt, Brace & Co., 1927.

"Peabody, Elizabeth Palmer." *D. A. B.* Vol. XIV.

Peabody, Elizabeth.
    1. MS letter to Miss Gay, on eve of departure for Newton, Mass., "with my brother Nathaniel—who has got a school there."
    2. MS letter, dated Salem, Feb. 26, 1838, to Mr. Robert C. Waterson: sends a message to Jones Very.
    (Margaret Brooks Collection in the Essex Institute.)

——— *Reminiscences of William Ellery Channing, D.D.* Boston:
Roberts Brothers, 1880.

"Peabody, Elizabeth Palmer." *The National Cyclopaedia of American
Biography,* XII, 350.

Perley, Sidney. *The History of Salem, Massachusetts.* Salem: 1924.

Pickard, Samuel T. *J. G. Whittier: His Life and Letters.* 2 vols. Boston and New York: Houghton, Mifflin & Co., 1894.

Records of the College Faculty, in Archives of Widener Library, at
Cambridge, Mass. Vol. XI (1829-1840).

Richardson, Charles F. *American Literature, 1607-1885.* 2 vols. New
York: G. P. Putnam's Sons, 1895. I, xii, 344; II, 233-234.

Ritter, Albert. *Jones Very—der Dichter des Christentums.* Linz, Wien,
Leipzig: Oesterreichische Verlagsanstalt, 1903. Critical biography of
Very, and translations of ninety-two of his poems.

Rusk, Ralph Leslie. *The Literature of the Middle Western Frontier.*
Vol. I, Chapter III, "Newspapers and Magazines." New York: Columbia University Press, 1926.

Russell, Phillips. *Emerson: The Wisest American.* New York: Bren-
tano's, 1929.

Salem *Gazette* articles:
    1. "School for Young Ladies," April 13, 1847.
    2. "Deaths: Washington Very," May 2, 1853.
    3. "Reminiscences of the Hacker School," March 19, 1875.
    4. "The Rev. Jones Very," May 11, 1880.
    5. "In Memoriam," May 14, 1880.
    6. "College Life of Jones Very," May 21, 1880. "A Pupil's Testi-
mony to Mr. Very as a Teacher" (same date).
    7. "Memorial to Jones Very," Dec. 17, 1880.
    8. "Jones Very," by Wm. P. Andrews, March 29, 1881.
    9. "To the Poet Very," Feb. 23, 1883.

Salem *Observer.* "Death of Rev. Jones Very, the Poet," May 15, 1880.

Salem *Post.* "Jones Very," May 12, 1880.

Salem *Register* articles:
    1. "The Hacker School House," June 26, 1865.
    2. "Obituary for Jones Very," May 10, 1880.
    3. "Mr. Very, the Poet," May 13, 1880.
    4. "Jones Very," May 20, 1880.

Sanborn, Franklin Benjamin. *Henry D. Thoreau.* "American Men of
Letters Series." Boston: Houghton, Mifflin & Co., 1882.

——— *Recollections of Seventy Years.* 2 vols. Vol II. Boston: Richard
G. Badger; The Gorham Press, 1909.

Santayana, George. *Interpretations of Poetry and Religion.* New York:
Charles Scribner's Sons, 1900.

Schonbach, Anton C. *Über Lesen und Bildung*. Graz: Leuschner & Lubensky's Universitäts-Buchhandlung, 1900. "Ralph Waldo Emerson und sein Kreis," pp. 81-133.

Shafer, Robert, ed. *From Beowulf to Thomas Hardy*. 2 vols. Vol. I, *From Beowulf to Doctor Johnson*.

Stedman, Edmund Clarence. *Poets of America*. Boston and New York: Houghton, Mifflin & Co., 1885.

Strong, Augustus Hopkins. *American Poets and Their Theology*. Philadelphia: The Griffith and Rowland Press, 1916.

Thomson, James. *The Seasons*. New York: Printed for Richard Scott, by D. and G. Bruce, 1811. Jones Very's copy, owned by W. I. Bartlett, Roanoke, Va.

Thoreau, Henry D. MS letter, dated Concord, Jan. 16, 1858, and addressed to "My dear Sir," who is probably Very. In possession of the Essex Institute, Salem, Mass.

Tracts by Josiah Quincy—President of Harvard University—1834.
   1. "Circular of the Senior Class."
   2. "Proceedings of the Overseers of Harvard University, the Report Accepted, and the Resolution Applied by Them on the 25th of August, 1834, Relative to the Late Disturbance in that Seminary."
   3. "President Quincy's Report of Result of Rebellion."

Underhill, Evelyn. *The Essentials of Mysticism and Other Essays*. New York: E. P. Dutton & Co., 1920.

"Very, Frank Washington." *Who's Who in America*. Vol. XIV (1926-27).

"Very, Jones." *D. A. B.,* Vol. XIX.

Very, Lydia L. A. *An Old-Fashioned Garden—and Walks and Musings Therein*. Salem: The Salem Press Co., 1900.

———— *A Strange Recluse*. Salem: The Salem Press Co., 1899.

———— *Poems*. Andover: W. F. Draper, 1856.

———— *Sayings and Doings among Insects and Flowers*. Salem: The Salem Press, 1897.

Visitor's Guide to Salem. Published by the Essex Institute. Salem: The Essex Institute, 1927.

Wheatland, Dr. Henry. Manuscripts XXVI, Genealogical R—W. (Essex Institute.)

Woodberry, George Edward. *Ralph Waldo Emerson*. New York: The Macmillan Co., 1907.

Woods, George Benjamin, ed. *English Poetry and Prose of the Romantic Movement*. New York: Scott, Foresman & Co., 1929.

ARTICLES IN MAGAZINES AND NEWSPAPERS

Andrews, William P. "An Inspired Life," *The Century Magazine,* II (Oct. 1, 1882), 859-862.

——— "Jones Very," *Harvard Register,* March, 1881, pp. 131-136.

Baker, Carlos. "Emerson and Jones Very," *The New England Quarterly,* VII (March, 1934), 90-99.

Batchelor, George. "A Poet of Transcendentalism." *The Dial* (Chicago), IV (July, 1883), 58.

Bradford, George, Jr. "Jones Very," *The Unitarian Review,* XXVII (Feb., 1887), 111-118.

Burns, Percy Pratt. "Jones Very," *Howard College Bulletin,* LXXX (June, 1922), 42-66.

Canby, Henry S. "Thoreau, the Great Eccentric," *Saturday Review of Literature,* IV (Nov. 26, 1927), 337-339.

Clarke, James Freeman. "Religious Sonnets—by Jones Very—Salem, Mass.," *The Western Messenger,* VI (March, 1839), 308-310.

Cooke, George Willis. "Emerson and Transcendentalism," *The New England Magazine,* N. S., XXVIII (1903), 264-280. Portrait of Very, p. 268; his connection with the Transcendental Club, and Very as contributor to *The Dial,* pp. 270-277.

"Death of Jones Very," Boston *Evening Transcript,* Tuesday, May 11, 1880.

Emerson, Ralph Waldo. "Chardon Street and Bible Conventions," *The Dial,* III (July, 1842), 100-102.

——— "Essays and Poems. By Jones Very. Boston: C. C. Little and James Brown," *The Dial,* II (July, 1841), 130-131.

Fuller, Margaret. "Literary Notices—Chat in Boston Bookstores.—No. I," *The Boston Quarterly Review,* III (Jan., 1840), 127-134.

Gohdes, Clarence. "Alcott's 'Conversation' on The Transcendental Club and *The Dial,*" *American Literature,* III (March, 1931), 14-28.

Hammell, Professor G. M. "Jones Very—A Son of the Spirit," *The Methodist Review,* LXXXIII (Jan., 1901), 20-30.

"Harvard University" (Valedictory Exercises—Jones Very's song quoted), Salem *Observer,* Saturday morning, July 23, 1836.

Hawthorne, Julian. "Such is Paradise," *The Century Magazine,* CXV (Dec., 1927), 157-169.

"Humanity and Benevolence," (Philadelphia) *American Daily Advertiser,* Sept. 17, 1818.

"Jones Very," *The Atlantic Monthly,* LII (July, 1883), 123 ff.

——— *Bulletin of the Essex Institute,* XII (Jan.-June, 1880), 74-75.

"Jones Very. The Finest Sonnet Writer in America. The Earth Life of a Mystic, Lately Ended. Characteristics of His Mind and Writings," Boston *Sunday Herald,* Sunday, May 16, 1880.

"Jones Very," *The Literary World* (Boston), XIV (June 30, 1883), 203.

Longfellow, Samuel. "Poems of Jones Very," *The Index,* IV (July 5, 1883-June 26, 1884), 10.

Nevins, Winfield S. "Jones Very, a Poet of Mysticism. A Strange and Interesting Man of Letters Whose Centenary Passed Almost Unnoticed," Boston *Evening Transcript*, Saturday, Oct. 25, 1913.

"New Publications," *The North American Review*, XLIX (Oct., 1839), 507.

"Poems. By Matthew Arnold. A New and Complete Edition," *The North American Review*, XCVI (Jan., 1863), 131-132.

"Salem's Famous Family," Boston *Globe*, Sept. 23, 1903.

Sanborn, Franklin Benjamin. "Emerson and His Friends," *The Literary World*, XI (May 22, 1880), 179.

"The Life and Services to Literature of Jones Very. A Memorial Meeting, Tuesday, Dec. 14, 1880," *Bulletin of the Essex Institute*, XIII (Jan.-June, 1881).

"The Poets and Poetry of America—by Griswold," *The North American Review*, LVIII (Jan., 1844), 1-39; LXXXII (Jan., 1856), 242-243.

Thompson, F. T. "Emerson's Theories and Practice of Poetry," *PMLA*, XLIII (Dec., 1928), 1170-1184.

Very, Lydia L. A. "Jones Very Again," Boston *Sunday Herald*, Sunday, June 6, 1880.

Very, Lydia Louisa Ann. "Old Corner in Salem," Boston *Evening Transcript*, Feb. 21, 1890.

"Very's Poetry" (from the *New York Tribune*), Boston *Evening Transcript*, Tuesday, Aug. 28, 1883.

Warfel, Harry R. "Margaret Fuller and Ralph Waldo Emerson," *PMLA*, L (June, 1935), 576-594.

Whittier, J. G. Letter "in my 84th year" to Lydia L. A. Very, concerning her poems. A newspaper clipping (in Birchbrook Mill and other clippings: Essex Institute files:– E:W625, 1894-2).

Winters, Yvor. "A New England Mystic," *The American Review*, VII (May, 1936), 159-178. This article is included in *Maule's Curse*, pp. 125-146, published in 1938, by New Directions, Norfolk, Conn.

INDEX

[229]